The Franks

The Peoples of Europe

General Editors
James Campbell and Barry Cunliffe

Already published
The Mongols
David Morgan
The Basques
Roger Collins
The Franks
Edward James

In preparation

The Thracians
Alexander Fol
The Picts
Charles Thomas
The Illyrians
John Wilkes
The Armenians
A. E. Redgate
The Bretons
Patrick Galliou and Michael Jones
The Celts
David Dumville

The Gypsies
Sir Angus Fraser
The Huns
E. A. Thompson
The Spanish
Roger Collins
The Turks
C. J. Heywood
The Sicilians
David Abulafia
The Goths
Peter Heather

The Early Germans
Malcolm Todd

The Franks

Edward James

Basil Blackwell

Copyright © Edward James, 1988

First published 1988
Reprinted 1988

Basil Blackwell Ltd
108 Cowley Road, Oxford OX4 1JF, UK

Basil Blackwell Inc.
432 Park Avenue South, Suite 1503,
New York, NY 10016, USA

British Library Cataloguing in Publication Data

James, Edward, 1947–
    The Franks. (The Peoples of Europe).
    1. Franks — History
    I. Title   II. Series
    944'.01   DC64
    ISBN 0–631–14872–8

Library of Congress Cataloging in Publication Data

James, Edward, 1947–
    The Franks / Edward James.
        p. cm. — (Peoples of Europe)
    Bibliography: p.
    Includes index
    ISBN 0–631–14872–8
    1. Franks—History. 2. Franks—France—History. 3. France–
–Church history—To 987. 4. Clovis, King of the Franks, ca.
466–511. I. Title. II. Series.
DC64.J36 1988
944—dc19

Typeset in 11 on 12.5 pt Sabon
by Opus, Oxford
Printed in Great Britain by
Butler & Tanner Ltd, Frome and London

To Columba

Contents

Preface

There is not enough space in the bibliography to acknowledge all my sources, direct and indirect, for what follows, although I have tried to list there the published work that has influenced me most. I would however like single out some people, to offer my profound thanks to the following, who have contributed directly and personally: the two dozen students in the Department of History at the University of York who, over three years, took my Special Subject on 'Gregory of Tours and His World', for good-humouredly helping me to appreciate Gregory; the students of 'Mortuary Behaviour' in the Department of Archaeology at York, for enduring my attempts to explain Merovingian cemeteries; three research students whom I currently supervise, Simon Burnell, Guy Halsall and Simon Loseby, for teaching me a great deal (with particular thanks to Guy, a survivor of my Special Subject course, for pointing out to me the source of inspiration for the artist of plate 47); Patrick Périn, for his friendship and hospitality on various trips to France, for doing his best to keep me up-to-date on Merovingian archaeology, and for encouraging me with *The Franks* even while he was busily writing his rival *Les Francs*; Ian Wood, for the constant stimulation of his ideas on Frankish history, and for commenting on a draft of *The Franks*; James Campbell, for the expert care and attention which he has given to the book; and my wife Columba, to whom I dedicate the book, for providing it with any stylistic niceties that it might have, and for offering so much love and understanding.

Acknowledgements

The author and publisher are grateful to the following for permission to use photographs in this book: the Ducal Library, Wolfenbüttel (1); the Bibliothèque Nationale, Paris (2) (Bib. Nat., MS Lat. 17654); Ann Münchow and the Hohe Domkirche, Trier (3); C. Pilet (4); the Römisch-Germanisches Museum and the Rheinisches Bildarchiv, Cologne (7); the Cabinet des Médailles of the Bibliothèque Nationale, Paris (8); H. W. Böhme (9); the Allgemeine Zeitung, Mainz (11); the Ashmolean Museum, Oxford (13); R. Brulet (14); the Musée des Antiquités Nationales, St-Germain-en-Laye (15); Editions Errance, Paris (16); R. Pirling and the Museum Burg Linn (17); the Institut Royale du Patrimoine Artistique, Brussels (18); L. Buchet of the Centre de Recherches Archéologiques, Sophia Antipolis (19); the British Museum (22); Maidstone Museums and the Kent Archaeological Society (23); the Musées Départementaux de la Seine-Maritime, Rouen (24); Editions Errance, Paris (25) and (26); the Rheinisches Landesmuseum, Bonn (27); the Römisch-Germanisches Museum and the Rheinisches Bildarchiv, Cologne (28); the Rheinisches Landesmuseum, Bonn (29) and (30); P. Demolon (31); the Erzbischöfliches Museum, Cologne (32); A. France-Lanord, of the Musée de l'Histoire du Fer, Nancy (33) and (34); the Archives Nationales, Paris (35) (MS K.4 no. 11); the Ashmolean Museum, Oxford (36), (38) and (39); the Cabinet des Médailles of the Bibliothèque Nationale, Paris (37); the British Museum (40); Ann Münchow and the Hohe Domkirche, Trier (41); J. Decaens and the Centre de Recherches Archéologiques Médiévales, Caen (42); the Musées Départementaux de la Seine-Maritime and the Musée Alfred-Bonno, Chelles (45); R. Pirling and the Museum Burg Linn (46).

The following plates were taken from these books: (5) from L. Lindenschmidt's *Handbuch der Deutschen Alterthumskunde* (1880–1889); (6) from K. Böhner's contribution to Fleury and Périn 1978 (see Bibliography for short references); (10) from T. Eck, *Les deux cimetières de Vermand et de Saint-Quentin* (1891); (12) from J. Chifflet, *Anastasis Childerici I* (1655); (20) and (21) from C. Boulanger, *Le mobilier funéraire gallo-romain et franc en Picardie et en Artois* (1902–1905). Plates 43 and 44 were taken by myself.

The following figures were adapted from drawings or maps in the following books: (3) from Périn 1980; (4) from C. Rostaing, *Les Noms de Lieux* (1945); (5) from Périn and Feffer 1987; (6) and (7) from Böhme 1974 (although (7) with some up-dating supplied by Dr Böhme); (8) from M. Müller-Wille, 'Königsgrab und Königsgrabkirche', *Bericht der Römisch-Germanischen Kommission* 63 1982; (13) from M. Martin, *Das fränkische Gräberfeld von Basel-Bernerring* (1976); (14) from Musset 1975; (15) from Prinz 1965; (16) from Werner 1964; (17) from M. Müller-Wille, *op. cit.*; (23) from Werner 1961; (24) from Vallet 1986.

Introduction: Who Were the Franks?

The political map of western Europe saw one of its greatest periods of change in the fifth and sixth centuries AD. The Western Roman Empire disappeared, and migrating or conquering peoples brought new names to many parts of Europe. The Scotti from Ireland settled in what became Scotland; the British from 'Great Britain' gave their name to 'Lesser Britain', or Brittany. The land settled by Angles, Saxons and Jutes came to be called *Englaland* (although in modern Irish 'England' remains 'Sasana', or 'Saxony'). The Burgundians migrated to Burgundy, the Lombards to Lombardy; the Vandals came to Andalusia. No such vestige survives of the most powerful of the Germanic peoples in the fifth century, the Goths, who by 500 controlled much of Spain, southern Gaul and Italy; 'Gothia', a regional name which survived for several centuries, has given way to 'Languedoc', and apart from a few village names in southern France and Spain the Goths survive on the map of Europe only in their homeland in Sweden, in the names of Gotland, Västergötland and Ostergötland. But in this history of name-giving perhaps the most successful people of all were the Franks: Brittany, Burgundy and Gothia all became, eventually, mere provinces of France, and such was the dominance of the Franks or French in the history of Europe that 'Firanja', from the Latin 'Francia', has come to mean 'Europe' in modern Arabic.

The story of how the Franks became the French and why they became so important in European history is one of the subjects of this book. We will see how a group of undistinguished

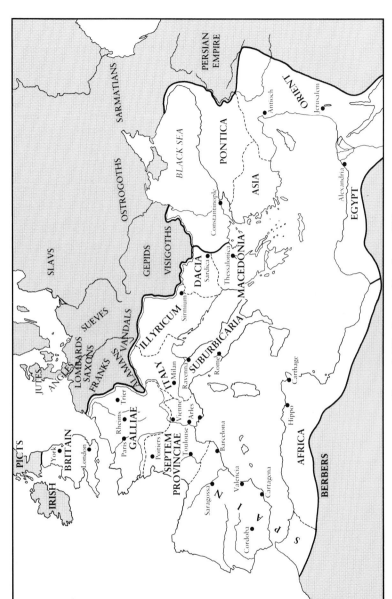

Figure 1 The Roman Empire, c. 300

barbarians from the marshy lowlands north and east of the Rhine frontier of the Roman Empire founded what was the most powerful and stable of all barbarian kingdoms in the period immediately after the collapse of the Western Empire in the fifth century. We shall concentrate above all on the dynasty which achieved this feat: the Frankish kings known as the Merovingians. We shall not follow the story in detail after the waning of that dynasty in the seventh century, though obviously an awareness of what happened to the Franks after the eighth century would emphasize their importance to European history. It was a Frank who was crowned in Rome in the year 800 and became the first Roman Emperor of Germanic origins. Franks began the reconquest of Spain from the Muslims, Franks led the Crusades against the Muslims in the eastern Mediterranean, and Franks spread their culture and fashions throughout Europe in the twelfth and thirteenth centuries. Despite what some Franks themselves, and some later historians, have thought, their success need not be seen as the result of special divine favour. Their importance in European history is due to their success in taking over, with its Roman structure largely intact, the wealthy and geographically central provinces of Roman Gaul. What historians and archaeologists can say about this process is the main theme of this book.   After the eighth century, of course, historians generally translate the Latin *Franci* by 'French'. The Franks became the French. They also became the inhabitants of the German province of Franken, or Franconia. From a linguistic point of view, their most direct descendants are the Dutch, and the Flemish-speakers of Belgium. It is tempting to ask at what point, chronologically, the Franks became French, Franconians, Dutch or Belgians, but a comparison with England may illustrate the knots into which the historian can tie himself if he applies these ethnic names carelessly. Britain was invaded, Bede tells us, by Angles, Saxons and Jutes. The Jutes settled in Kent. The areas over which the invading kings ruled almost certainly included large numbers of British. (Many of these may have called themselves Romans; the English newcomers simply called them 'foreigners' – 'Welsh'). At the end of the sixth century, St Augustine came to *Jutish* Kent and became the head of the church of the *Angles*. A generation later the Church came to Anglian Northumbria (which one of

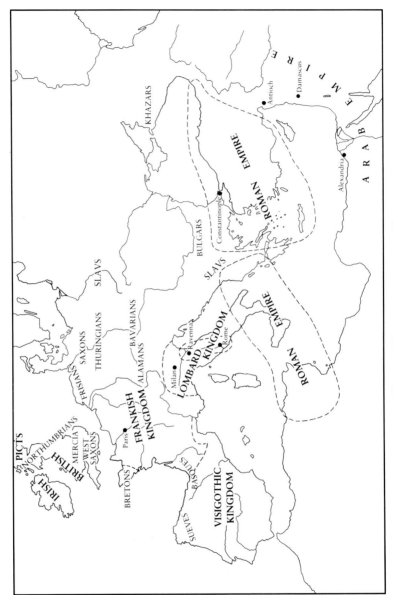

Figure 2 The post-Roman World, c. 650

its own earliest writers called *Saxonia*). The *Anglian* kingdoms were all taken over in the ninth century by the Vikings; but the Viking kingdoms were themselves defeated by the West Saxons, whose kings called themselves 'Kings of the Angles'. The confusion further north in Britain is just as marked, and is perhaps best captured by Sellar and Yeatman:

The Scots (originally Irish, but by now Scotch) were at this time inhabiting Ireland, having driven the Irish (Picts) out of Scotland; while the Picts (originally Scots) were now Irish (living in brackets) and *vice versa*. It is essential to keep these distinctions clearly in mind (and *verce visa*).[1]

The confusion still survives, and the English and others still annoy the Scots and the Welsh by talking of 'English' when they mean 'British' (and *vice versa*).

These confusions exist largely because we have fixed and anachronistic ideas of what constitutes a people or a nation. The theorists of nationalism in the nineteenth century, who influenced historians of the Middle Ages at the time and who still condition our own thinking, imagined that a people was a group of men and women with a common language, a common culture and a common racial type, who could be clearly distinguished from their neighbours. They portrayed the settlement of the Anglo-Saxons in Britain, and that of the Franks in Gaul, as an invasion of a long-skulled 'Nordic' race into an area inhabited by broad-skulled 'Celts'. As we shall see in more detail in the last section of this book, some believed that the French monarchy and aristocracy could trace their origins directly back to the military race of the Franks: the French Revolution was 'the final victory of the Gauls over the Franks'. That is why some historians of the Franks have been so interested in establishing whether particular individuals in sixth- or seventh-century Gaul had 'Frankish blood', whether a particular institution was 'Roman', 'Gallic' or 'Frankish', or by what stage the two races of Gauls and Franks had largely 'fused' through intermarriage. But historians today can see that 'peoples' are much more fluid than were once thought: they can combine into new groups, take on new names, or impose those

---

[1] W. C. Sellar and R. J. Yeatman, *1066 and All That* (Harmondsworth, 1960): *Important Note* to p. 13.

names onto others. Early medieval peoples are not biological entities, like races; sometimes they appear to be no more than men and women who are temporarily grouped together, by others, by themselves or, more commonly, by their leaders. They may have a common language, a common culture, a common way of dressing (which can be discovered by the archaeologist), but if they have, all these things may have been imposed on them by conquest or cultural domination, as happened to the Celts in pre-Roman times. Moreover, the Celts did not call themselves 'Celts'. We often have to cope also with the problem that a people might conceive of itself and refer to itself in one way, and outsiders might refer to it in another. We must always remember that ethnic names are but labels. They may be applied to people who would not use that name of themselves; they may gather together groups of people who would not think of themselves as constituting one group.

The answer to the question 'who were the Franks?' thus demands at least two more questions in reply: 'What period do you want to know about?' and 'Do you want to know about it from the point of view of insiders or outsiders?' The name itself presumably originates with the Franks themselves, since 'Frank' meant something like 'fierce' in their own Germanic language, and came to mean 'free' – the origin of our own English adjective 'frank'. But for the first two and a half centuries of the history of the Frankish people we have to rely on the perceptions of outsiders as to who were Franks and who were not: we have only Roman sources to inform us. These sources imply that the Franks were originally a confederation of peoples who spoke, or whose leaders spoke, a Germanic language, and who lived north and east of the northernmost part of the Rhine frontier of the Roman Empire. They took part in the barbarian raids on the Empire in the third century, and Roman Emperors led several campaigns against them in the fourth century. In that century also a number of people whom Romans called Franks reached high military and civil positions within the Roman Empire. In the mid-fourth century some Franks were settled within the Empire, just west of the Rhine estuaries. In the fifth century the Franks appear infrequently in the sources, but mostly as allies of the Romans. Finally, at the beginning of the sixth century, comes the first historical source which might actually have been written by a Frank: the earliest version of their law-code, called the *Pactus Legis Salicae* by those modern historians who have tried to reconstruct it. But the *Pactus Legis Salicae* does not use the word 'Frank' at all. The people for whom the *Pactus* was intended were Salians, one group within the Frankish people. Probably at that time the Franks still conceived of themselves primarily as members of one or other of various smaller peoples or tribes which were collectively called 'the Franks'. Perhaps the word 'Frank' was used when referring to their membership of a political confederation, or when they wished to contrast themselves with other groups, such as Romans or Alamans. Their own primary feelings of loyalty may have been to their tribal group. Loyalty to the tribe, rather than to the whole confederation, may have lasted among some Franks, particularly those who remained east of the Rhine, until as late as the eighth century.

The crucial period for the development of the idea of the Franks as a unified people was almost certainly the reign of Clovis (*c.* 481–*c.* 511). It was he who destroyed the political independence of most or all of the tribes, and it was he, as king of the Franks, not king of the Salians, who led his people into a series of succesful military campaigns that made the Franks into one of the most powerful of the Germanic peoples. Thereafter those who owed their position to Clovis's descendants (the Merovingian kings) included the Gallo-Roman clerics who produced nearly all the historical sources we have, and they had an interest in stressing the unity of the Frankish people.

In the time of Clovis it was probably fairly easy for a Gallo-Roman cleric to know who was a Frank and who was not. They could probably be distinguished by dress, by name, by social position and function, and perhaps by language (although some Frankish families may have been living among Romans and speaking Latin for generations). Gregory of Tours (d. 594) wrote the *Ten Books of Histories*, our major source for the history of Gaul in the sixth century. He wrote about the Frankish kings and the deeds of their agents and subjects. The only time he mentions the ethnic identity of a particular German is when he points out that he is a Saxon, a Thuringian, or a Burgundian: we are perhaps right to assume that most of the others with Germanic names were Franks. But it is also clear that Gregory does not consider it necessary constantly to point out 'this man is a Frank, this man is a Gallo-Roman'. We cannot even be sure who was the first Frank to become a bishop. It may have been Bertechramnus (Bertram) of Bordeaux, because Gregory mentions almost as an aside that he was related to the Frankish kings. However, Bertram may have been the product of a 'mixed marriage'. His Frankish name alone does not indicate Frankish parentage, for by the sixth century it was becoming quite fashionable for Romans, even aristocratic Romans, to take Germanic names: Gregory himself had a great-uncle called Gundulf. Patrick Geary has recently argued how fluid ethnic categories were in the eighth century:

No one characteristic, be it law, language, custom, or birth, can be considered a sufficient index by which to assign ethnicity, nor was it any different for contemporaries. Self-perception, and perception of others, represented a choice in a variety of somewhat arbitrary characteristics, which could be seen differently by different people. The real, although not entirely impenetrable, barriers were between slave and free, free and noble. Within the elite a person or faction could be Burgundian by birth, Roman by language, and Frankish by dress. Likewise, someone born of a father from Francia and a mother from Alamannia could properly be termed a Frank or an Alamannian by different authors considering him from different perspectives. His own perception of himself might change during his lifetime, depending on how he viewed his relationship to the Frankish king and his local faction.[2]

The 'racial' hostility assumed by nineteenth-century historians (natural perhaps to Germans in the wake of Napoleon or to Frenchmen after the Franco-Prussian War) could hardly have existed given such subjectivity and fluidity: the long-standing prejudice that Romans had had against barbarians must have declined in the face of the new political and social conditions.

Two developments acted together to change the meaning of the word 'Frank' in the course of the sixth and seventh centuries. Firstly, Gallo-Romans and other subjects of the Frankish kings adopted Frankish customs, such as Frankish personal names, while many Franks adopted the Latin language and Roman ways: this blurred the old ethnic divisions so much

---

[2] P. J. Geary, *Aristocracy in Provence: The Rhône Basin at the Dawn of the Carolingian Age* (Stuttgart, 1985), p. 111.

that they became meaningless. Secondly, the continued political dominance of the *reges Francorum*, the 'kings of the Franks', and their Mayors of the Palace, began to make their subjects, of whatever origin, think of themselves as Franks. The kingdom was 'Francia', and those who lived in it quite naturally took on the new name; it identified political allegiance rather than ethnic identity. By the mid-eighth century it seems that most inhabitants of northern Gaul (whose actual ethnic origins were predominantly Gallo-Roman) probably called themselves, and were certainly called by others, 'Franks'. An eighth-century saint's life refers to aristocrats in the Trier region, who had clearly Roman names and who obviously still preserved some of their Roman traditions, as 'senators of the *Franks*'. People in southern Gaul, however, because they were increasingly independent of the power of the Frankish kings, used different ethnic words of themselves: those in Aquitaine, for instance, known as 'Romani' by the Franks, called themselves 'Aquitani'.

This distinction between north and south made no difference to what ethnic words foreigners used of people in Gaul. For someone in Spain or in Italy, anyone coming from Gaul or Francia was a Frank, a subject of the Frankish king, regardless of what he would have called himself. Even in the twelfth or thirteenth century an inhabitant of southern Gaul or 'France' might have resented being called 'French'; the south had been conquered three times by the northerners, in the sixth, the eighth, and the thirteenth centuries, but still they preferred to keep their own identity. Yet the word 'Francus' was used by Latin writers in Italy or Britain to refer to those in the south as well as in the north. And it was in this period, the age of the Crusades, that the words 'Frank' and 'Francia' entered Arabic and came to mean 'European' and 'Europe'.

Some of the problems of writing a study of 'the Franks' have, I hope, emerged. 'The Franks' is a term that has no absolute meaning, but one which changes according to time or circumstance. The problem has been ignored by some historians and archaeologists, and circumvented by others. Erich Zöllner, for instance, stops his *Geschichte der Franken* in 550, when it is still possible to distinguish a Frank from a Gallo-Roman in the historical sources (although it would be optimistic to assume that the two can be so easily distinguished from the archaeological record). Other historians (such as G. Fournier in *Les Mérovingiens*) equally sensibly use the dynastic label 'Merovingian' to refer to the civilization produced jointly by Frank and Gallo-Roman, and do not waste time trying to make ethnic distinctions. In what follows I shall try to steer an unhappy course between these two compromises. Since I see the primary meaning of 'the Franks' to be a Germanic people who were a powerful force upon their Roman and German neighbours in late Antiquity, I shall attempt, where possible, to isolate their own achievement, and to distinguish it from that of their neighbours and subjects. That means that the story finishes in the seventh century, during which period 'Frank' ceased to be a word applied primarily to a Germanic-speaking people. Conveniently that coincides with the point at which the Merovingians began to be superseded as effective rulers of the Franks by the Carolingians, and at which the archaeological record – or that part of it which has so far been adequately studied – begins to be much less extensive and informative. The story is thus contained within the period from the third to the seventh century, now commonly known to historians as 'late Antiquity'. It also means that the geographical focus of the work will be, in modern terms, northern France, north-west Germany and the Low Countries. The Franks made extensive conquests, but this area remained their homeland. Inevitably I shall also be dealing at times with material which is not strictly 'Frankish' at all, but which is a product of the 'Merovingian' world. To do otherwise would be to ignore important facets of the world of the Franks.

1

The Sources

Everything we know about the past comes from what has chanced to survive. There are manuscripts in parchment or papyrus recording aspects of Frankish history which mostly were protected in monastic libraries; there are the bodies of tens of thousands of Franks, buried with what their relatives chose to put in their graves; there are a few pitiful remains of the houses in which they lived and the churches in which they worshipped; and there are traces of their presence fossilized in the language and place-names of France, the Low Countries and north-west Germany. Each of these types of evidence requires careful analysis before any certain conclusions about the history of the Franks can be reached. In this chapter we shall look at the kinds of evidence which is available, and how historians, archaeologists and philologists can make sense of it.

Historical Sources

If the Franks were a prehistoric people we should no doubt call them the 'Row-Grave People', after what has been seen as their most distinctive archaeological feature, the laying out of graves in neat rows: indeed German archaeologists do on occasion refer to the *Reihengräberzivilisation*. However, the Franks are a people with a name, who are known through historical sources, and it is sensible to start with those written sources. Immediately we come across our first major problem: through-

out nearly the whole of the period of Frankish history with
which we are concerned, from the third century down to the
seventh century, historical sources are written not by Franks but
by foreigners, viewing the Franks from the outside, often in
ignorance and with incomprehension. The Franks first appear
in Roman sources, written in Italy or elsewhere in the
Mediterranean world by men for whom the Franks were just
another group of northern barbarians, characterized by the
same stereotypes as other northern barbarians. In the sixth
century, when the Franks had established themselves as the
major political power in Europe, very few, if any, of our sources
actually emanate from the Franks themselves; they are nearly all
written outside the main area of Frankish settlement, by men
who, if they met Franks at all, generally met the Frankish
aristocracy, who favoured a Roman lifestyle. The only possible
exception to this is the *Pactus Legis Salicae*, the earliest
formulation of Frankish law, but this too was written down in
Latin, not Frankish, and perhaps by men better versed in
Roman provincial law than in Frankish customary law. Even
when our first clearly Frankish authors appear, in the seventh
century, they viewed their fellow-Franks partly through Roman
eyes; they wrote in Latin, not Frankish, and had learnt the art of
writing in a clerical school. A Frank who joined the Church,
said a seventh-century Frankish law-code, was no longer a
Frank: he lived by Roman law, and thus was legally a Roman.

It is likely that the historical sources which we can now read
represent only a tiny proportion of what had once been written
down. In general, what has survived has done so either because
of its literary value or its practical use. Thus, some of the
panegyrics declaimed before Roman emperors, a valuable
source of information on Roman military encounters with the
Franks, have been preserved because they were valued as
poetry. The books of letters written by Sidonius Apollinaris,
bishop of Clermont from *c.* 469 to the early 480s, are
invaluable documents for fifth-century Gallic history; they were
collected together by Sidonius and preserved as literary models
for those writing Latin prose. The decisions of Frankish church
councils, on the other hand, were preserved because those
decisions were legally binding, and were hence of practical use
to the Church in later centuries. Likewise, documents recording

the gift of land to a monastery by a wealthy benefactor were often treasured by a monastery for very practical reasons. Because some of those monasteries survived, with their archives and libraries more or less intact, right down to the eighteenth century or later, those documents have also survived. Monasteries were not the only institutions with archives and libraries in the sixth or seventh centuries: kings, bishops, wealthy and not-so-wealthy laymen, even town councils, also had them. In Merovingian Gaul official acts and private transactions alike were probably conducted by means of the written word. But very little of this secular written material has been preserved, because of all these archives and libraries only monasteries, and then only a few monasteries, had an uninterrupted history down to modern times. Monasteries also had the resources to copy the manuscripts they valued, to disseminate them and thus to increase their chances of survival. Our surviving sources, then, inevitably have a clerical bias; for the most part they are works which were of interest or use to clerics. We are fortunate, indeed, that clerics in the eighth and ninth centuries became much more deeply involved in government and administration than they had been in the sixth or seventh centuries; thus were preserved, in monastic libraries, some secular documents of earlier times.

Most documents survive to this day only in later copies of the original, or copies of copies, and so on. The first task of historical research often has to be to attempt a reconstruction of what the original might have looked like, just as the archaeologist will call on specialist help to restore a badly damaged and corroded artefact. The historian has to deduce where a scribe may have made mistakes in copying an earlier document, or to determine whether a later scribe has deliberately altered the document, adding a few phrases to a charter, for instance, so as to lay claim to more property or privileges. Indeed, in the case of charters or other texts which give or enumerate privileges, the historian always has to reckon with the possibility that the whole text may be a later forgery. An extreme case of the kind of things which can happen to a genuine text is that of the *Pactus Legis Salicae*. Internal evidence suggests that this was drawn up under King Clovis, between 507 and 511. There are 87 manuscripts, only one of which is as early as even the eighth

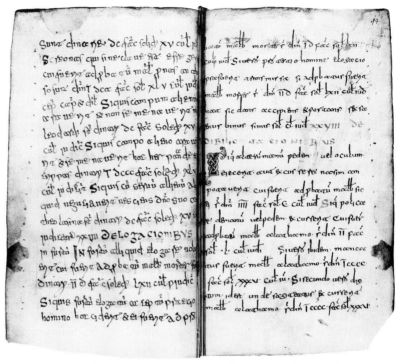

Plate 1 The earliest surviving manuscript of Lex Salica, *from the late eighth century. This opening shows where one scribe ended and another began.*

century (see plate 1). All 87 manuscripts differ from one another to a greater or lesser extent. Law is a living thing, of course; each time the law-code was copied by a scribe he included clauses added by Clovis's successors, or excluded clauses that were quite out-of-date. The modern printed text which can be read in the great series now produced in Munich, the *Monumenta Germaniae Historica,* corresponds exactly to none of these manuscripts; it is merely the modern editor's idea of how the text might originally have read in its various promulgations from the time of Clovis onwards.

None of these problems seriously affects the works of the greatest of all writers of Merovingian Gaul: Georgius Florentius, better known as Gregory, bishop of Tours. His works are known from manuscripts which are not far removed in time from his day (see plate 2), and offer only minor textual

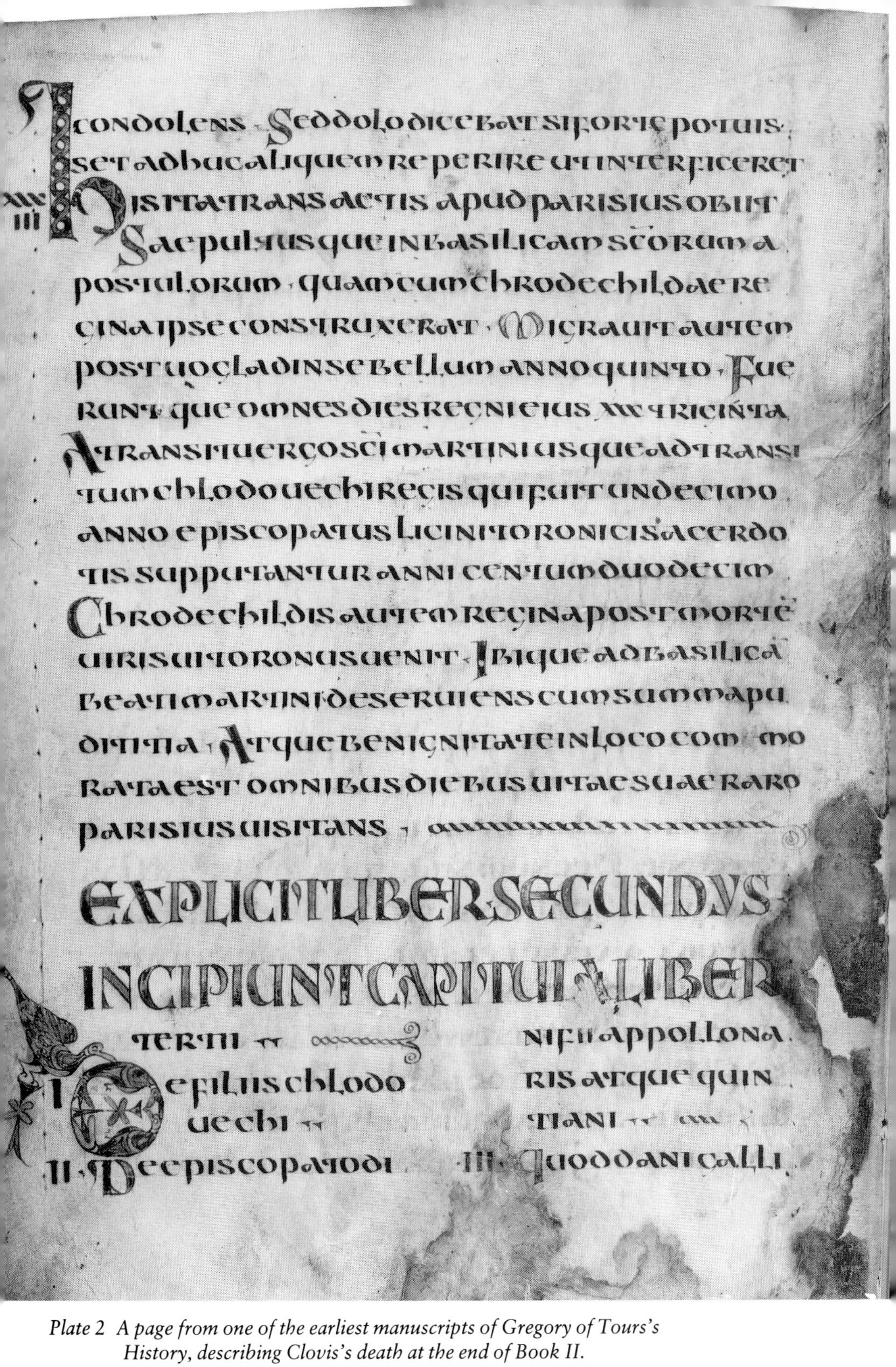

condolens seddolodicebat siforte potuis
set adhuc aliquem reperire utinterficeret
his itatransactis apudparisius obiit
Sepulsusque inbasilicam sctorum a
postulorum quamcumchrodechildae re
ginaipseconstruxerat migrauit autem
postuocladinsebellum anno quinto fue
runt que omnesdiesregnieius xxxriciñta
Atransituerçosci martini usquedtransi
tum chlodouechiregis quifuit undecimo
anno episcopatus licinitoronicisacerdo
tis supputantur anni centumduodecim
Chrodechildis autem reginapostmorte
uiriscuitoronusuenit ibique adbasilica
beatimartinideseruiens cumsummapu
dititia Atque benignitateinloco com mo
rataest omnibusdiebus uitaesuae raro
parisius uisitans

EXPLICIT LIBER SECUNDUS

INCIPIUNT CAPITULA LIBER

TERTII
I Defiliuschlodo
uechi
II Deepiscopatodi

NIFII APPOLLONA
RIS ATQUE QUIN
TIANI
III Quoddanicalli

---

*Plate 2 A page from one of the earliest manuscripts of Gregory of Tours's
History, describing Clovis's death at the end of Book II.*

problems. Gregory was a member of a distinguished Gallo-Roman family, which had already produced several bishops, including St Gregory of Langres, from whom Gregory took his name. The family had its estates in the *civitas* or city-territory of the Arverni, corresponding closely to the modern province of the Auvergne, with its capital at Clermont. He was born there around 540, some 10 years after the brutal Frankish attack on the Auvergne. He was trained for the clergy from an early age, and in 573 was chosen by the king to succeed his mother's cousin Eufronius as bishop of Tours, a see which several other relatives had held. In the course of his episcopate he wrote several works, books of miracles worked by the patron saint of his see, Martin of Tours, and collections of stories about other saints, some of whom were his relatives or predecessors. All that we know about his life comes from his own works, most notably from the *Ten Books of Histories*, finished not long before his death in 594. This is the work known since the eighth century as the *History of the Franks*, since its main concern is with the doings of the Frankish kings, particularly those kings with whom Gregory himself dealt: half the work, Books VI to X, is concerned with the events of the 10 years of Gregory's maturity, from 581 to 591. But Gregory himself was proud of his Roman and Christian traditions, and he exhibits little knowledge of the Frankish people itself. Only a handful of Germanic words creeps into his text, and very little information about Frankish institutions and customs. Even had he known much about ordinary Franks, he would probably not have told us any more; history, before the nineteenth century, was about Great Men – mostly, for Gregory, kings and saints.

Historians writing histories of the early Franks since Gregory have tended to be little more than recapitulations of Gregory: the habit was established as early as the seventh century, when Fredegar wrote four books of history, three of which consisted of a summary of the six books of Gregory to which he had access. Gregory's judgments on the kings and queens of his day have, on the whole, been generally accepted. His assessment of the wicked King Chilperic, his numerous allegations of murder levelled at Chilperic's queen, Fredegund, his picture of the political life of Merovingian Gaul as one of almost unrelieved civil war and brutal crime, have all been taken at face value, and have been a powerful factor in establishing a particular image of the Franks in the historical consciousness. It is only recently that historians have begun to question the assumption that 'he was at pains to be an impartial writer. . .; he concealed nothing and invented nothing, and we can correct his judgments by his own narrative', as Charles Pfister wrote in the eleventh edition of the *Encyclopedia Britannica* (1910). We can certainly try to correct his judgments by his own narrative; but we cannot correct his facts, for usually we have no other source of information. Gregory was not a participant in most of the events which he described; he was a collector of reports, of hearsay and rumour, whose truth he may not always have tried to untangle. He was anxious to tell a good story; he was even more anxious to draw a good moral. His *Histories* begin with a confession of faith, followed by an account of Genesis; his task was to unfold the mystery of God's providence, and to tell of the rewards granted to good men and the punishments meted out to the wicked. Because of the mistakes he makes in his Latin and his apparently uncritical acceptance of miracle stories, modern historians have often been prepared to regard him as artless and naive, and hence someone who 'concealed nothing and invented nothing'. But in fact Gregory's work has to be used very carefully by the modern historian; he was a skilled and artful writer, with particular theological and literary goals in mind.

This often holds true also for that other large category of narrative material surviving from the period, to which Gregory himself contributed: lives of saints. The writer of a saint's life, the hagiographer, is not so much a biographer as a writer of sermons. He wants to present his hero as someone who represents the Christian virtues, and lives the life of Christ and his apostles on earth. If the virtues, the anecdotes and the miracle-stories become stereotypes, that is, in a sense, what the hagiographer intends: it is a stereotypical saint which he wishes to present. The hagiographer may borrow his motifs from other hagiographers; he may invent or embellish if it suits his moral and theological purpose. Clearly we cannot treat a saint's life as historical narrative. Nor can we treat them in a crudely rationalist way, dismissing the miracles which bulk so large in these lives, or finding supposed scientific or other explanations for them, and accepting the rest as historical. Nevertheless,

Plate 3 An ivory plaque now in Trier shows the ceremonial reception of relics in a sixth-century town.

there is much incidental detail in these works which the historian can use in reconstructing the world in which the Franks lived. We might wonder, for instance, whether a man who stole the end of a bell-rope from the bell-tower of a church of St Martin, because he wanted a health-giving relic but could not get into the church, really was struck down by the miraculous power of the saint. Perhaps the social and psychological pressures of guilt could produce physical effects. We are still left with something much more secure: an invaluable piece of evidence for the existence of bell-towers with external access in sixth-century Gaul. Thus, with care, we can use Gregory and other literary writers of his time as sources of information about many aspects of Merovingian life. Margarethe Weidemann has used Gregory in this way to write a valuable 'cultural history' of sixth-century Gaul, and May Vieillard-Troiekouroff has written a book on the ecclesiastical architecture of Gregory's day, drawing far more information from Gregory's writings than she was able to do from archaeology.

Other types of documentary evidence survive from the period, and are subject to the same problems of analysis as are familar to historians of other periods. Legislative material, for instance, is valuable evidence for the desires of legislators, but is difficult to use as social history. We can never be sure that the problems which the legislation was designed to solve were real and widespread, or if they existed largely in the legislator's imagination, nor can we know whether the legislation did actually solve those problems, for we can never be sure of the efficacy of enforcement. The relationship between ideal and reality is at the heart of the problems of studying the historical sources of the period; there are some who feel that the only way to be certain of getting at the reality is to look at the concrete evidence studied by archaeologists.

Archaeological Evidence

Most of what survives from the past to inform us about the Franks consists of artefacts, things made by human hand. (In the future 'ecofacts' – evidence about the natural environment – may become more important.) In theory the study of ancient artefacts is the province of the archaeologist. In practice what are in historians' terms the most important artefacts of all – the actual manuscripts – are studied by palaeographers; inscriptions on stone are studied by epigraphers; inscriptions and other aspects of coins by numismatists; paintings and other objects with iconographic decoration by art historians; and so on. Each of these types of artefact can be studied by means of techniques used also by the archaeologist. Scientific or iconographic analysis of manuscripts may reveal date or provenance, just as it might for pottery or jewellery. Many of the disciplines for studying ancient artefacts which have grown up in the past century, which frequently operate in isolation from one another, are in fact closer in their aims and methods than might be supposed.

There are nevertheless obvious differences between studying words which have survived on ancient manuscripts and studying other, non-written, artefacts. The historian, studying words, can study personalities and events. The archaeologist can rarely if ever do either; he is often studying very general and gradual changes, changes which are often not detectable through the written sources, and which cannot normally be fitted neatly into the known historical framework. Frankish historians and, sometimes, archaeologists have been too fond of assuming that a particular archaeological find, for example evidence of the destruction of a building, must date from the time of a known historical event; archaeologists have been too ready to assume that the historical framework is well known and immutable. The historical evidence in fact has very many gaps, and it is unlikely that any important manuscripts concerning Frankish history are waiting to be discovered – although certainly many are waiting to be edited and analyzed properly. Things are very different in the discipline of archaeology. There is not only a considerable amount of previously discovered and as yet unpublished archaeological material, but new discoveries, any of which could change currently accepted ideas, are being made almost every day. In an archaeological context the word 'artefact' has to be interpreted very broadly. It includes gold and silver jewellery, swords, pottery and other things with which we are familar from museum displays. But earthworks, wall-foundations, graves, slight discolorations of earth surfaces which reveal the existence of postholes, all these are artefacts which can be just as significant to the archaeologist.

Plate 4 An aerial view of the cemetery of Frénouville (Calvados) after excavation.

Frankish archaeology was born in 1653, when workmen restoring the church of St Brice in Tournai discovered the grave of King Childeric (see below p. 59). Had it not been for his seal-ring it is unlikely that the grave would have been identified as early Merovingian; for another two centuries, in fact, Merovingian cemeteries were frequently thought to be Celtic or Roman. But the event of 1653 set the tone for the next three centuries and more: Frankish archaeology was very largely synonymous with cemetery archaeology. Because Franks (and other peoples) in the Merovingian period had the custom of burying the dead fully clothed, with their clothes-fastenings and other jewellery, and because they often placed other objects, such as weapons or vessels of pottery, glass or metal, in the grave, Frankish cemeteries were a relatively easy and attractive source of precious objects for museums and private collectors. They were also found quite easily, by constructors of railways, roads and new housing, and, as they no doubt had been for centuries, by farm-workers. What was new, from the mid-nineteenth century onwards, was that accidental discoveries were often reported to the local societies of antiquaries which were being founded all over western Europe, thus bringing cemeteries to the attention of excavators. Unfortunately their enthusiasm was seldom joined to any scholarly awareness of the need to record or publish anything but the more spectacular objects.

Although settlement sites have begun to be excavated in increasing numbers, cemeteries still provide the Frankish archaeologist with the bulk of his evidence. It is there that most of the products of Frankish craftsmen, of smiths, goldsmiths, potters, glass-makers, even wood-turners and weavers, are to be found. It is cemeteries which, so far, provide us with our strongest evidence for individual Frankish communities: evidence on size of community, health and mortality, age structure, perhaps even social structure or religious belief.

Given the importance of cemetery excavations for our knowledge of the Franks from the fourth or fifth century through to the seventh, some introduction to the different ways in which cemetery evidence can be used may be helpful here. The first and most obvious type of evidence consists of the objects placed in the graves themselves, the grave-goods. These are to be found in large numbers in the display-cases and store-rooms of museums all

Plate 5 A romanticized nineteenth-century view of Childeric's treasure when discovered in 1653.

over western Europe, and, indeed, in North America as well. Much of this material was excavated a long time ago, without adequate recording. Some of it is of unknown provenance, while much of the rest comes from cemeteries that were not adequately excavated or recorded. Many facts which could be of vital interest are often quite unknown: the position of the object in the grave, the nature of the other objects placed in the grave with it, the state of the accompanying skeleton, the nature of the grave itself and what could be detected of the funerary ritual, the position of the grave within the cemetery and its relation to other graves. We are left with the objects themselves, which can be studied from an art-historical or technological point of view, and which can, if we know their provenance, provide the archaeologist with useful dots on his or her distribution map.

The drawing up of distribution maps (like those on page 45 or 201) illustrating the find-spots of similar objects is still, for some archaeologists, a major aim. Interpreted carefully, such maps can indeed yield significant information. A map may show very clearly the major centre of production of a particular object: outlying dots may indicate the spread of these objects from that central area, by trade, exchange, migration or other means. But in the main such maps show the distribution of objects which have been found in cemeteries and then been preserved in museums or published. They may thus show the distribution of hyperactive nineteenth-century archaeologists (some of whom could pillage dozens of graves a day), or of well-organized local archaeological societies or museums. More significantly, they may show the distribution of particular burial customs. If a distribution map appears to show that a particular fifth-century clothes fastening was restricted to northern Gaul, it does not prove that that was the main area of its manufacture or use: it was not the custom in southern Gaul in the fifth century to bury the dead fully dressed.

The archaeologist, like the historian, is primarily interested in studying development through time. He needs to establish some sort of chronology for the objects which he is studying. He might be able to establish a *relative* chronology, in which certain objects are established as older than others, by working out a typology, that is, a history of the development of a particular type of object, from more primitive and simple to more developed and complex (or, sometimes, from more primitive and complex to more developed and simple). But to establish an *absolute* chronology he needs actual dates, which are very rare: the grave which established the study of Frankish archaeology in 1653, the grave of Childeric I (d. 481/2), is still the only one which provides a certain and absolute date. Increasingly, however, archaeologists can date graves in which fragments of wood survive, by analyzing the tree-rings. With luck (in particular, with the survival of the tree-rings nearest the bark) the year in which the tree was felled can be pinpointed. We cannot, of course, be sure that the wood was not stored for some time, or used in another context before being buried. Some graves contain coins, which, particularly if they are Roman imperial coins, can be dated fairly precisely. A coin, like a piece of wood, can provide a *terminus post quem*, a date after which the burial must have taken place. (This is not necessarily very helpful. Childeric's own grave contained a coin of Alexander the Great, and we do not need proof that Childeric's burial took place after 323 BC!)

Fundamental to the gradual working out of a chronology for Frankish grave-goods was Joachim Werner's *Münzdatierte Austrasische Grabfunde* (1935), a study of those graves in Austrasia, the eastern part of the Frankish kingdom, which contained a relevant and datable coin and which were also recorded well enough that all the contents of the grave were known. The next milestone was Kurt Böhner's *Die fränkische Altertümer des Trierer Landes* (1958), in which he worked out a chronology for the grave-goods found in the Merovingian cemeteries in the region of Trier. Böhner studied only those graves which contained two or more types of objects. Each of these sets of grave-goods he regarded as a contemporary assemblage; by comparing assemblages he was able to put them into some kind of relative order, to work out when different types of object appeared on or vanished from the scene, and eventually to suggest a scheme of succeeding phases or *Stufe*, to which (with the help of only a very few coin-dated graves) he assigned absolute dates (see plate 6). Böhner's chronology received some criticism (notably from Werner), and has been refined by scholars such as Hermann Ament, but it is still widely used as a basis for an absolute chronology of Merovingian-period graves – despite the warnings of Böhner himself of the dangers of applying it uncritically outside the Rhineland area. Patrick Périn's *La Datation des Tombes Mérovingiennes* (1980), the most recent and exhaustive study of the methodological problems of dating, largely confirms the accuracy of Böhner's framework, while suggesting ways of refining it and generalizing it still further.

Recent investigations of chronology, such as Périn's, have used computer techniques to bring more precision to Böhner's methods of comparing assemblages, in order to establish relative chronologies within individual cemeteries. Computer techniques are, of course, best attempted with cemeteries which have been dug in their entirety and recorded properly, in modern times, and in cemeteries which have not suffered deliberate pillaging or unintentional damage: there are not many cemeteries which fulfil both these conditions. Numerous cemeteries are known from which most of the grave-goods were pillaged within a generation or so of the deaths of the individuals: it has been suggested that this was no illicit

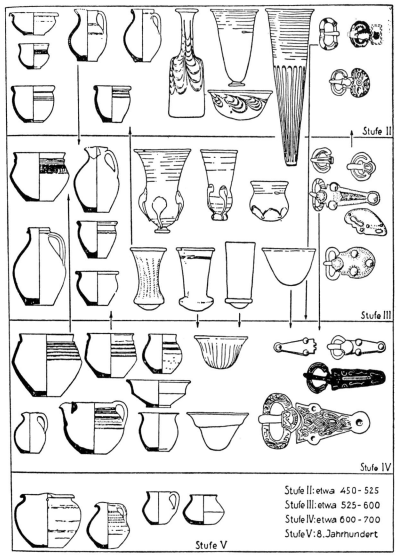

Plate 6 Kurt Böhner's four Merovingian Stufe (periods) seen in terms of the development of pottery, glass and buckles. II: c. 450–525; III: c. 525–600; IV: c. 600–700; V: 8th century.

pillaging, but the socially acceptable recovery by relatives of the objects which they themselves had employed in the funerary ritual. The study of grave-robbing is interesting in its own right,

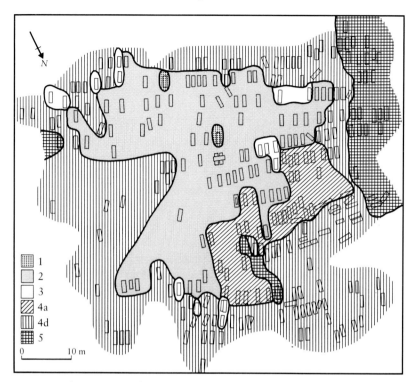

*Figure 3 The cemetery of Mazerny (Ardennes), illustrating its development: 1.
c. 525; 2. c. 525–c. 600; 3. c. 580–620; 4. c. 600–c. 650; 5. c. 650–c. 700.*

but robbed cemeteries do not usually provide sufficient evidence
for full-scale analysis. If there is enough data for the computer
to work on, however, very useful results can be obtained.
Confirmation of the computer analysis may perhaps be found
by looking at the stratigraphy, that is, by studying which graves
were overlaid by other, later, graves, or, more probably, by
studying the 'horizontal stratigraphy' of the cemetery, that is, by
looking at the ways in which site developed during its
generations of use. As is seen in figure 3, the earliest
archaeological material is usually found in the central core of
the cemetery, with graves being added concentrically around the
core over the ensuing generations of use, so that the most recent
material is on the periphery. Establishing a chronology is, of
course, only a means to an end. Once a clear view of the
chronological development of the cemetery has been gained,

then a history of the changing material culture of the community to which the cemetery belonged can be attempted. A formula can be used to calculate the likely size of that community at any one time, if the cemetery size and duration are known; if the skeletons survive to be studied, some assessment of the average life-span of men and women could be reached, and, indeed, something of the diseases from which they suffered.

In an ideal world we might hope to investigate not only the cemetery, but also the buildings in which the community lived, and even the fields in which they worked. So far this has not been possible. Settlement sites have been excavated, although in small numbers compared to the thousands of known cemetery sites. They are not so easy to recognize as cemeteries, and demand more of the excavators; moreover, many of them are largely inaccessible, lying as they do under modern villages or towns. So far, wherever settlement sites have been excavated, their associated cemetery (or cemeteries) has not been excavated as well. It would be very instructive to be able to compare the results of the investigation of these two different survivals of a community. To reconstruct the material culture of a community from how that community chooses to dispose of and honour the dead is inevitably a chancy business: a cemetery may be a very poor reflector of a particular community's economy, social structure and life-style. The excavation of a settlement site, while perhaps providing evidence which is unlikely to be found in a cemetery, such as evidence of diet, may provide few clues to, for instance, the relative wealth of the members of the community. Clearly the ideal, as yet unattained, would be an excavation to reveal as many facets of the same community as possible, in life as well as in death; here, perhaps, is the greatest challenge facing the Frankish archaeologist.

Linguistic evidence

We have looked at some of the problems of the historian and the archaeologist. The third specialist who can study the Franks is the philologist, who can look at the Frankish language and the way in which it spread in the period of the invasions, as well as studying the Franks through their personal names and the place-names which appear to be associated with them. Philologists too are dependent on their sources, which may well be in the very same documents that historians are studying. In studying place-names, for instance, it is dangerous to proceed from the modern forms and spellings of place-names, which may successfully conceal the original form and hence the vital clues as to the date of the formation of the word; the philologist needs to look for the earliest occurrence of the word in the historical sources. Just as the earliest surviving manuscript of an historical text may date from several centuries after the death of the author, so the earliest written record of a place-name is seldom chronologically very close to its formation.

Place-names are therefore almost never very closely datable, even though a broad chronological time-span might be suggested. As an example we may take one of the very commonest forms of French place-name ending, that derived from the Latin *-iacus* or *-iniacus*. Place-names with this suffix normally have a prefix derived from a Roman personal name: the original must have meant 'the estate, or farm, of so-and-so'. The modern form varies according to the different regional evolutions of Latin into modern Romance dialects, as can be seen in figure 4. Thus *Conniacus*, the estate of Connius, becomes Cognac in southwest France, Cogny in central France, and Coigny in the north. But we cannot assume that all these place-names with *-iacus* go back into the Roman period, because some at least are formed by adding that suffix to a Frankish personal name e.g. Landouzy (Aisne) from *Landwald* + *iacus*, or Busigny (Nord) from *Boso* + *iniacus*. (There is often room for doubt, however. Is Attigny (Ardennes), for instance, formed with the Germanic Hatto or the Roman Attius?) That place-name formations using a Frankish personal name are more common in the north-east, the main area of Frankish settlement, does not necessarily show that the men thus commemorated were all Franks, for it became fashionable among Romans in northern Gaul to take Frankish names. But it does show us that place-names were still being formed according to Roman habits in the Frankish period. Other Latin place-name elements became much more common in the Frankish period, however; the majority of French place-names formed with *-ville* and *-court* (Latin *villa* and *curtis*, both meaning 'estate' or 'farm') contain personal names

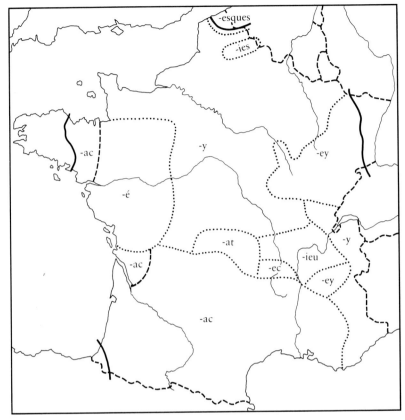

Figure 4 *Place-name endings derived from Gallo-Roman estate-names ending in -*acum *and -*iacum. *The thick lines exclude those areas of modern France where the main language is not derived from Latin.*

of Germanic origin, like Charleville (from Karl or Carolus), Thionville (from Theudo) or Aboncourt (from Abbo), all three from the département of Moselle. Sometimes it is likely that these new names are renamings of estates which had existed in the Roman period; in other cases they may indicate new settlements, made perhaps in newly cleared forests. Examining the patterning of place-names of different periods in an individual area may give valuable clues as its settlement history.

One major cause of the changing character of place-names in Frankish Gaul was the arrival of a new selection of personal names, which rapidly took over from the Roman ones in northern Gaul. These Frankish names predominated there until later in the Middle Ages, when the custom of naming children after saints became dominant. The characteristic Frankish name consisted of two elements, each with a meaning of its own: thus Sigebert = Shining (*-berht*) Victory (*Sige-*) or Childeric = Powerful (*-ric*) in Battle (*Childe-*). Common name-endings for men were *-bald* (bold), *-frid* (peace), *-wald* (command) and *-wulf* (wolf), while women's names might end in *-berga* (protection), *-rada* (counsel), and *-gund* or *-hild* (both meaning 'battle'). These particles could however just as easily be found at the beginnings of names, and seem to have been used quite arbitrarily. Thus, the ninth-century Frankish historian Nithard had a brother Hartnit; and one wonders whether anyone paid much attention to the paradoxical meaning of Queen Fredegund's name (= peace-battle). A number of the early Frankish personal names began in gutturals which were later lost, thus making unfamiliar names appear much more familiar. Thus *Chlodowechus* (in royal names generally modernized as 'Clovis') was, by the ninth century, pronounced and written *Lodowechus* = Lodovic, Fr. Louis; Charibert became Herbert; and so on. As with later English, a number of these compound names had well-known hypocorisms, or shortened forms; thus men whose names began with *Berht-* were often called Berto or Betto; Bernhardus (Bernard) was often shortened to Benno. It is clear that the coming of the Franks into the former Roman Empire made many Romans familiar with these name-giving habits even if they remained quite ignorant of the Frankish language.

The language itself was a west Germanic dialect, distinct from Gothic (East Germanic) or Old Norse (North Germanic). During the early Middle Ages the language frontier between Latin and Frankish moved westwards, indeed, much further west than the modern language frontier in Belgium: the partial recovery of Romance (i.e. a Latin-derived language) at the expense of the Germanic gains was a phenomenon of the central and later Middle Ages. It may be that the frontier between the Germanic-speaking Flemings and the Romance-speaking Walloons (a Frankish word meaning the same as the English word 'Welsh'), which still causes bitterness and division in Belgium today, is the most obvious modern result of the Frankish invasions; as we shall see, however (p. 118), this is a matter of debate among scholars. But clearly the Frankish conquests in Gaul brought about a period of linguistic change, both for Gallo-Romans and for the Franks themselves. Some of the latter must have become Romance-speaking; others, particularly perhaps kings and aristocrats, must have remained bilingual. (It has been suggested that the first king of France to speak only Romance (French) was Hugh Capet, who came to the throne in 987.)

Through those bilinguals, perhaps, came many of the Frankish words which have entered the French language. These words themselves tell us something about the nature of Frankish settlement, and the role adopted by the Franks within the former Roman Empire. They are associated above all with a few specific areas of life. Often they have English equivalents, either because of the similiarities between Old English and Frankish, or because they were introduced into English by the French-speaking Normans after 1066. Some are associated with government and court-life: names for figures like the marshal, the seneschal, the baron, the chamberlain, *échanson* (cup-bearer), and *échevin* (municipal magistrate). Others relate to the law: *plège* (pledge), *ordalie* (ordeal), *rachimbourg* (legal adviser), *fief*, *alleu* (allod: inherited property). As one might expect, French borrowings from Frankish also include words relating to warfare: *brogne* (byrnie, cuirass), *épieu* (pike), *étrier* (stirrup), *heaume* (helmet) (along with many other French words beginning with *h*), *fourreau* (scabbard), *flèche* (arrow), *garder* (to guard), and *guetter* (to lie in wait). Rather more surprising is the large number of words associated with agriculture and country-life, where Frankish words must have replaced Latin words in current use: *cresson* (cress), *haie* (hedge), *hêtre* (beech), *houblon* (hops), *houx* (holly), *osier* and *saule* (willow), *roseau* (reed), *troène* (privet) and *bouc* (billy-goat); *freux* (rook), *hanneton* (may-bug), *mésange* (tit), and *blé* (corn); *bois* (wood), *forêt* (forest), *fourrage* (fodder), *jardin* (garden), and *gerbe* (sheaf). Even words connected with the body: *échine* (spine), *flanc*, *fronce* (wrinkle), *hanche* (hip); with clothing: *feutre* (felt), *froc* (cowl, frock), *gant* (glove), *poche* (pocket); or with colours: *blanc*, *brun*, *bleu*, *gris*; came into French from Frankish. There is a similar phenomenon in English, where a number of very common words were introduced into English by the Scandinavian settlers of the Viking period. Numbers of newcomers do not have to be large to produce such linguistic innovations. But these innovations do give a hint as to the depth and importance of the Frankish impact on the inhabitants of Roman Gaul.

2

The Franks before Clovis

In the course of the Roman conquest of Gaul, in the second and first centuries BC, the Romans came into contact with the Germans for the first time. When the Gauls (or, as the Greeks called them, Celts) ceased to be a threat, and became loyal subjects of the Empire, the stereotypical barbarian in Roman eyes came to be a German rather than a Gaul. In the process some of the features of that stereotype – notably height, fierceness, blond hair, the warrior ethos – became associated with the new enemy as well. Indeed the two peoples were probably not so easily distinguishable; some of the Germans Julius Caesar met in the region of the Rhine may have been Gauls, and the very name *Germani* is itself a Celtic word. Few Teutonic-speaking 'Germans' could in fact be found further west than the river Elbe in Caesar's day. The Rhine did not form any kind of ethnic boundary, although, when it became obvious that the Empire was not going to expand further, it was useful politically to maintain that it was. The German barbarians were beyond the Rhine; the Romans, and civilization, were this side of it. Naturally that is to view it solely through Roman eyes. It is very difficult to do anything else. The first Germans to write about themselves did so centuries after the Roman Empire had disappeared from Europe – and even then they wrote in Latin, and preserved concepts of German 'barbarism' and Roman 'civilization'.

The Confederation of the Franks

The two Romans to write extensively about the Germans, Tacitus and Pliny, mention the names of many German tribes, but do not name the Franks at all. Franks appear first in the Roman sources in the middle of the third century, when they are among the Germans who are raiding across the Roman frontiers. A Roman marching-song joyfully celebrating the deaths of thousands of Franks, recorded in a fourth-century source, is associated with the 260s; but the Franks' first appearance in a contemporary source was in 289. The Franks were not the only new ethnic name to appear in those years; several of the groups who were to play an important part in the dismemberment of the Roman Empire in the fifth century first appear in the third. The raids, caused partly by political crisis within the Empire, must have brought about political changes and regroupings and even social upheaval beyond the Rhine too. *Franci*, a word probably meaning 'bold, fierce, courageous', was used to refer to various Germanic peoples living just north and east of the lower Rhine in what are now the Netherlands and the north-western part of West Germany (see figure 5). Different peoples may have belonged to the 'Frankish confederation', or were assumed by Romans to belong to it, at different times. The Chamavi were mentioned as a Frankish people as early as 289, the Bructeri from 307, the Chattuari from 306–15, the Salii or Salians from 357, and the Amsivarii and Tubantes from *c.* 364–75. The Chauci, neighbours of the Saxons, seem to have broken up under Saxon attack in the third century, and groups may have joined Frankish peoples such as the Salians. Other peoples like Herules and Frisians may from time to time have been counted as Franks too; indeed the Frisians of the northern coast of the Netherlands seem often to have been confused with the Franks. The Chamavi were the first mentioned, and, perhaps, the people around whom other Frankish peoples grouped. The Roman map known as the Peutinger Map has an inscription north of the Rhine: *Hamavi qui et Franci*, which could be translated 'the Chamavi who are also called Franks'. It is interesting that this group still preserved its own sense of identity within the Frankish people as late as

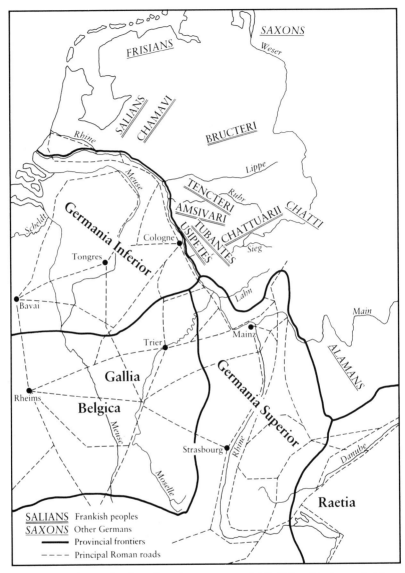

*Figure 5 The north Rhine frontier area around AD 300, with the probable
homelands of the various Frankish tribes.*

the ninth century, when they are given their own law code.
Their name survives in the area of *Hamaland*, between the
Lower Rhine and the Ijssel.

It has been suggested by Von Uslar that Franks can be identified archaeologically by the distribution of a certain type of pottery, labelled therefore 'proto-Frankish', which could be found in the second and third centuries AD in a triangle of territory formed by Nijmegen and Koblenz on the Rhine eastwards to beyond the Weser. Much more certain archaeologically is the impact the Franks made upon the north-west region of Roman Gaul in the third century. The large number of coin hoards deposited in the ground between the 250s and the 270s, and never recovered by their owners, is witness to the troubled times caused in large part by the raids of Franks and others. One of the worst attacks came in 274–75, when Franks and Alamans overran almost the whole country. Two hundred and thirty-eight coin-hoards in Gaul have been dated to the 270s, although we cannot know whether they are all connected with this one incursion. At one time it was almost traditional for archaeologists to date any destruction layer in their excavation to 275; this too is pure assumption.

Enough emerges from the historical sources to be certain that these raids, mostly by Franks and Alamans, were highly destructive and geographically quite wide-ranging. One source says that the Emperor Probus (276–82) had to restore 60 towns (out of the 115 or so in Gaul). Many Roman fortifications, inland as well as along the frontiers, date from this period. The attacks were not by land alone; Frankish ships raided the Channel coasts and penetrated into the heart of Gaul via the river systems – just as the Vikings were to do six centuries later – and, if we are to believe our sources, some Franks went much further than Gaul. Aurelius Victor says that 'Frankish bands, having sacked Gaul, occupied Spain, sacked Tarragona and took ships across to Africa'[3] – anticipating the journey of the Vandals nearly two centuries later. The Frankish pirate base in Africa lasted from *c.* 260 to 272. The extraordinary exploits of some of these Franks seem to have wrung unwilling admiration even from Romans. A Roman panegyric recalls what happened to some of the Franks deported to the East by the Emperor: it speaks of

---

[3] Aurelius Victor, *Liber de Caesaribus*, 33: ed F. Pichlmayr and R. Gründel (Leipzig, 1961).

the unbelievable audacity and unworthy success of a small group of Frankish prisoners who, under the divine Probus, left the Black Sea on ships they had captured, ravaged Greece and Asia, pillaged at almost every point on the Libyan coast, and finally took the town of Syracuse. . . and having accomplished their long voyage, they entered the Atlantic Ocean. . . proving by the success of their bold enterprise that no country is sheltered from the fury of pirates, whenever it is within reach of a ship.[4]

Franks in the Roman Empire

Postumus, the general who made himself Emperor in Gaul in 260 in order to restore the border and repel the attacks of Franks and other Germans, did so with the help of other Franks. The Emperor Maximian's admiral Carausius was in charge of defending northern Gaul and southern Britain against the Franks (and, according to later authors, the Saxons as well). He too seems to have come to an agreement with Franks, and it was with Frankish support that he managed to set himself up as Emperor in Britain. Both he and his successor in Britain, Allectus, used Frankish troops. This ambiguous relationship between Romans and Franks continued during the next two centuries, during which time they were by turns enemies and allies. This is no comment on the fickleness of the Franks (or Romans), for if it is true that the Franks were a recognized group of smaller tribes, it is equally true that at no time before the sixth century did they form a political unit. Different groups of Franks may well have been pursuing their own internal feuds and rivalries by taking pro- or anti-Roman positions; little or none of this appears explicitly in our sources, however.

Our main sources for the Franks in the late third and early fourth centuries are the panegyrics written in praise of Emperors such as Constantius Chlorus and his son Constantine. By the nature of these sources, any information we may glean from them is going to be problematical. Dangers are going to be exaggerated, so that victories may seem more glorious; we are going to hear more of victories than of defeats, and so on. We hear how Maximian defeated Frankish 'pirates' in 287, and

---

[4] Panegyric to Constantius Chlorus, 18.3, in *Panégyriques Latins*, ed E. Galletier (Paris, 1949), pp. 96–7.

forced the submission of the first known Frankish king, Gennobaudes. We hear of Constantius Chlorus settling defeated Franks within the Empire, in the *civitates* (city-territories) of Trier, Amiens, Langres and elsewhere, as *laeti* – that is, prisoners-of-war granted land in return for military service. Such settlements were made by several Emperors during the fourth century and they involved many barbarian peoples; the settlements occasionally leave traces in modern place-names, or in villages named in medieval documents, and the naming of whole areas after these groups (such as the Frankish groups commemorated by the territory-names of *pagus (Ch)Amavorum* and *pagus (Ch)Attuariorum* in Burgundy) may indicate quite large-scale settlements. (For the debate over whether these settlements can be recognized archaeologically, see below pp. 44–51.) The panegyric of Constantius Chlorus vaunts the benefits of these arrangements:

Under the porticoes of every city sit rows of barbarian prisoners. . . All of them, shared out among the inhabitants of your provinces in order to serve them, wait to be led to the deserted lands which they must restore to growth. . . Now it is for me that the Chamavian and the Frisian work. This vagabond and this pillager work ceaselessly to bring my land under cultivation. . . What is more, if they are called up into the army, they hurry to join, they are brought to heel by army discipline. . . and they congratulate themselves for having served us as a Roman soldier.[5]

Around 307 Constantine the Great attacked the Frankish tribe of the Bructeri, and built the fortress of Deutz, at the bridgehead over the Rhine from Cologne, 'in the land of the Franks' (see plate 7). He threw two Frankish princes, presumably Bructeri, called Ascaricus and Merogaisus, to the wild beasts in the arena at Trier. The heavy involvement of Franks in the Roman army probably began during Constantine's reign (306–37). We can get some idea of this involvement from the *Notitia Dignitatum* of the early fifth century, which itemizes the various sections of the Roman army; it lists several *cohortes* and *alae* of Franks, as well as detachments of Amsivarii, Bructeri, Chamavi, Chattuarii, Salii and Tubantes. There are Salii in Gaul and in Spain; there are detachments of Franks at Apollonos and Diospolis in Egypt, in Asia Minor and in Mesopotamia.

[5] Panegyric to Constantius Chlorus, 9.3, in *Panégyriques Latins* ed E. Galletier (Paris, 1949), p. 89.

Das römische "Kastell Deutz" um 310 n. Chr.

Plate 7 Reconstruction of Roman fort at Deutz, east of the Rhine from Cologne.

Plate 8 A gold coin of Constantine the Great, minted to celebrate a victory over a weeping Francia.

Frankish involvement in the Roman army was not only at the level of individual recruits or auxiliary regiments: some Franks reached high position. The usurper Magnentius (350–53) had joined the army as a *laetus* according to one source, and, according to another, was born in the *civitas* of Amiens as the son of a British father and a Frankish mother. He was proclaimed Emperor by part of the army in the West, but was defeated by the Eastern army of the Emperor Constantius II, after his Frankish general Silvanus deserted him on the battlefield. He committed suicide at Lyons in 353.

Silvanus himself had an almost equally ambitious and disastrous career. He was the son of Bonitus, who had distinguished himself in the campaign against Constantine's imperial rival Licinius; although Bonitus was a Frank, like Magnentius he took a Roman name. Silvanus followed him in a military career, became *magister militum* (Master of the

Soldiers, the senior military position under the Emperor) and successfully defended the imperial frontiers against his fellow-Franks. When he heard that the ever-suspicious Emperor Constantius suspected him of disloyalty (falsely, said the historian Ammianus Marcellinus), he allowed himself to be persuaded by officers in the Roman army, themselves of Frankish birth, to usurp the imperial throne. He reigned in 355, for 28 days. The next Roman Emperor of Frankish origins was to be Charlemagne, inaugurated in an equally illegitimate fashion in the year 800. Significantly, Silvanus's first impulse on hearing of the Emperor's suspicions had been to flee to the Franks living outside the Empire; one of his tribunes, another Frank, persuaded him that if he did so his fellow-Franks would either kill him or sell him back to the Empire. No story illustrates better the diverse experience of the Franks in the fourth century. But there is one text which nicely encapsulates the problem of identity faced by these Franks. It is an epitaph, which reads *Francus ego civis, Romanus miles in armis*: 'I am a Frankish citizen, and a Roman soldier under arms.'[6]

Silvanus was not the last, nor the most distinguished, of those Franks who served the Empire. There was Charietto, who fought his fellow Franks on the Rhine, and was appointed count of both the Germanies by Julian. The Frank Merobaudes served Julian on the Persian campaign of 363, was *magister peditum* (Master of the Infantry) in the West from 375 to 388, served as consul twice, in 377 and 382, and seems to have been appointed to the consulship for a third time, a great honour, shortly before his death. Another Merobaudes was *dux Aegypti*, commander of the army in Egypt. Bauto was *magister militum* in the West in the early 380s, and was appointed consul in 385 (the young St Augustine pronounced his panegyric), and effectively acted as regent to the young Valentinian II. After his death, his daughter Eudoxia married the Emperor Arcadius. That great tenth-century compiler of imperial ceremonial lore, the Emperor Constantine Porphyrogenitos, recalled that it was laid down in the fourth century, and inscribed on stone, that a Roman emperor could never marry a German, unless she was a Frank, because of their glory and prowess: a memory, perhaps, of this exceptional marriage.

[6] *Corpus Inscriptionum Latinum*, XIII no. 3576.

Richomer, the Frank who become consul in 384 and was the supreme military commander in the East from 388 to 393, may have been related to Bauto. The historian Ammianus Marcellinus delivered Richomer's panegyric in Constantinople at the beginning of his consulate, and spoke warmly of their friendship; it is possible that it was their paganism which united them, for the pagan orator Libanius, several of whose letters to Richomer survive, speaks of this bond he had with the Frankish general. In the West it was Richomer's nephew Arbogast who succeeded Bauto and acted as *magister militum* – thus briefly giving this one Frankish family immense influence in both halves of the Empire in the years on either side of 390. A fragment of a lost history by Sulpicius Alexander (preserved by Gregory of Tours, LH II. 9) claims that 'The Emperor Valentinian was shut up in his palace at Vienne, and almost reduced to the status of a private citizen; the control of the army was handed over to Franks, and civilian offices went to those in Arbogast's following.' In 392 Valentinian II eventually attempted to regain his freedom, and dismissed his Frankish general; Arbogast tore up the letter of dismissal in the Emperor's presence. Valentinian's death (murder or suicide?) took place after a suspiciously short interval; Arbogast then took it upon himself to proclaim a Roman, Eugenius, as Emperor. Both Eugenius and Arbogast were pagans, and their brief and ill-fated partnership was the last attempt by pagans to wrest control of the Empire from the Christians. Theodosius I sent the eastern army (its cavalry led by Richomer) against the West (led by Arbogast). However, the two Franks never met in battle to decide the leadership of the Roman Empire between them. Richomer died before the battle of Frigeridus in 394, and was replaced by another German, the Vandal Stilicho. In the battle Richomer's nephew Arbogast was defeated and killed. Not coincidentally, this battle also marks the end of the great period of Frankish influence within the Empire.

While these great figures dominate the stage, the history of the bulk of the Frankish people continues its obscure course. The Frankish nationality of these generals and consuls was, perhaps, almost an accident, and arguably quite without effect upon the Franks themselves. We may remember Silvanus, who was warned by his fellow Franks of the danger of returning to his homeland; it seems that they thought that Franks outside the Roman Empire would regard him as a turncoat. The only high-ranking Frank within the Roman army who seems to have returned to Francia was Mallobaudes. He was a general under Gratian, who later became *rex Francorum* – king of Franks beyond the Rhine – and led his people to victory against the Alamans in 378. We know nothing of how he got to be recognised as king of the Franks, nor how much Roman money it took to secure this recognition as a way of attacking the Alamans. For the most part the Frankish generals we meet in the Roman sources had probably largely adopted the culture and the outlook of their Roman colleagues. To them as well, perhaps, Franks living east of the Rhine were barbarians.

Frankish cemeteries in Roman Gaul?

There were, however, many Franks who lived west of the Rhine. Some of these were *laeti*, as we have seen, settled in various places in Gaul from the reign of Probus onwards. The *Notitia*

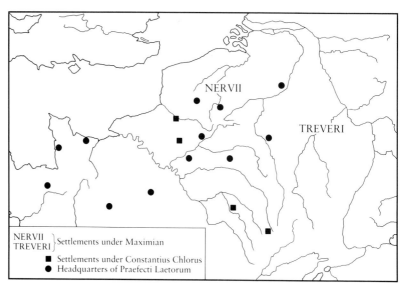

Figure 6 The historical evidence for the settlement of laeti *and for the headquarters of the Roman officials in charge of them.*

Dignitatum records where the dozen *praefecti laetorum* were stationed in northern Gaul *c.* 400. These prefects were the Roman military officials responsible for administering the *laeti* and their recruitment into the army (see figure 6). And scattered between the Rhine and the Loire are several dozen cemeteries which may represent the physical remains of these communities of *laeti*. The burials which they contain resemble those of contemporary Gallo-Romans in a number of ways. They are inhumation burials; inhumation had begun to replace cremation in northern Gaul from the early fourth century. The bodies are often buried together with vessels of pottery or glass of Roman manufacture. However, the male graves often contain weapons – spears, axes (including throwing axes), sometimes swords – as well as bronze fittings for belts and harness (see figure 7). There is nothing to suggest that any of these things were necessarily of Germanic manufacture, but the idea of burial with weapons was not customary among Romans (civilians could not carry arms, and Roman soldiers did not own their own weapons). Nor, indeed, was it common among Germans at this time, although the richest of German chiefs in

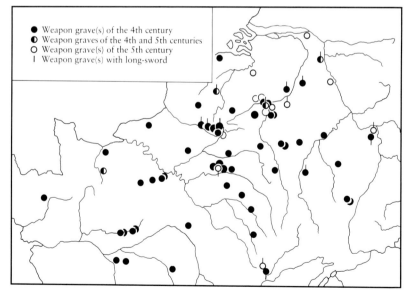

Figure 7 *Male burials with weapons from the period 300 to 450.*

the third century and later were often buried with their weapons and a great variety of vessels and other possessions. What makes these men's graves almost certainly Germanic is that they are found next to women's graves which are clearly not Gallo-Roman. These women's graves contain typically Germanic jewellery, notably tall conical bronze brooches (tutulus brooches), usually worn one on each shoulder and cross-bow brooches, often worn in pairs on the chest (see plate 9). These brooches are found, not only in these north Gallic burials but also, in quite large numbers, in cemeteries in a very restricted area, between the mouths of the Elbe and the Weser, in what is now Lower Saxony. It is clear that they are Germanic in manufacture, since both their prototypes and their more evolved forms are found in Saxony (and the later ones in Anglo-Saxon England) and not in Gaul. Furthermore, it is highly unlikely that they were imports, to be worn by Gallo-Roman women. They are often worn in precisely the same way in both Saxony and northern Gaul, the two brooches on the shoulder, sometimes connected by chains, and two other brooches on the chest: thus these women in northern Gaul are almost certainly wearing the same kind of clothes as the women in Saxony, fastened in the same fashion. There is a further link between these cemeteries in northern Gaul and those in Lower Saxony; some of the men's belt-fittings and other items of Roman manufacture have been found in Lower Saxony. These too could be items of trade, but are perhaps more likely to represent Germans returning to Germany after serving in the Roman army.

These belt-fittings and brooches range in date from *c.* 350 to *c.* 450, with the bulk of them from the last decades of the fourth century and beginning of the fifth. Distribution maps of these objects strongly suggests that northern Gaul had a scattered population of people coming from Lower Saxony. But distribution maps are notorious for being misleading in a variety of ways. These particular distribution maps only show the distribution of excavated graves in which these objects have been buried. The virtual blank in the distribution of most of these objects in the region between the Elbe and the Rhine, or beyond to the Somme, does not mean that the Germans in this region – mostly Franks – did not use these objects, or even make

Plate 9 Germanic-style brooches, including the tall conical tutulus brooches, from female grave no. 88 at Oudenburg (Belgium)

them; it simply means that they did not bury them with the dead. In fact the Franks in their homeland in the fourth century did not bury their dead dressed and equipped with weapons; this was a fashion they did not take up until the end of the fifth century. But it is not impossible that some or even most of these 'Germanic' graves in northern Gaul were the graves of Franks, who were frequently used by Romans in their armies. The one fact that might support this hypothesis is that these men's graves commonly contain throwing-axes. Later, in the sixth century, throwing-axes are only found in Frankish areas, and are regarded as peculiarly Frankish: indeed they come to have the name *francisca* for that reason. None have been found in the men's graves of Lower Saxony.

The question remains, do these graves contain the bodies of *laeti* and their families? This is one of the questions to which the researches of H.W. Böhme have been directed. He concluded first of all that these communities of Germans, with wives and dependents, are being used by the Romans for military purposes. Some of the Germanic graves are in Roman cemeteries outside Roman military camps, such as Vermand, Oudenburg on the Belgian coast, and Krefeld-Gellep on the Rhine. Some other smaller cemeteries, where the Germanic graves form a much higher percentage of the total burials, are associated with militarily strategic sites, such as Furfooz, by a fortified spur in the Ardennes: here 70 per cent of the men's graves contain weapons, and there are very few women, which suggests a military post.

Lemant and others have recently studied one of these cemeteries, Vireux-Molhain (Meuse); we can get some idea of the history of one of these Frankish communities in northern Gaul. Vireux-Wallerand is the modern name of a Gallo-Roman *vicus* or village on the right bank of the Meuse. After the Frankish raids of the 260s, these Romans fortified a spur on the opposite bank of the Meuse, in the modern commune of Vireux-Molhain. The fortification was a simple one, and seems to have been used only sporadically until around 350. Then it was refortified, by a rampart of dressed stone one metre thick. The nearby cemetery reveals the same burial customs that have been identified as Germanic. There are some 50 or 60 tombs, dating from the period *c.* 375 to *c.* 425, representing 25 or so men and women per generation. If this represents the garrison it was clearly a small one; perhaps other temporary members of the garrison were buried elsewhere. Like Furfooz the cemetery, and hence presumably the garrison came to an end before the middle of the fifth century.

Another recently-studied example is Vron (Somme), excavated by Claude Seillier. This appears to have belonged to a settlement of Germans, which began around 370–375. Vron is north of the Somme, very close to the Channel coast; Seillier associates it with Valentinian I's reorganization of the Saxon Shore, the defensive system designed to protect Gaul from Saxon pirates. Unlike Vireux-Molhain, this cemetery continues beyond 450, although there are some changes at that time; a displacement of the site of the cemetery, and a slight impoverishment of the grave-goods. A significant number of Anglo-Saxon objects remind us that it was not only Franks who settled in that part of Roman Gaul in the fifth century. There is neverthless between the late fourth and early sixth centuries a gradual evolution in terms of burial customs and material culture, so that by the early sixth century it has the appearance of a typical Frankish cemetery. Vron is one of the best examples of that relatively rare commodity: a site displaying continuity between the Roman and Frankish periods. Other examples are Samson and Haillot, both in the region of Namur.

Not all of these cemeteries can be associated with specifically military sites. Others, such as Abbeville-Homblières, are rural settlements, associated with Roman villas, and containing a few Germanic-style burials with rich grave-goods and a high proportion of burials without grave-goods. Abbeville-Homblières has four children's graves with a variety of grave-goods; one boy about seven years old was equipped with an axe. Böhme suggests that such settlements were small villas still farmed by Roman tenants but under Germanic proprietorship. One can compare this with the cemetery outside Vermand, with its 429 graves. The Germanic-style graves here were scattered all over the cemetery, and formed perhaps as much as 20 per cent of the total. These Germans can hardly have been a subordinate group within this small town; their grave-goods are often rich, including objects in gold and silver. The chief whose grave was found, with his elaborately

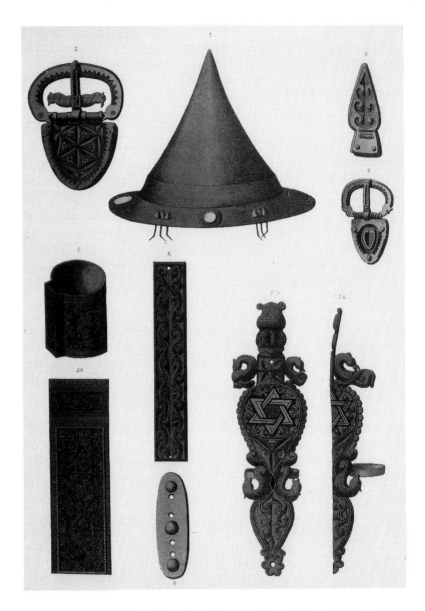

Plate 10 The shield-boss, buckles and silver-gilt spear-fittings of the Germanic chief buried at Vermand.

decorated belt-fitting and spear-ornament (see plate 10) must have been an important figure within the local community. The social position of these Germans suggested by such cemeteries as Abbeville-Homblières and Vermand makes it unlikely that the Germans we are dealing with are *laeti*, prisoners-of-war, or descendants of prisoners-of-war, under Roman authority. They were surely free soldiers fighting in or alongside the Roman army, who had come into northern Gaul with their families: what Romans called *foederati*, *dedicitii*, *gentiles*, among other terms. Some of these cemeteries seem to have been continuously used from the late fourth through to the early sixth century and beyond: these Franco-Roman settlements survived to be incorporated into the new kingdom of France. The presence of Germanic, perhaps largely Frankish, communities within northern Gaul already by the fourth century is an important fact, particularly when we consider that archaeologically, in terms of burial customs and material culture, they prefigure the Merovingian culture which was to emerge in northern Gaul around AD 500, neither German nor Roman but a mixed culture: in Böhme's phrase, a 'gallisch-germanische Mischzivilisation'.

The Franks from 350 to 450

Except for a brief Frankish incursion into the Empire during a squabble between two Emperors in 341, there seems to have been quite a lengthy peace on the frontier after the 320 campaign. The Franks took part in a large scale incursion of Germanic groups in 350, however, and it was not until 356, it seems, that the area around Cologne was recovered by the Emperor Constantius's nephew Julian. In 357 and 358 Julian campaigned against the Quadi, Chamavi, Chattuari and Salii, all Frankish tribes. Peace was made with the Salii, the Salians, who were given land within the Empire on which to settle: Toxandria, probably an area just west of the mouths of the Rhine. The Salians, who were later to take over the leadership of the Franks, settled down within the Roman Empire, and remained there in obscurity and hence, presumably, at peace, until the mid-fifth century. Small-scale, but bloody, campaigns against the other groups continued for several years, mostly conducted by the German general Charietto (a Salian?) acting together with some Salians in Julian's name. Peace was made, but only after a large fleet had been sent from Britain to intimidate these other Frankish groups. Julian concluded his campaign by fortifying and refortifying, and the peace which followed suggests how successful he had been. He was then ordered by his uncle Constantius to bring his élite troops to the East. Neither Gallo-Romans nor Franks wanted to leave Gaul to the mercy of the Alamans, and in protest they acclaimed Julian Emperor, and raised him on a shield, a Germanic custom which was soon to become part of imperial ceremonial. Julian did leave Gaul with some of his Frankish troops, to win the whole Empire from Constantius. The Franks insisted on bringing their families with them, and most of them may have stayed. The *Notitia Dignitatum* records detachments of *Galli* in the East, but their symbol in the illustrations to the text of the *Notitia* suggests that in reality they were Franks: it was the *securis*, the *francisca* or throwing-axe, the Frankish weapon *par excellence*.

It was nearly 20 years before the next (recorded) hostilities took place. This time our informant is Sulpicius Alexander, fragments of whose lost History are preserved in the *Histories* of Gregory of Tours. Gregory is a little puzzled that the Franks do not seem to have kings; instead there are *duces*, or 'leaders', named as Gennobaudes, Marcomer and Sunno. The latter led the Franks westwards across the frontier, where they ravaged and killed. The Romans slaughtered many in the *Silva Carbonaria* (a forest in eastern Belgium), and then argued over the best course of action. One Roman general decided it was futile to attack the Franks in their homeland; another, Quintinus, crossed the Rhine, and lost almost his entire army in the forests and marshes east of Neuss. Later, according to Sulpicius Alexander, Arbogast, a Frankish general in the Roman army (see p. 43 above) urged the Emperor to punish the Franks – *gentilibus odiis insectans*, perhaps to be translated as 'urged on by tribal hatreds'. Arbogast had talks with Marcomer and Sunno, the *regales* (royal leaders?) of the Franks, and, the following winter, led an army against these *subreguli* (sub-kings); he crossed the Rhine and 'laid waste the land nearest to the bank, where the Bructeri lived, and the region occupied by

Plate 11 Excavating one of the eleven Roman naval ships found at the site of the Mainz Hilton.

the Chamavi. He did this without meeting any opposition, except that a few Amsivarii and Chatti showed themselves on the far-distant ridges of the hills, with Marcomer as their *dux*, or warleader'. Finally, losing all patience with Sulpicius Alexander's constantly changing words for the Frankish leaders, Gregory of Tours goes on to say that Sulpicius reported a treaty between Eugenius and the *reges* or kings of the Alamanni and the Franks, but omitted to record their names. These are our first clues to the internal political life of the Franks: valuable but inconclusive. In *c.* 395 a new treaty was made with the Frankish leaders; Marcomer later contravened this treaty and was captured, tried in Milan and exiled to Etruria. Sunno took his place briefly, but was killed by his own people, or so says the poet Claudian; perhaps he was the leader of one group of Franks, murdered by the group who had been led by Marcomer when he tried to usurp Marcomer's position.

What happened to the Franks in the early fifth century is still more obscure. They do not seem to have played a role in the great invasion across the Rhine frontier in 406–07, after which the Vandals, Alans and Sueves all reached Spain, and the former founded a kingdom in North Africa. The administrative capital of Gaul was moved from Trier, near the Frankish homeland, to Arles in the far south, and what was left of the frontier troops were joined to the field armies. There are reports of conflicts with the Franks in 413, 420 and 428. Indeed Franks are recorded as successfully fighting against the Vandals, on the side of the Romans, and groups of Franks are to be found as Roman allies throughout the last years of the Empire in Gaul. Events in Gaul in the first decade and a half of the century are confusing in the extreme; various Roman usurpers used different groups of barbarians against legitimate authorities, and those fighting for the legitimate Emperors also used barbarian support. At times it must have been as difficult for the barbarians involved to have known whether they were fighting 'for' or 'against' the Empire as it is for modern historians.

The barbarian invasions of 406–07 caused a major crisis for the Roman authorities; that crisis in turn inspired a number of attempts by Roman generals to gain the imperial throne, and gave an opportunity for rebellion and social disturbance which affected wide areas of western Gaul. Some of these problems were resolved in the course of the second decade of the fifth century. The barbarian problem was partially solved, at least as far as Gallo-Romans were concerned, by the migration of the Vandals and others into Spain. Local revolts were crushed, and imperial authority reasserted. The Visigoths were settled in south-west Gaul in 418, and the Burgundians in south-east Gaul in 443, under the terms of a treaty or *foedus*, which involved a settlement of the people, under their king, in return for military service. The precise conditions of the *foedus* are unclear; it is a matter for debate (and has been for well over a century) whether the *foederati*, the Visigothic and the Burgundian federates, were actually given land (and if so whether they settled on it or lived from rents), or whether instead, as Walter Goffart argues, the Roman government ceded them the right to collect taxation. The two peoples certainly abided by the spirit of their treaty, the Visigoths, for instance, fighting at Rome's request against the Vandals in Spain; but inevitably such action resulted in an extension of the power and influence of the Germanic settlers. They began to act more and more as political authorities in their own right, and increasingly Romans in Gaul began to look to them rather than the Roman authorities for protection and employment. The vindication of Roman policy can however be seen in 451, when Gaul had to face the invasion by Attila and his Huns. The Burgundians and the Visigoths both fought on Rome's side and contributed crucially to Attila's defeat in the battle of the Catalaunian Fields.

The Roman general largely responsible for Roman policy in the two decades leading up to this battle was Aëtius. He maintained the alliance with the Visigoths, destroyed the Rhine kingdom of the Burgundians in 437 (with the help of his Hunnic allies) and re-established the Burgundians, in 443, in the area of Geneva. In 446 he became consul for the third time, an event celebrated in a panegyric by Flavius Merobaudes. Merobaudes was a Roman soldier turned orator, brought up in Spain, but very probably a descendant of the Frankish general Merobaudes mentioned above (p. 42). His panegyric is even vaguer than its fourth-century predecessors, but the remark that 'the Rhine has bestowed pacts making the wintry world Rome's servant, and, content to be guided by western reins, rejoices that the Tiber's domain swells for it from both banks'[7] *might* refer to campaigns

[7] Panegyric II, translated in F. M. Clover, 'Flavius Merobaudes: a Translation and Historical Commentary', *Trans. American Philosophical Soc.* **61** (i) 1971, p. 13.

against Franks as well as Burgundians. If so, it probably relates to the tribes of Franks settled on the middle Rhine, rather than to those living west of the lower Rhine, the Salians. Perhaps Aëtius campaigned against the Franks who had sacked Trier *c.* 440. This sacking was described by Salvian, a priest who wrote not long after, from a safe refuge in Marseilles: 'There lay all about the torn and naked bodies of both sexes, a sight that I myself endured. These were a pollution to the eyes of the city, as they lay there lacerated by birds and dogs. The stench of the dead brought pestilence on the living; death breathed out death.'[8] What was the response of those men of rank who had survived this disaster, asked Salvian? They demanded circuses from the Emperors. By *c.* 445 Aëtius appears to be minting coins in Trier once more; that could be in celebration of the victory implied by Merobaudes's panegyric. But Merobaudes also refers to treaties concluded between Aëtius and the Rhineland Franks. It is possible that there was an agreement whereby these Franks were entrusted with the defence of the middle Rhine.

There is support for the idea that Rhineland Franks became Roman federates from one of the most celebrated of Frankish excavations, at Krefeld-Gellep. Gellep is a village now forming part of the town of Krefeld, on the Rhine north of Cologne; once it was the Roman fort of Gelduba, part of the defensive system on the Rhine frontier. Excavations began in the cemetery here in 1934, and still continue, now under the directorship of Renate Pirling, over 5000 graves later. First used in the early Roman period, the cemetery (and hence presumably the settlement/garrison) began to expand from the early fourth century. Many of the dead were buried with pottery vessels, which is common in Roman graves, and three with weapons, which is not. Around the middle of the fourth century the graves take on a new orientation: they are aligned west-east, rather than south-north, and at the same time the grave-goods almost, but not quite, disappear. The fact that some grave-goods are still buried with the dead enables the areas of the cemetery used in the late fourth and fifth centuries to be identified; in many other places in northern Gaul the custom of burying grave-

[8] Salvian, *On the Governance of God* VI.15, translated by E. M. Sanford (New York, 1930), p. 183.

goods disappears altogether, which makes identification of late Roman graves almost impossible. Among these late Roman graves at Krefeld-Gellep are a number of weapon-graves side by side with women's graves containing Germanic-style jewellery (cf. p. 46). These seem to appear first of all in the period after 425, with the richest of them, grave 43, being datable to around 450. These types of graves in the fourth century have been associated, as we have seen, with Frankish federates; it is tempting to see this as evidence for this part of the Rhine defenses being entrusted to Franks. This may have been the origin of the Rhineland Frankish kingdom with its capital at Cologne, which was to be a dangerous rival of the Salian Frankish kings.

Around 450, the Salian Franks attacked the *civitas* of Arras, and Aëtius fought them at a place called *Vicus Helena*. Sidonius Apollinaris informs us of his great victory in the panegyric for the Emperor Majorian, which also allows us to conclude it was only a minor skirmish. The Roman army in fact broke up a Frankish wedding party, where:

amid Scythian [i.e. barbarian] dance and chorus a yellow-haired bridegroom was wedding a young bride of like colouring. . . the enemy was forced to flee. Then might be seen the jumbled adornments of the nuptials gleaming red in the waggons, and captured salvers and viands flung together pell-mell and servants crowned with fragrant garlands carrying wine-bowls on their oily top-knots. (Carm. V. 219–29)

This passage also provides our earliest physical description of the Franks, whom Sidonius compares poetically to the monsters defeated by the Centaurs:

for this youth likewise subdues monsters, on the crown of whose pates lies the hair that has been drawn toward the front, while the neck, exposed by the loss of its covering, shows bright. Their eyes are faint and pale, with a glimmer of greyish blue. Their faces are shaven all round, and instead of beards they have thin moustaches which they run through with a comb. Close-fitting garments confine the long limbs of the men; they are drawn up high so as to expose the knees, and a broad belt supports their narrow waist. It is their sport to send axes hurtling through the vast void, and know beforehand where the blow will fall, to whirl their shields, to outstrip with leaps and bounds the spears they have hurled, and reach the enemy first. Even in boyhood's years the love of fighting is full-grown. (Carm. V. 237–50)

According to Sidonius, the Franks who seized the *civitas* of Arras were led by Cloio, whom Gregory of Tours calls Chlogio. He is the only known ruler of the Franks in the mid-fifth century. Gregory reported that 'some people say' he was the ancestor of Merovech and the Merovingian family who later monopolized royal power in Gaul, and adds that he lived at *Dispargum. . .in terminum Thuringorum*, 'in the land of the Thuringians' (a non-Frankish but German people beyond the Rhine); it has been suggested that it is much more likely this originally read *in terminum Tungrorum*, 'in the *civitas* of Tongres' (in modern Belgium). Gregory also says that Chlogio captured Cambrai (near Tongres) and then 'occupied the country up to the Somme'. There is no evidence that this occupation was ever given up. The next we hear of any Franks they appear to be on good terms with Aëtius: a Frankish king died (we do not know of which Frankish tribe he was king) and Aëtius supported the claims of the younger son, who was then in Rome on an embassy. The Roman general adopted him as his son, and sent him back loaded with gifts. It was a typical piece of Roman policy towards the barbarians, and it may have borne fruit in 451, when the Huns invaded. In that battle Salians fought on Aëtius's side; characteristically, it seems, some Rhineland Franks also fought on Rome's side, while others, named as Bructeri, on Attila's. Aëtius himself was assassinated three years later, on the orders of Valentinian III. In 455 two of Aëtius' loyal (Germanic?) bodyguards killed Valentinian in revenge. It was the end of the Theodosian dynasty that had ruled in the West for over half a century, and the end of stable imperial rule. In the next half-century the Franks would seize their opportunity to replace the Romans in Gaul altogether.

King Childeric's Grave

Gregory alone gives us details of the reigns of the two great Frankish kings who dominate the later fifth century, Childeric and Clovis. Like any historian, he was at the mercy of his interests, his preconceptions, his prejudices, and, above all, his sources of information. In the late twentieth century we do have rather more information about what was happening in the fifth

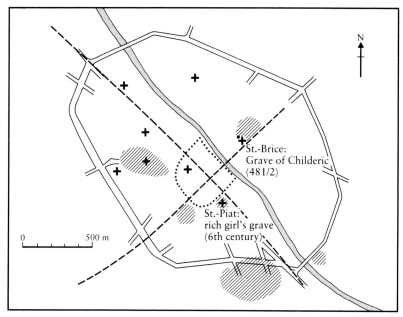

Figure 8 Tournai in the late Roman period. The dotted line indicates the walls of the Roman town; the shaded areas the Roman and Frankish cemeteries.

century than Gregory did, and so it is really no longer necessary to view these two kings entirely through Gregory's eyes.

There is no better way to begin an evaluation of Childeric than with a brief account of the event which put him on the scholarly map: the discovery in 1653 of his grave, in the Belgian town of Tournai, just north of the River Scheldt (see figure 8). Not the least remarkable thing about the find was the speed and great thoroughness of the publication of the treasure: *Anastasis Childerici Primi*, 'The Resurrection of Childeric I', by Jacques Chifflet, which appeared in 1655. It was the first grave of early medieval date to be recognized as such and published; it remains the only early medieval grave on the Continent which can be dated by reference to historical sources to within a year or two. Chifflet's publication was not perfect, of course, partly because he himself did not arrive at the graveside immediately; he was dependent on the accounts of those who had been present when the discovery was made – by a deaf-mute stone mason called Adrien Quinquin. It is almost certain that some of

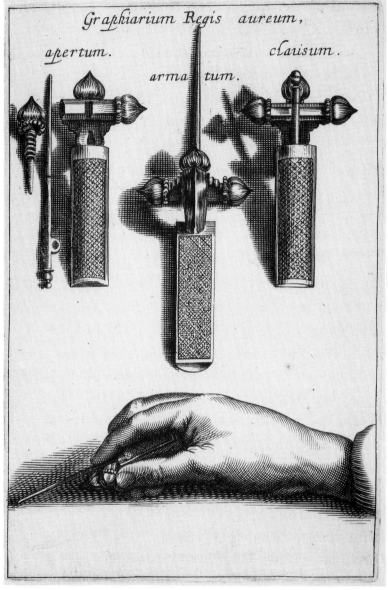

Plate 12 *The gold fibula of Roman type found in Childeric's burial, and Chifflet's idea of how it may have been used — as a stylus.*

the objects whose engravings he published were not found in the grave of the Frankish king, but in nearby and perhaps associated graves. Thus the crystal ball, found otherwise only in female graves, probably came from a relatively humble, and somewhat more recent, grave nearby. It is also very likely that some objects were pilfered from the royal grave before ducal officials arrived on the scene.

Despite the problems, we can see in Chifflet's drawings a fairly coherent assemblage of material not at all out of place in a wealthy late fifth-century grave. There are gold-and-garnet belt and equipment fittings; gold buckles and a gold arm-ring, as found in numerous wealthy Germanic graves of the Roman and early medieval period; a brooch of the type worn on the right shoulder by high Roman officials, which Chifflet mistook for a writing-stylus (see plate 12); a Frankish throwing-axe, or *francisca*; the fittings for a sword or scramasax (a single-edged sword); the famous gold bees which Napoleon took to be a symbol of French royalty, and which led him to wear a cloak bejewelled with such bees at his imperial coronation. (They may, in fact, together with the golden bull's head, have decorated the harness of Childeric's horse, a fact which would have amused many Europeans in 1804, had they known.) There were also coins in the grave, and, finally, the crucial find, Childeric's seal-ring, with its inscription CHILDERICI REGIS ('belonging to King Childeric'), and its portrayal of the long-haired king wearing Roman-style military dress and bearing a lance. The whole concept of a seal-ring, of course, implying the use of written documents, is Roman rather than Frankish. The seal-ring does not make the identification of the grave with Childeric absolutely certain, but it does make it highly likely.

On the night of the 5th/6th of November 1831, a thief broke into the Cabinet des Médailles, and so very little of Childeric's treasure survives today. The French police sent a diving bell into the Seine and recovered the small portion of the gold treasure which had not been melted down: a gold buckle; some of the gold bees; and portions of the gold-and-garnet fittings of the sword and scabbard. The ring can be reconstructed with the aid of a plaster impression made before 1831 (see plate 13).

More light has been thrown onto the grave in recent years, by

Plate 13 A reconstruction of the gold seal-ring which identified Childeric's tomb.

artefact research and by further excavation in Tournai. The polychrome fashion in gold-and-garnet jewellery was once thought to have come to the West from the Black Sea area, thanks to the migrations of the Goths, Alans and Huns, but now archaeologists are beginning to see that it originated in Pannonia, in the heart of Attila's Hunnic Empire, in the early part of the fifth century. In the second half of the fifth century it became virtually an international aristocratic style among the barbarian peoples, a style which spread, perhaps, because of the close connections between many Germanic leaders within the Roman army. The rich tomb of Pouan (Aube) was once thought to have yielded the earliest examples of this style in the West; it was even suggested that the tomb of Pouan was that of the Visigothic king Theodoric I, who died in the great battle against Attila in 451. Recent researches, such as those of Michel Kazanski, incline to the view that Pouan and Tournai are virtually contemporary. The jewellery of Tournai, however exotic it may have looked in Gaul in the later fifth century, may indeed have been made there, though perhaps by goldsmiths from the East.

In 1983, in the aftermath of the commemorations for the 1500th anniversary of Childeric's death and Clovis's accession,

Plate 14 One of the three pits containing horses found some 15 metres from Childeric's grave. The pit is cut across by a later Merovingian burial.

excavations began again in the area of St-Brice in Tournai, conducted by Raymond Brulet. They have shown that Childeric's grave was not an isolated one, but was in the midst of, and perhaps formed the earliest grave in, a Frankish cemetery that was used down to the seventh century. But much more intriguing was the totally unexpected discovery of three large pits each containing ten or so skeletons of horses. They were only 20 metres from the site of Childeric's burial; they were dated by the radiocarbon dating method (C_{14}) to *c.* 490 plus or minus 50 years; they were cut into by two graves of the sixth century (see plate 14). It is very tempting to see these horse-burials as connected with the funeral ceremonies of Childeric himself. The custom of horse burial in the Germanic world is well known to archaeologists. It is generally regarded as a pagan ritual; indeed the sacrifice of horses (and the eating of horse-flesh) was a custom fiercely denounced by the early medieval church for this very reason. And this lavish slaughter of a herd of horses, if these three pits are contemporary, throws a different light on the very Roman-looking burial of the king himself.

The Historical Sources for Childeric's Reign

Who was the man revealed so tantalisingly by the grave-goods? What kind of authority did he bequeath to his son? What was the extent of his power? Looking closely at how we derive our information about Childeric gives a revealing insight into the problems of our sources for early Frankish history. First of all, we may note that Childeric's name is not mentioned by any contemporary. Historians often say that he first appears in the historical sources in 463. It is not nearly so straightforward as that. Three sources, the Chronicle of the Spanish bishop Hydatius and the Gallic Chronicle, both written in the fifth century, and the sixth-century Chronicle of Marius of Avenches, all mention a battle in 463, in which the Visigoths were defeated, and Frederic, the brother of King Theodoric II of the Visigoths, was killed. Marius said that it took place near Orleans, *inter Ligerem et Ligericinum*, between the rivers Loire and Loir, and that it was fought between Aegidius and the Goths. Hydatius says that Aegidius fought the battle, and describes the occasion as an uprising against him in Armorica, led by Frederic. The Greek historian Priscus must be referring to this campaign when he wrote that 'disagreement with the Goths in Gaul deterred Aegidius from war against the Italians. Being at odds with them about the land bordering theirs, he fought valiantly, displaying in that war the noblest actions of a brave man'.[9] The Gallic Chronicle, on the other hand, does not mention Aegidius; it says that Frederic was killed near the Loire while fighting the Franks. If it is possible to reconcile these sources, we might understand that Aegidius was a Roman general who relied extensively or exclusively upon Frankish troops. It is only with Gregory of Tours, at the end of the sixth century, that we seem to discover that it was not Aegidius who led those Franks, when we read the bald statement 'Childeric

---

[9] Priscus, fragment 30, translated in C. D. Gordon, *The Age of Attila*, p. 119.

fought a battle at Orleans'. Historians have suggested that Childeric and Aegidius were closely cooperating during this campaign; or that Childeric and his Franks were fighting on behalf of the Romans. Perhaps it was just that Gregory read that the Franks fought at Orleans, and assumed they must have been led by Childeric. Whatever conclusion we may reach we must not forget that this is the only event mentioned in contemporary sources with which it is possible to associate Childeric.

The other document from before Gregory's time which mentions Childeric does so only obliquely, but with rather more certainty. This is the famous letter from Bishop Remigius of Rheims to the young King Clovis. 'A strong report has come to us that you have taken over the administration of the Second Belgic Province. There is nothing new in that you now begin to be what your parents always were.'[10] Thus, assuming that Gregory is right in naming Childeric as Clovis's father, we know that Childeric had the administration of Belgica Secunda. Remigius implies by his 'always' that Childeric had been in this position of authority within Belgica Secunda for a long time. This province had Remigius's own see of Rheims as its metropolis, and included Tournai, where Childeric was buried, and Soissons (see figure 9). We need not assume that Belgica Secunda was the only province which Childeric and Clovis administered: Remigius mentions it because he is writing as the senior bishop of that particular province. Later in the letter Remigius refers to 'your bishops' and 'your citizens', and advises the young pagan to listen to the advice of 'your bishops'. Perhaps this is what his father Childeric had done. A legal text known as the *Praeceptio Chlotharii* says that Chlothar's grandfather had founded churches and given them immunities. Historians have generally thought that this *Praeceptio* was issued by Chlothar II, on the sole grounds that Chlothar I's grandfather – Childeric – could not have founded churches. It is not surprising that a pagan king should deal cannily and even generously with the Catholic hierarchy, just as the Burgundian kings, who were Arian heretics, were doing at the same time in south-east Gaul. And indeed this is a conclusion supported, from another viewpoint, in the *Life of St Genevieve*. There is

[10] Translated in J. N. Hillgarth, *Christianity and Paganism*, p. 76.

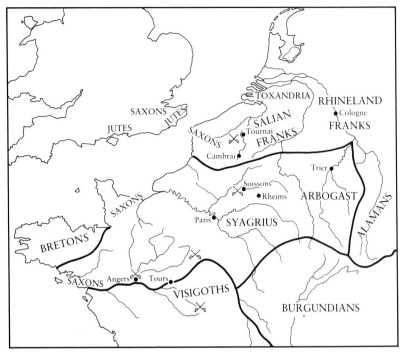

*Figure 9 The traditional view of Syagrius's kingdom, stretching across most
of northern Gaul.*

increasing agreement that this text was originally written down
in the early sixth century, and not wholly concocted in the
eighth or ninth century. Genovefa was born in the *civitas* of
Paris, perhaps, interestingly, to parents of Frankish origin, for
she has a Frankish name. The *Life* tells how Childeric laid siege
to Paris over a period of ten years, which may mean no more
than that his troops dominated the countryside around Paris, or
produced a state of insecurity which forced Genevieve to
organize famine relief, just as so many others (mostly bishops)
did in Christ's name in the fifth century. But Genevieve's
hagiographer mentions Childeric in another context: 'the pagan
Childeric, king of the Franks, loved her with a veneration that I
cannot express'. Even pagans can recognize the importance of
placating those with spiritual power.

Contemporary sources thus suggest that Childeric, who had
perhaps fought beside the Roman general Aegidius, had won for

himself some official or semi-official position within the Roman structure in northern Gaul some time before his death. He had a basis for authority over the Romans as well as over his own Franks, as indeed the gold cruciform brooch with which he was buried (see above plate 12) clearly suggests, and he worked to gain their active support. Later traditions (Gregory of Tours (d. 594) or the further embroideries of Fredegar (d. 642) and the *Liber Historiae Francorum*, of the eighth century) all associate Childeric closely with Aegidius, and also bring Aegidius's son Syagrius into the picture. Clearly if we wish to discover Childeric's own significance we need to know about these two Romans as well.

Aegidius and Syagrius

Aegidius, 'a man of great renown', according to the chronicler Hydatius, 'and pleasing to God for his good works', first appears in the contemporary sources in 458, when he took Lyons from the Burgundians in the name of the new Emperor Majorian. He then moved to Arles, where he was besieged by Theodoric's Visigoths: Majorian came to Gaul and drove away the besiegers. In 461 Majorian returned to Italy, where he was immediately murdered by his German general Ricimer, and replaced by a puppet Emperor. In the following year, according to Hydatius, a certain Count Agrippinus surrendered Narbonne to King Theodoric in order to gain Visigothic help against Aegidius. It may well be that Agrippinus, who elsewhere is called *magister militum*, had been replaced in that office by Aegidius when Majorian became Emperor, and was now using the long-established treaty between the Visigoths and the Empire to rid himself of a rival who refused to recognize the new Emperor. Aegidius retired to northern Gaul, and in the following year we find him with the Franks fighting the Visigoths at Orleans; as Priscus said, it was only that struggle that prevented him from going to Italy to take revenge for Majorian's murder. The Visigoths were thus acting, at Agrippinus's urging, on behalf of the legitimate Emperor Libius Severus. Hydatius wrote that the Visigoths led a rebellion in Armorica against Aegidius; he might with more justice have said that they were persuading the Romans of the north-west to fight for the Emperor against the rebel Aegidius. Hydatius also tells us that in 465 Aegidius sent envoys to the Vandal king Geiseric 'by the Atlantic sea-route'; not being able to send envoys through a hostile southern Gaul he had to send them from a port such as Nantes, to reach Geiseric's Vandal kingdom in North Africa via the Straits of Gibraltar. Presumably these envoys were going to negotiate an alliance against Ricimer and the Emperor. But in that same year (again according to Hydatius), Aegidius died, 'some say in an ambush, others by poison'.

That is all we can know, or surmise, about Aegidius from the contemporary sources. Everything else must come from Gregory of Tours, from his colourful anecdote concerning Childeric and Aegidius in Book II chapter 12 of his *Histories* and from the bald, ill-connected and probably ill-understood statements about the activities of the Romans and others in the Loire region, reported in Book II chapters 18 and 19. First, the colourful anecdote. The Franks were annoyed at the way Childeric was chasing after their daughters, and chose Aegidius as king, sending Childeric to exile in Thuringia. He returned after eight years, bringing with him as his wife Basina, whom he had stolen from her royal Thuringian husband Bisinus. There may be some historical core to this fairy-tale. Gregory might have heard some misunderstood memory of the Franks fighting under Roman leadership, which would lead him to assume that the Franks had elected a Roman as their military leader, as their *rex*. We may remember that fifth-century sources imply that Aegidius was leading the Franks at the battle of Orleans in 463. The later addition by the historian Fredegar, that the Franks eventually revolted against Aegidius's rule because he attempted to impose taxes on them, might also have some basis in fifth-century events; the *Liber Historiae Francorum* places a similar story under an Emperor Valentinian. Some historians have used Gregory's story to establish a chronology for Childeric and Aegidius, postulating the beginning of Childeric's reign in the early- to mid-450s to allow him his eight-year exile before returning for the battle of Orleans in 463: this probably allows more credibility to the story than is justified.

The information which Gregory supplies in LH II. 18 and 19

is of a very different kind, and much more credible. It is not anecdotal, but consists of short statements, only loosely connected together, and ambiguous both in terms of chronology and of cause and effect. As has long been recognized, the information was no doubt taken from a single annalistic source, probably compiled in Angers: it has been dubbed the *Annales Andecavenses*. Gregory made no attempt to compile his own plausible story from this source; he seems to quote it verbatim.

Childeric fought a battle at Orleans [enemy unspecified]. Adovacrius came with his Saxons to Angers. A great plague killed many people. Aegidius died, and left a son called Syagrius. . ... The Britons [Bretons] were expelled from Bourges by the Goths. Count Paul, with Romans and Franks, attacked the Goths and took booty from them. Adovacrius came to Angers. Childeric arrived on the following day. Count Paul was killed and Childeric took the city.

Both Fredegar and the author of the *Liber Historiae Francorum*, who had read Gregory, assumed that Gregory meant that Count Paul had been killed by Childeric. This is perfectly possible, although it has been rejected by modern commentators on the grounds that Childeric was on the Roman side, and hence an ally of Paul, whom they see as the heir to Aegidius's power in the north. However, as we have seen, there were at least two factions among the Romans, and Paul's Romans were not necessarily Aegidius's Romans, nor, indeed, was Childeric ever necessarily an ally of Aegidius: all that depends on the supposition that they had fought side by side at Orleans.

In the following chapter Gregory tells us that Odovacrius allied with Childeric against the Alamans who had invaded part of Italy, and defeated them. Historians have usually amended 'Alamans' to 'Alans', an Asiatic people known to have been active in that same Loire region in which Adovacrius and Childeric were campaigning, on the grounds that Childeric could hardly have been fighting in Italy, and on the assumption that the Adovacrius of chapter 18 is the same as the Odovacrius of chapter 19. But the latter is almost certainly the Odovacer or Odoacer who became ruler of Italy in 476: we must either conclude they are two different men, active in different parts of the western Empire, or that King Odoacer, born of a Hunnic father and a Skirian mother, had once been a leader of Saxons on the Loire. In either case we should surely conclude also that Childeric and his Franks were indeed playing an important political role in the Empire in the 460s and 470s, not, as most historians have argued, spending their time in unimportant skirmishes near the Loire.

Aegidius died in 464 or 465 and left a son called Syagrius. It is a name used in aristocratic families in the Lyons region from the fourth right down to the eighth centuries; this may be a hint that Aegidius originally hailed from there. We do not know how young Syagrius was at the time, or if he was under the protection of Count Paul, or, indeed, if he was protected by Childeric against Count Paul and his faction. We know very little about Syagrius at all, but this has not prevented historians from assuming a great deal. All that we do know comes from Gregory of Tours; Syagrius is not mentioned by a single contemporary source. We read in Gregory that he was the son of Aegidius; that he had his residence at Soissons; that he was defeated by Childeric's son Clovis, and killed by him after attempting to find political asylum in Alaric II's Visigothic kingdom. He was, says Gregory, *rex Romanorum*, 'king of the Romans'. Gregory never uses the phrase 'kingdom of Soissons', a political entity constructed by modern historians by analogy with the contemporary Visigothic 'kingdom of Toulouse'. Gregory said that Soissons was the seat of Syagrius, and that it had formerly been held by Aegidius. We do not need to conclude from this that Aegidius had the 'capital' of his 'kingdom' at Soissons; the detail about Aegidius being at Soissons may have been added by Gregory simply to explain why Syagrius should be at Soissons at all.

What do we know about the extent of Syagrius's kingdom or the nature of his power? Unfortunately, nothing. The assumption made by many historians is that Syagrius held sway over a large territory from Soissons in the east to the borders of Brittany in the west and the Visigothic kingdom in the south (see figure 9), but this is based on nothing more than a desire to fill this political blank with some plausible authority, and a feeling that Gregory would not have used the word *rex* if there was not a *regnum* of some reasonable size. Syagrius has thus been promoted to the position of a major political force in late fifth-century Gaul. For G. Kurth, he was responsible for the gradual diminution of Childeric's power, so that Childeric when he died possessed little more than the territory around and to the north of Tournai. (Perhaps Kurth could not imagine why Childeric would want to die at Tournai unless he had to; there is the very common assumption that Tournai was the centre of Childeric's power, when all that we know about his connection with the town was that he was buried there.) For most historians, Syagrius has figured as a bulwark of *Romanitas*, against whom Clovis had to fight before Frankish power could extend over the rest of Gaul. Even those who argue that Childeric had been an important figure argue that Syagrius was later to confine Childeric's power to some extent and keep him in the north-east.

We may doubt whether this ghostly 'kingdom' ever existed. In what way was it a kingdom? Gregory could have used the word *rex* of Syagrius for a number of reasons. Franks at the time might have seen him as another *rex*, an ethnic ruler. Syagrius's Roman subjects might have seen him as a *rex*. Or Gregory might have intended by the use of that word to give an impression of Syagrius's independence of the Empire. He was not a *comes* or a *patricius* or a *magister militum*, because he did not hold an imperial appointment; indeed, it is possible that he did not recognize the legitimacy of any of the Emperors. It might be significant that Gregory's invention of the suitable title of *rex* for him is rejected by Fredegar, who calls him *patricius* in his version of Gregory's *Histories*. As Marc Bloch noted 60 years ago, Gregory often did not understand his sources, oral or written: 'Subject of a Frankish king, how could the good bishop have an accurate and clear idea of the political situation, in reality extraordinarily complex, of a piece of Romania in the late fifth century?'[11] Without Gregory's *rex*, Syagrius appears as no more significant than his contemporary Arbogast, count of Trier. Perhaps he was in reality no more than Count of Soissons, count of a town, therefore, lying within the province which, according to Bishop Remigius, had 'always' been administered by Childeric. However, Gregory may, as we shall see (p. 79), have had reasons for inflating Syagrius' position, since it also inflated Clovis's victory over him.

[11] Marc Bloch, 'Observations sur la conquête de la Gaule romaine par les rois francs' (*Revue Historique* 154 1927), pp. 75–6 of the reprinted version in Bloch, *Mélanges Historiques* I (Paris, 1963).

Northern Gaul at the time of Childeric's Death

The destruction of the kingdom of Syagrius, that is, the elimination of the historical myth of the kingdom, obviously affects any assessment of Childeric's career. Picture the great bulwark of the kingdom of Syagrius, a figment of the modern historical imagination rather than of Gregory's, removed from the historical maps (compare figures 9 and 10). What takes its place? That question may well have occurred to Gregory himself; if Syagrius, *rex Romanorum*, did not rule the Romans of northern Gaul, who did?

It is doubtful if, in the period 465 to 481, there would have been any clear answer to that question. To some extent the *civitates* might have been able to function independently, with the help of their bishops and the local aristocracy. Armies led by or made up of the British immigrants who were coming from

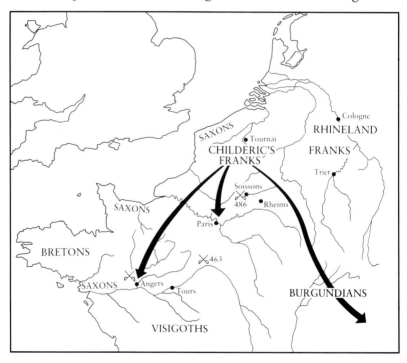

Figure 10 Suggested map of North Gaul in c. 480 illustrating Childeric's campaigns

south-west Britain were influential far beyond the later boundaries of Brittany: their best known general was Riothamus
(whom one historian, Geoffrey Ashe, has recently tried to
identify as the original King Arthur). Britons may have served to
protect bishops and other Roman authorities over much of the
north-west. The campaigns of Childeric may not have put an
end to Saxon or Anglo-Saxon power in the Loire region; there is
evidence for Saxons in the region of Bayeux and Boulogne as
well. There were Alans and probably other Germanic groups in
northern Gaul too. But over much of the north of Gaul it was
Franks who were militarily dominant, and hence politically
powerful; Roman authorities may have continued to exist with
their support and cooperation.

We know the name of one Roman official, apart from
Syagrius, who managed to survive: Arbogast, count of Trier,
recipient of a verse letter from Bishop Auspicius of Toul and,
around 477, of a prose letter from Sidonius Apollinaris.
Auspicius's letter calls him the son of Arigius, but seems to show
that he was a descendant of the Frankish Arbogast who had
commanded the western Roman armies in the 390s. Sidonius
thought Arbogast fully Romanized.

You have drunk deep from the spring of Roman eloquence and, dwelling
by the Moselle, you speak the true Latin of the Tiber. . . The splendour of
the Roman speech, if it exists anywhere, has survived in you, though it has
long been wiped out from the Belgian and Rhenish lands: with you and
your eloquence surviving, even though Roman law has perished at our
border, the Roman speech does not falter. (Ep. IV. 17)

The language used by both Sidonius and Auspicius implies
that Arbogast was indeed a Roman aristocrat and official,
successor in his office to his father Arigius, and not a Frankish
ruler dignified by Roman title. Yet Roman law had vanished
from Arbogast's lands, says Sidonius; perhaps he ruled on his
own authority, on the basis of his family's local wealth and
influence. It is not impossible that he survived as a Roman ruler
with the help of barbarian, Frankish, troops. His territory was
very close to that of the Rhineland Franks, who had already
taken Trier on four occasions and must have been a considerable power in the region. Perhaps that relationship came to an
abrupt end: if Count Arbogast is the same person as the Bishop

Arbogast of Chartres who flourished *c.* 490, then perhaps he had been chased out of Trier by the Franks. But Auspicius's letter claims that Arbogast had a desire to retire to a spiritual life, as so many of his aristocratic contemporaries did, like Sidonius Apollinaris himself, and he may have taken up that see voluntarily. It may be that the Rhineland Franks were just as interested in working out means for a peaceful takeover of the Roman system as Childeric and the Salians seem to have been.

Very little is known of the inhabitants of *Francia Rinensis*, as a late Roman geographer calls their territory. As we have seen they seem to have taken over Cologne, which became the main residence of their kings, by the mid-fifth century. Their kingdom seems to have been more unified than the kingdom of the western, Salian, Franks was in the fifth century, and it was surely an important power. It appears that they were wooed by Ricimer and the Burgundians to form an alliance against the Alamans – a wooing which may have had the practical result of a marriage alliance with the Burgundian dynasty around 469. Sidonius Apollinaris saw the Frankish prince Sigismer as he travelled to meet his bride:

Before him went a horse gaily caparisoned: other horses laden with flashing jewels preceded or followed him. But the most gracious sight in the procession was the prince himself, marching on foot amidst his runners and footmen, clad in gleaming scarlet, ruddy gold and pure-white silk, while his fair hair, glowing cheeks and white skin matched the colours of such bright dress. The chiefs and companions who escorted him presented an aspect terrifying even in peacetime. Their feet from toe to ankle were laced in hairy shoes; knees, shins and calves were uncovered: above this was a tight-fitting many-coloured garment, drawn up high and hardly descending to their bare thighs, the sleeves covering only the upper part of the arm. They wore green mantles with crimson borders. Their swords suspended from the shoulders by baldrics pressed against sides girded with studded deer-skins. This equipment adorned and armed them at the same time. Barbed lances and throwing-axes filled their right hands; and their left sides were protected by shields, the gleam of which, golden on the central bosses and silvery white around the rims, betrayed at once the wearers' wealth and ruling passion. (Ep. IV. 20)

This passage is an interesting corrective to the view that late Romans viewed barbarians with distaste. Such men as Sidonius described had formed the backbone of the Roman armies in northern Gaul for a long time, and Sidonius seems to be describing these Franks with the enthusiasm of many civilians for a well-turned out troop of soldiers. It may well have been with the help of soldiers such as these that Arbogast maintained his authority in Trier, just as Roman officials in Gaul had done in the Empire of the fourth century.

Britons in the West and Rhineland Franks in the East were two military powers in northern Gaul in the second half of the fifth century. The third was Childeric himself. And it is tempting to see him as the most important of them all. He was active militarily on a broad front, from the mouths of the Loire across to the borders with the Alamans. Did he have the same authority over a section of northern Gaul as the Burgundian and Visigothic kings had in the south? It is not impossible that Childeric had arranged a *foedus* with the Roman authorities. If Professor Goffart is right (see p. 55), under such a treaty barbarian kings and their followers were given the authority to collect taxes for their own use, rather than being paid for their military help by taxes raised (with difficulty and expense) by the Roman bureaucracy. Such an agreement need not have involved any Frankish settlement in the area between the Somme and Loire but would have had important political consequences, for the impersonal link that the average Gallo-Roman had with a distant Emperor would have been replaced by a very direct relationship to a Frankish warrior. There is no evidence for such an arrangement under the Franks, however. It is more likely that Childeric's authority was much more piecemeal. He was dignified by an official Roman title (as is implied by the letter of Remigius, p. 65 above, and the fibula with which he was buried, which resembled Roman badges of office), but he had to struggle for recognition in an area in which there were numerous competing authorities. The situation revealed in the *Life of St Genevieve* is not unlike that revealed for the western Danube provinces at exactly the same period, in Eugippius's *Life of St Severinus*: a patchwork of surviving Roman authorities in the towns, with little military power behind them, and a countryside dominated by the barbarians.

One might hope that archaeology could provide the answer to the problem of whether Frankish domination of northern Gaul arrived under Childeric rather than Clovis. The problem

Plate 15 A sword from tomb 1276 at Arcy-Ste-Restitue (Aisne) with a hilt covered with gold foil and a guard of gold and garnets. The ornamented disc hung from the scabbard as decoration.

is, of course, the virtual impossibility of differentiating between Gallo-Romans and Franks from the archaeological evidence. The skeletal evidence is of no help, and neither is the material culture found, in no great quantity, in fifth-century graves. Indeed apparently Frankish grave-goods witnessing to an apparently Frankish material culture owe as much to provincial Roman antecedents as to Germanic ones. Archaeologists agree that it was not until the time of Clovis that this material culture, expressed in types of objects and in burial-customs, spread south of the Somme into the whole area between the Rhine and the Seine, and beyond, to the Loire and even, to a limited extent, into Aquitaine and Burgundy. This dating could be questioned. There is the one fixed date of Childeric's own grave, of course, but in practice Childeric's own grave-goods are too exceptional and too rich to be very much use in establishing a firm chronological series; all they can do is to link Childeric with a series of rich warriors' or chieftains' graves belonging to the so-called 'Flonheim-Gültlingen' group, characterized, among other things, by the same sort of gold-and-garnet decoration on sword-fittings as Childeric himself had (see plate 15). These aristocratic graves are assumed to be later than Childeric. Why? For a purely historical reason: some of them are found south of the Somme and the Ardennes, behind which the Franks were supposedly retained until the destruction of the kingdom of Soissons in 486: they must thus belong to Clovis's reign and not Childeric's. Precisely the same chronological argument has been used of the earliest cemeteries to display the new burial customs and grave-goods: those south and west of Soissons cannot be earlier than 486 because of Syagrius. If we dismiss Syagrius as a significant political force, then we might be able to redate the early Frankish graves south of the Somme. But we still cannot know anything more of the political or military process by which Childeric's Franks moved into northern Gaul. All we can do is to suspect that by the time Childeric died he had already laid the firm foundations on which his energetic and ruthless son could build.

3

The Conquests

Gregory of Tours wrote a curious preface to Book V of his *Histories*, in which he berated the kings of his own day:

The Franks ought, indeed, to have been warned by the sad fate of earlier kings, who, through their inability ever to agree with one another, were killed by their enemies. . . Just think of all Clovis achieved, Clovis, the founder of your victorious country, who slaughtered those rulers who opposed him, conquered hostile peoples and captured their territories, thus bequeathing to you absolute and unquestioned dominion over them! At the time when he accomplished all this, he possessed neither gold nor silver such as you have in your treasure houses! But you, what are you doing?. . . you cannot keep peace, and therefore you do not know the grace of God.

We have the apparent inconsistency that Gregory was here urging his own kings to refrain from civil war and to imitate Clovis, while in his account of Clovis's reign Gregory had dwelt at some length on the way in which Clovis slaughtered his fellow Frankish kings, some of whom were his own relatives. But it illustrates the way in which our main source for Clovis's reign views 'the founder of (his) glorious country'. It is thanks to Gregory that Childeric's son Clovis has been seen as the founder of Frankish power in western Europe: the king who united the Franks under his rule, led them in a series of largely successful campaigns against other powers, and brought them to Catholic Christianity. The significance of Clovis's conversion we shall leave until chapter 4, but it is necessary to make one point about it now. Gregory, a determinedly Catholic bishop of Tours, naturally saw Clovis's adoption of Catholicism as a central point for his *Histories*; his conviction that Clovis 'knew the grace of God' may have led him to show some of Clovis's sordid crimes in what seems to us to be an oddly favourable light. But the paradox may also be resolved by bearing two things in mind: that Gregory liked a good story (and Clovis's life offered several), and that often Gregory did not make his moral stance explicit, preferring a not easily detectable ironic tone.

Clovis and his Conquests

Historians have devoted a great deal of energy to sorting out the dates for Clovis's reign. Gregory gives none himself, except at the end of Book II when he says that Clovis died five years after the battle of Vouillé, 112 years after the death of St Martin, and in the 11th year of the episcopate of Licinius of Tours. He used a local dating system, as was only natural in the years before the BC/AD system was accepted. Translating Gregory's three Tours-based dates into our terms, therefore, Clovis died, respectively, in 512, 509 and 517 AD. In fact whenever Gregory's dates for Clovis's reign can be checked by external sources, Gregory is wrong. For various very good reasons historians reckon Clovis to have died in November 511, after a reign which began in 481/2, though it is worth noting that this latter date, and hence the date of Childeric's grave, is worked out from Gregory's unverifiable statement that Clovis reigned for 30 years. But let us leave an unprofitable line of inquiry: for the moment we are interested in *what* Clovis did rather than *when*.

Gregory starts his story of Clovis's reign with Clovis's attack (486?) on Soissons, ruled by Syagrius, *rex Romanorum*. As was suggested above (pp. 70–71), Syagrius was probably not an important political figure, and may have been inserted at this point in the *Histories* for literary reasons. Gregory may have felt that he needed to symbolize the Frankish takeover of northern Gaul by portraying it as a campaign of conquest against a single adversary. For Gregory, barbarians won their position within the Empire by conquest; there is little understanding of the way in which they were ceded titles and powers by the Emperors

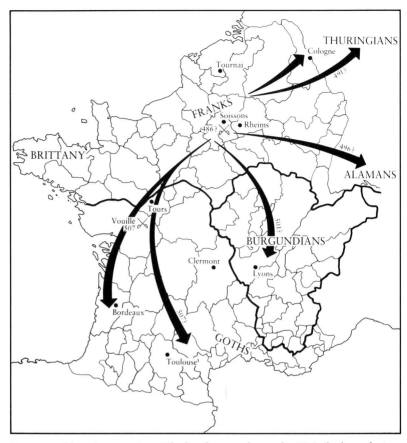

Figure 11 Clovis's campaigns. The borders are those of c. 506; the boundaries of the individual civitates (city territories) of Gaul are also marked.

themselves. Gregory's whole account of Clovis's reign is a simplified and dramatized version of history: the no doubt prolonged war against the Alamans is summed up as if it were one battle; the war against the Visigoths (which certainly lasted from the 490s down to the 510s and beyond) is again portrayed in terms of the one campaign of 507; the takeover of *Romania* is likewise symbolized in the defeat of one person, Syagrius. Gregory may also have wanted some plausible context for the anecdote he had to hand concerning Clovis and the soldier who objected to Clovis's return of part of the war-booty to an unnamed bishop. If that bishop was in fact Remigius of Rheims

Plate 16 A nineteenth-century image of Clovis.

(as Fredegar thought), we have the possibility that most of what Gregory knew of the Syagrius campaign came from this anecdote which he read in the now lost *Life of St Remigius*, a copy of which Gregory tells us he had.

This story of 'le vase de Soissons' is as famous in French popular tradition as that of Alfred's cakes is in England. Clovis's pagan army plundered many churches on this campaign, and among many other things stole a vessel 'of great size and wondrous worksmanship'. The bishop asked for the return of the vessel, and Clovis invited him to Soissons where the booty was going to be distributed. Clovis asked his men to let him have the vessel over and above his share; most agreed, saying 'everything in front of us is yours; our very persons are yours to command' (LH II. 27). But one soldier in anger broke the vessel to pieces with his axe, telling Clovis that he should have no more than his fair share. Later that year Clovis was inspecting the state of his soldiers' equipment on the parade-ground; he complained about this particular soldier's axe, and threw it to the ground. As the man picked it up Clovis split his skull in two with his own axe, shouting 'that's what you did to my vessel in Soissons!' It is an instructive story, if it is reliable, which seems to give us a view of someone who was more Roman general than Frankish king: the parade inspection (on what the Franks called, until the eighth century, the *campus Martius*) is one clue, and the second, some would argue, is the idea of the equal division of booty, regardless of rank. It is interesting too in showing Clovis taking the trouble to mollify church leaders. We may compare it to the most crucial contemporary document for Clovis's reign, referred to on p. 65: the letter in which Bishop Remigius congratulated Clovis on taking over the administration of Belgica Secunda and recommended that he follow the advice of 'his' bishops.

Gregory tells us at least some of the consequences of Clovis's victory. He says that Syagrius's army was destroyed, that Syagrius fled to Alaric II of the Visigoths, and that Clovis put pressure on Alaric to hand him over, which he did, 'for the Goths are a timorous race', and Syagrius was killed by Clovis. The implication of Gregory's account is that Clovis's victory led to the extension of Frankish power over much of northern Gaul. A curious passage in the *History of the Gothic Wars* by the

Greek historian Procopius has often been related to this process. Procopius explains more than once that the Germans 'are now called Franks', but he continues to use the more classical word 'German'. He tells how the Germans went against their neighbours the Arborychoi, whom most commentators believe to be the Armoricans, the inhabitants of north-west Gaul.

But the Arborychoi proved their valour and loyalty to the Romans and showed themselves brave men in this war, and since the Germans were not able to overcome them by force, they wished to win them over and make the two peoples kin by intermarriage. This suggestion the Arborychoi received not at all unwillingly; for both, as it happened, were Christians. And in this way they were united into one people, and came to have great power. Now other Roman soldiers had been stationed at the frontiers of Gaul to serve as guards... (They) gave themselves, together with their military standards and the land which they had long been guarding for the Romans, to the Arborychoi and Germans; and they handed down to their offspring all the customs of their fathers, which were thus preserved, and this people has held them in sufficient reverence to guard them even up to my time. For even at the present day they are clearly recognised as belonging to the legions to which they were assigned when they served in ancient times, and they always carry their own standards when they enter battle, and always follow the customs of their fathers. And they preserve the dress of the Romans in every particular, even as regards their shoes. (*Gothic Wars* V. xii. 13–19)

Procopius is not the most reliable of observers, above all when it comes to the customs of barbarian peoples, but if this strange story relates to anything, it must refer to the Franks at the time of Childeric and/or Clovis. (Procopius himself seems to place it before the accession of Clovis, except that he portrays the Franks as Christians.) But although we know nothing about the process, we must assume that one of the most important developments of Clovis's reign was the consolidation of his power in northern Gaul. By the time he fixed his residence at Paris, towards the end of his reign, his authority over most of that area must have been unquestioned, and the Seine basin was henceforth to be the centre of Merovingian power. Even if Procopius describes the process in a wholly fanciful way, the consequences he described were probably perfectly real. The Frankish kings in the sixth century were the heirs of Roman generals like Aëtius; they continued the traditions of the Roman army (as we see in the story about the vessel of Soissons), and they recruited Gallo-Roman soldiers from the *civitates* of Gaul to swell their armies of conquest. The acceptance by Gallo-Romans of the Franks as the heirs of Rome is perhaps the main secret of Frankish success.

After the Soissons campaign, according to Gregory, Clovis's next major achievement was to subject the Thuringians to his rule, in *c.* 491. The Thuringians were, like the Franks, a relatively recent confederation of Germanic peoples, including probably the Warni, some Angli, some Suevi. Around the year 400 they were to be found between the middle Elbe and the Main rivers, but after the collapse of the Hunnic Empire in the 450s they began to extend their territory further south and west, into areas contested by the Franks (see figure 11). Clovis's campaign against the Thuringians, whereby he 'subjected them to his rule', according to Gregory, does not seem to have had lasting effects; after Clovis's death Thuringia was ruled by three royal brothers, and had to be conquered afresh by Clovis's sons. Thuringia, like Francia in Clovis's day, was a land ruled by various tribal kings, and hence much less easy to subdue than the more centralised and organised territories of the Roman Empire.

It was about this time that Clovis married Chrodechildis, or Clotilde in modern French, the daughter of the former Burgundian king Chilperic. She was a Catholic Christian (unlike her family, who were Arians, not believing in the equality of the persons in the Trinity), and Gregory saw Clotilde as responsible for initiating the process of Clovis's conversion. Another element in that process, again according to Gregory, was a battle which Clovis fought against the Alamanni (*c.* 496, according to Gregory's chronology). In the midst of a battle which was going badly for the Franks, Clovis called upon Jesus Christ and promised to be baptised if he won the battle, which he duly did. There has been fruitless discussion over whether this campaign was the same as that mentioned in a letter of 506, or whether Clovis led two campaigns against the Alamans, in 496 and 506. There were probably several campaigns. But this letter suggests that 506 was the crucial one. It was from Theodoric the Great of the Ostrogoths, who had ruled Italy since 493 and was keen to establish himself as an elder statesman among the barbarian kings of the West, partly via numerous marriage alliances: he had himself married Clovis's sister. His letter congratulated Clovis on his crushing victory over the Alamans, but warned him not to pursue his campaign against those Alamans who lived south of the Danube. At this time Theodoric may have settled the Germanic people called the Baiovarii (Bavarians) on the Danube, to provide further protection to the Alpine passes, and he clearly wished to extend his patronage over the remaining Alamans, and to secure the Danube as a border between himself and the Franks. However, the bulk of the Alamannic kingdom seems to have been taken over by the Franks. Excavations at the Runde Berg near Urach (Würtemberg), an important political centre in Alamannia, have revealed a hill-fort with its workshops and dwellings, and have demonstrated wide-ranging commercial relations, above all with Italy; the excavators are convinced that the evidence demonstrates that it was destroyed in 506. Indeed, none of the fourth- and fifth-century fortified sites in south-west Germany that have so far been excavated continue much beyond 500, although there are examples of ordinary rural cemeteries which show no break at all. Clearly there was some major social upheaval, which affected above all the social élite, and the Frankish attacks are the obvious explanation. Clovis was not necessarily the only Frankish leader engaged in fighting the Alamans. The Rhineland Franks, whose territory bordered Alamannia, were certainly involved. Gregory tells us that their king, Sigibert the Lame, was so called because of an injury he had received while fighting the Alamans at Tolbiacum. Since Tolbiacum (Zülpich) is only 25 km from Cologne, we must assume that the Alamans were on the offensive. It was obviously in Clovis's interests to check the expansion of the Alamans, but his involvement in the wars against them may also have been intended to prevent Sigibert increasing his power by waging successful warfare.

The marriage alliance with the Burgundian princess Clotild turned Clovis's attention towards the Burgundian kings. His anger may have been aroused, as Gregory said, by the treatment that Clotild's family had received; if he was a more cynical politician than Gregory allows, then at least the story that Clotilde's parents had been murdered by King Gundobad of the

Burgundians served the Franks as useful propaganda for many years. Gregory recounts how King Godegisil secretly called Clovis south to help him against his brother King Gundobad. The campaign was successful, and Gundobad was forced to agree to pay tribute to Clovis. Not long afterwards Gundobad revenged himself upon Godegisil, killing him and all his chief supporters and uniting the Burgundian kingdom under his rule. Some time after that Gundobad apparently refused to pay any more tribute to the Franks; nevertheless, some kind of alliance remained or was renegotiated, for the Burgundians joined forces with the Franks to attack the Visigoths in 507.

Clovis's most significant military success was against the Visigoths in south-west Gaul. Again Gregory has dramatized and personalized the war. Far from being confined to the one campaign of 507, as Gregory maintained, contemporary annals relate how the Visigoths retook Saintes from the Franks in 496 and how the Franks took Bordeaux in 498. Perhaps Clovis took Tours also at this time; there was a tradition half a century later (very oddly *not* reported by Gregory of Tours) that Clovis converted to Christianity because he was so impressed by the miracles he had seen taking place at the tomb of St Martin at Tours. There was a temporary peace in 502, agreed by the two kings when they met at Amboise, on an island in the river which by then separated their two kingdoms, the Loire. It is possible that Alaric agreed to pay tribute to Clovis at this time; this would help explain the remark made by Avitus of Vienne that the downfall of the Visigothic kingdom had been due to the drastic debasement of the Visigothic coinage. If Alaric paid Clovis in debased coin, it is hardly surprising that Clovis invaded his kingdom.

Whatever the reason for Clovis's invasion, we are probably right to query the motive that Gregory imputes to Clovis. He portrays Clovis as a Catholic king inspired by religious zeal against the Arian Visigoths, and shows how signs of heavenly favour were bestowed on Clovis's army as it passed by the churches of St Martin of Tours and St Hilary of Poitiers. It was ten miles outside Poitiers, at Vouillé, that Clovis's army met Alaric II's, and the Visigoths fled 'as they usually did'. Alaric was killed, along with a large number of Gallo-Roman senators, said Gregory of Tours, leaving us to assume (probably wrongly) that these senators were fighting on Clovis's side rather than the Arian Alaric's. Clovis was aided by the son of King Sigibert the Lame, and his Burgundian ally Gundobad attacked Visigothic territory in the east, although he was badly beaten once Theodoric the Great sent his Ostrogoths from Italy in to help his fellow Goths. For another generation the Ostrogoths had a large say in Visigothic affairs. After maintaining themselves at Narbonne for a few years, the Visigothic kings moved to Spain, which would be the seat of their kingdom until it was destroyed by the Arab invasion of 711. Clovis's eldest son Theuderic was sent to mop up the western portion of Aquitaine, particularly Auvergne; as a result, when Theuderic inherited the north-east portion of the Frankish kingdom, later called Austrasia, in 511, he also took Auvergne as his share, and for another century and more this *civitas* remained an outlying annexe of the Austrasian kingdom. Clovis himself secured Bordeaux, Toulouse and Angoulême before going back north to Tours. Although there was still some fighting between Franks and Visigoths after Clovis's death, before an accepted border could be established between Frankish Aquitaine and Visigothic Septimania, Clovis's campaign may have almost doubled the territory in Gaul subject to him, as well as adding a rich and highly Romanized region to his kingdom.

There were other consequences of this successful campaign. It led to an alliance with the Emperor Anastasius, who was by 508 at war with Theodoric in Italy; while Clovis was in Tours, on his return from the campaign, he seems to have received letters from Constantinople which conferred the consulate on him, and, like a good Roman, he rode along the way from St Martin's to the cathedral showering gold and silver coins on the populace. From that time, Gregory says, he was called *consul aut augustus*. Whether that *aut* translates as 'and' or 'or' the story seems equally unlikely. Anastasius could not have made him Augustus, a fellow Emperor, nor does Clovis seem ever to have used the title. Gregory may be reporting a story current in Tours (he could easily have spoken to people whose parents were in that crowd being showered with coins) which misreported or misremembered what actually happened: the celebration of an honorary consulate. The ceremony may indeed have been repeated elsewhere; it would be natural enough for Clovis to use his alliance with Anastasius to display himself as the official and legitimate ruler of Romans as well as his own Franks. Clovis himself recognized the change that his victory over the Visigoths had made to the basis of his power: on his return north, after his enigmatic visit to Tours, he established his residence at Paris. To this day, except briefly under the Carolingians, Paris has remained the centre, symbolic or actual, of French political power.

The Unification of the Franks

It was after the battle of Vouillé also, according to Gregory, that Clovis felt his position among the Franks to be strong enough to move against other Frankish kings. We might suspect that Clovis had been gradually ridding himself of these rivals throughout his reign, without waiting until his last five years. The first mentioned by Gregory does indeed seem to have been disposed of after 507, perhaps because he was the most formidable of all. This was Sigibert the Lame, king of the Rhineland (or Ripuarian) Franks, who as far as we know had enjoyed good relations with Clovis up until then. His son Chloderic had fought alongside Clovis in the campaign against the Visigoths, possibly in return for Clovis's help against the Alamans. Not long after the Visigothic campaign, Gregory tells us, Clovis persuaded Chloderic to kill his father as he was walking in the forest outside Cologne. While Chloderic was selecting his reward from his father's treasure-chest, one of Clovis's Franks split his skull with an axe. Clovis announced to the Rhineland Franks that Chloderic had killed his father and had in his turn been killed; they clashed their shields, shouted their approval and made Clovis their king. Gregory commented (ironically?) that this was God's will, for Clovis 'walked before Him with an upright heart and did what was pleasing in His sight'.

The incorporation of *Francia Rinensis* into his kingdom was an extremely important political achievement. Until the late fifth century the Rhineland Franks were just as powerful, perhaps more so, than the Salians; had this still pagan and much less Romanised group of Franks won dominance, the history of

Plate 17 The helmet found in the prince's grave (no. 1782) at Krefeld-Gellep, made of iron with gilt copper appliqué plates.

Gaul, and of Europe, might have been very different. Yet the independent traditions of these Franks were recognized. The *Pactus Legis Salicae* (see above p. 13), the earliest Frankish law-code, applied to those Franks between the Loire and the *Silva Carbonaria*, the area known in the seventh century as *Neustria*: it did not apply to the Rhineland Franks. Whenever there was a partition of the Merovingian kingdom, the kingdom of the Rhineland Franks, known by the seventh century as *Austrasia*, kept its unity; when there was only one Merovingian king, in Neustria, the Rhineland Franks petitioned for their own king. It was under an Austrasian Merovingian king, Dagobert I, that the *Lex Ribvaria* was issued: the legal customs of the

Rhineland Franks, as applied to at least one part of their kingdom (the area of their former capital Cologne) were written down. The Rhineland Franks or Austrasians remained largely Frankish-speaking, while many of the Salian Franks or Neustrians became Latin-speaking. It was from the Austrasians that the second great dynasty of Frankish kings came: the Carolingians.

The Salian amalgamation with the Ripuarian kingdom may be archaeologically visible, in a number of wealthy aristocratic graves from the first quarter of the sixth century. Krefeld-Gellep is again (as on p. 56) a good example. From the later fifth century there are graves with vessels of various kinds (in Roman fashion), with weapon-sets and, in the women's graves, rich jewellery, including pairs of Germanic-style brooches. This would seem to be evidence of the use of this Roman fort by the Rhineland Franks themselves. Graves continue in this section of the cemetery into the seventh century. But, early in the sixth century, burials start appearing some 200 metres from the earlier ones. One of the earliest graves in this new area is no. 1782, one of the richest graves known from the period immediately following Childeric's burial. This dead 'prince' was buried with a gilded helmet (see plate 17), a full set of weapons including long-sword, barbed spear and throwing axe, a golden finger-ring with an antique gem, gold and garnet cloisonné jewellery, including fittings for a saddle, eating-knives with delicate gold filigree decoration on the handles, and, among other items, vessels including a glass bowl and glass jug. The exceptional nature of the find, its date, around 525, and its position as the 'founder-grave' of a new part of the cemetery make it tempting to associate it with Clovis's conquest of the area. Renate Pirling suggests that the camp of Gelduba, formerly Roman imperial property, fell to Clovis, as the new king, and that this 'prince' was one of Clovis's followers, appointed to administer the region in the king's name.

In Gregory's account the next Frankish king to die was Chararic, who had made the mistake of not supporting Clovis in his campaign against Syagrius. Clovis ordered Chararic and his son to be tonsured and ordained clerics; this suggests these events happened after Clovis's conversion.[12] Clovis heard that

[12] I have hidden away some thoughts on the symbolism of hair and forcible tonsure among the Franks in 'Bede and the Tonsure Question', *Peritia* 3 (1984), pp. 85–98.

Chararic's son was threatening to kill Clovis (as soon as his hair had grown again). So he had both Chararic and his son beheaded, and took over their kingdom. Next he had some arm-rings of bronze gilded to look like solid gold, and used these to bribe the *leudes* (sworn followers) of Ragnachar, king of the Franks around Cambrai. These *leudes* handed Ragnachar and his brother Ricchar over to Clovis: Clovis killed them both with his axe, and then berated the hapless *leudes* for betraying their lord. Ragnachar's other brother, Rignomer, who was at Le Mans, was also put to death. All three were relatives of Clovis, Gregory says, and 'in the same way he encompassed the death of many other kings and blood-relations of his whom he suspected of conspiring against his kingdom'. He is said to have remarked at an assembly how sad he was that none of his relatives was left to help him in times of crisis: 'he said this because. . . in his own cunning way he hoped to find some relative still in the land of the living whom he could kill.' We are in the dark as to who these relatives were, how close their kinship with Clovis was, and what their position in the Frankish kingdoms had been, but it was surely Clovis's greatest political achievement to have united the hitherto divided Franks under one king. No doubt his other military successes persuaded Franks living under other kings that he could offer them more than any other leader, but there is no reason to doubt Gregory's idea that the unification of the Franks involved a good deal of bloodshed and civil strife: we come back to the paradox with which this chapter began.

The Conquests under Clovis's Descendents – The South

When Clovis died in 511 the kingdom was divided among his four sons. Traditionally historians have said that this was merely following Frankish inheritance customs. But, as Ian Wood has argued, it may rather have been an expedient forced by Queen Clotild, to prevent Clovis's eldest son Theuderic (her step-son) from cutting her own three young sons, Childebert, Chlodomer and Chlothar, out of their inheritance completely.

As we have seen, the greater part of Gaul had been added to the Frankish kingdom by Clovis himself. But it was in the half

century after Clovis's death, under Clovis's sons, that the
Franks and their Merovingian dynasty extended their power
and influence over much of western Europe, and became the
dominant Germanic successor kingdom to the Roman Empire.
When King Theudebert wrote to the Emperor Justinian,
probably around 540, he was able to present himself as ruler
over many peoples, including Visigoths, Thuringians, Saxons,
Jutes and *Norsavi*, and as lord over Francia, Pannonia and the
northern seaboard of Italy, extending from the Danube and the
frontiers of Pannonia to the Ocean. Similar claims may lie
behind the panegyric written by Venantius Fortunatus for
Chilperic, which said that Goths, Basques, Danes, Jutes, Saxons
and Bretons all trembled before him; Chilperic was 'the terror
of the Frisians and Sueves' (see below, p. 166).

Our sources for this important process are, regrettably, not
without their problems. Gregory of Tours is still a basic source,
but he seems to have known little about the activities of Clovis's
sons: the entire fifty years of their rule is dealt with in fewer
than fifty short chapters. And although Gregory is well-
informed about affairs in his part of Gaul, he knows very little
about the lands beyond the Alps, Pyrenees, Rhine or the
Channel. Non-Gallic sources are hardly more helpful; Isidore's
History of the Kings of the Goths tells us little about Frankish
intervention in Spain, and although Procopius's *History of the
Gothic Wars* is very valuable for details of Frankish involvement in Italy, it is difficult to know how much it can be trusted.

The first concern of the heirs of Clovis, after the partition of
the kingdom had been agreed, may have been the consolidation
of Clovis's conquest of Aquitaine. There is some evidence in
saints' lives and elsewhere of continued action against the
Visigoths in the far south, and the occasional exchange of
territory. It may not have been until the 530s or 540s that the
'frontier' was established in the south between Frank and
Visigoth which gave the Visigoths the coastal strip known today
as Bas-Languedoc, and known then variously as Septimania,
Gothia (to the Franks) or Gallia (to the Spanish). Most of the
campaigns which helped define those borders may have been
small-scale local ones, but there were at least two which
involved the kings themselves. The first was the attack on
Visigothic territory made by Childebert I in 531, to avenge the

wrongs done to his sister Clotild by her husband, the Arian King Amalaric of the Visigoths. Amalaric was defeated near Narbonne, and forced to retire to Barcelona, where he was killed, in the forum. Childebert achieved his aim of rescuing Clotild, but she died on her way home to Paris: she was buried there, alongside her father Clovis. Less than three years later Theuderic sent his son Theudebert, with Chlothar's son Gunthar, to win back territory from the Goths; Theudebert advanced as far as Béziers, near which he met Deuteria, the Gallo-Roman woman he was shortly to marry, to the annoyance of his Frankish subjects. There were subsequent Frankish attacks on Septimania, but it remained under control from Spain (first with the Visigoths and then with the Arabs) until the mid-eighth century. The two strongholds of Nîmes and Carcassonne successfully guarded the territory against Frankish incursion at its two most vulnerable points, the gap between the Pyrenees and the Cévennes and the gap between the Central Massif and the sea.

Childebert does not seem to have entered Spain itself in 531, but exactly ten years later, together with his brother Chlothar I, he launched a major attack across the Pyrenees. The Frankish armies devastated the province of Tarraconensis, and besieged Saragossa. The Franks retreated in fright on seeing the tunic of St Vincent of Saragossa paraded on the walls, according to Gregory of Tours: 'however, they succeeded in conquering a large part of Spain and they returned to Gaul with immense booty'. Spanish sources, more plausibly, record a massive defeat of the Franks, after a Visigothic army had blockaded the Pyrenean passes; only a few Franks managed to bribe their way to safety in Gaul. If the campaign had been the success claimed by Gregory, it is odd that the Franks did not invade Spain again for another ninety years. Clearly, in that direction expansion was not practical.

Their best alternative was towards the south-east, into that part of Gaul still occupied by the Burgundians. Gregory's account of all this is rather confused. According to him the inspiration for the attack came from Clovis's widow Clotild (a Burgundian herself), who called her three sons together and asked them to avenge her parents' death (see above p. 85); this seems to have happened in 523 or 524. The brothers marched against the two reigning Burgundian kings, Sigismund and Godomar, Gundobad's sons; Sigismund was captured by Chlodomer, but Godomar fled and managed to prevent the Franks from conquering the kingdom. Some time later Chlodomer decided to invade again. First he had Sigismund, with his wife and children, murdered and thrown down a well (thus inadvertently turning the murdered king into a saint). Then he persuaded his half-brother Theuderic to join him in the fresh attack on Burgundy; Godomar was defeated, but Chlodomer himself was killed in the battle, and again Godomar was able to regain his kingdom. According to Gregory, Childebert and Chlothar then decided to attack Burgundy together. Theuderic refused to join them, although his men were so keen for booty that he was forced to take them against the *civitas* of Auvergne instead, where one group of Gallo-Roman senators had attempted to remove their territory from his kingdom. The devastation wrought in Auvergne was considerable, if the bitter memories preserved by Gregory of this attack on his own homeland are anything to go by. Gregory's narrative puts this attack on Auvergne in 532; other evidence strongly suggests that the attack on Auvergne was *c.* 525. If these events were linked with an attack on Burgundy, therefore, it was not the final attack on Burgundy, as Gregory thought. The final attack took place in 534. According to the sixth-century chronicler Marius of Avenches, Theuderic's son Theudebert joined in with his uncles Childebert and Chlothar in the conquest and partition of the realm. Henceforth Burgundy was part of the Frankish kingdom, although the surviving Burgundians were allowed to keep their own law and, for the most part, the Frankish kings who ruled the area did so from the north. It is interesting that Chlothar gave one of his sons the Burgundian name of Guntram, and that Guntram was given the portion of Burgundy when the Frankish kingdom was partitioned again in 561 (see figure 18 p. 171). Guntram named his own son Gundobad, after the greatest of the Burgundian kings. Clearly there were still Burgundian sensibilities which the Merovingians found it worth their while to placate.

To the south of Burgundy was *Provincia*, the province of Provence, held by the Ostrogoths since the time they had intervened in Gaul to help the Visigoths against Clovis. The

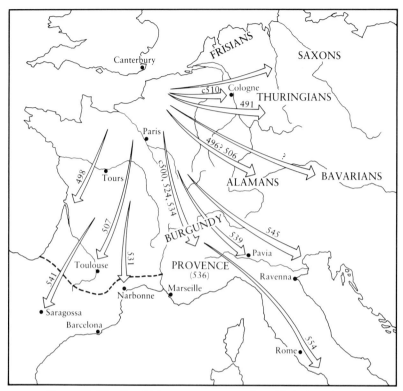

Figure 12 The Frankish conquests up to the mid-sixth century.

success of the Franks here was a result less of their own endeavours than of the war between the Ostrogoths and the Emperor in Italy. The Ostrogoths, under Theodoric the Great (493–526), had been sent into Italy by the Emperor Anastasius, to rescue it from its Germanic king, Odoacer. But Ostrogothic Italy was just as independent of the Empire as Odoacer's Italy had been. The Emperor Justinian saw his chance after the death of Theodoric, and the suspicious death of his daughter Amalasuntha. In 536 Justinian's great general Belisarius landed in Italy to begin a traumatic quarter-century of wars of reconquest. Both Justinian and the Ostrogothic king Theodahad attempted to buy Frankish alliance; Gregory, always keen to view international relations in terms of family morality, put it that the Frankish kings threatened Theodahad with punishment for his shameful murder of Queen Amalasuntha, and thereby

obtained 50,000 gold pieces. When his successor Witigis came
to power in Italy in 536 one of his first acts was to seek Frankish
alliance by giving them Provence, part of Raetia (an Alpine
province), and 2000 pounds of gold. The three Frankish kings,
Childebert, Chlothar and Theudebert (who had succeeded his
father in 534) agreed to send troops to help Witigis in Italy, but
non-Frankish troops, so as not to contravene the treaty they had
made with the Emperor. The acquisition of Provence was a
great boon to the Merovingians, as it gave them access to Arles
and Marseilles, the two main Mediterranean ports: 'so as
gentlemen of leisure they view the horse races at Arles',
commented Procopius. Of rather more importance than horse
races were the tolls which they could exact on the trade that
passed through these ports (see pp. 193–194). Marseilles in
particular seems to have been of great importance. Several
incidents in Gregory of Tours's *Histories* show how Frankish
kings were very concerned about their control of this town,
which suggests that its trade was still considerable.

If Witigis's gift of Provence was of great profit to the Frankish
kings, so was the continuing war between Goth and Roman in
Italy which had occasioned the gift. Alamans and Burgundians
under Frankish authority were the first to take advantage of the
situation, in 538, the former invading Venetia and the latter
taking Milan. In 539 the Franks themselves invaded, under
Theudebert, together with their Alaman and Saxon allies. The
Greek historian Procopius (General Belisarius's secretary) put it
this way:

The Franks, hearing that both Goths and Romans had suffered severely by
the war, and thinking for this reason that they could with the greatest of
ease gain the larger part of Italy for themselves, began to think it
preposterous that others should carry on a war for such a length of time •
for the rule of a land which was so near their own, while they themselves
remained quiet and stood aside for both. So, forgetting for the moment
their oaths and the treaties they had made a little before with both the
Romans and the Goths (for this nation in matters of trust is the most
treacherous in the world), they straightway gathered to the number of one
hundred thousand under the leadership of Theudebert, and marched into
Italy. They had a small body of cavalry about their leader, and these were
the only ones armed with spears, while all the rest were foot-soldiers
having neither bows nor spears, but each man carried a sword and shield

and one axe. Now the iron head of this weapon was thick and exceedingly sharp on both sides, while the wooden handle was very short. And they are accustomed always to throw these axes at one signal in the first charge, and thus to shatter the shields of the enemy and kill the men. (*Gothic Wars*, VI. xxv. 1–4)

They came into Italy as supposed allies of the Goths, and entered the Gothic capital, Pavia. They immediately slew all the Gothic women and children they could find, throwing them into the river. 'These barbarians,' commented Procopius, 'though they have become Christians, preserve the greater part of their ancient religion; for they still make human sacrifices and other sacrifices of an unholy nature, and it is in connection with these that they make their prophecies'. Whether the Franks, a generation and more after the conversion of their kings, did indeed behave thus, or whether it was their certainly pagan German allies, or whether it was Procopius's acceptance of wild rumour or war propaganda, it is now quite impossible to say. The Franks routed the Gothic army, and then went on to defeat the Roman army too. According to Procopius, however, they had come to Italy without sufficient provisions, and soon they succumbed to the Italian secret weapons which even now decimate the invading hordes: diarrhoea and dysentery. Theudebert was persuaded by his Franks to leave Italy, although they continued to hold the crucial Alpine passes.

It may be that the Frankish kings were aiming at no more than the mere extortion of bullion from the powers struggling for domination of Italy. Their ambition may well have been much more extensive, however. Around 545 the Franks seemed to have gained 'the largest part of Venetia' (*Gothic Wars* VII. xxxiii. 7); in around 546 Theudebert invaded Italy again and made 'some parts of Liguria and the Cottian Alps and most of Venetia' subject to him: 'and the Goths indeed had a few fortresses left in Venetia, while the Romans held the coast towns; but the Franks had brought all the others under their sway' (VIII. xxiv. 6–8). When Theudebert died in 548 Justinian's ambassador tried to restore the alliance that the Empire had had with the Franks, and the heir Theudebald ingenuously insisted that if he had taken anything from the *Empire* he would return it. The implication was that he would not in fact return any territory, since he had won it from the

Goths – 'and upon this the Emperor Justinian should certainly have congratulated the Franks' (VIII. xxiv. 27). In 552 when a Roman general besieged Verona the Frankish generals on the scene were in a position to forbid him to reunite it to the Empire; since most of the fortresses in northern Italy were held by the Franks, they said, the land was rightfully theirs. The last Ostrogothic king in Italy failed to win Frankish help because the Franks were 'eager to acquire Italy for themselves'. (VIII. xxxiv. 18)

The history of this Frankish domination in northern Italy fades into obscurity. Procopius stops writing in the mid-550s, and Gregory of Tours was clearly ill-informed about the whole Italian episode. Gregory does say that Theudebert's general Buccelin, or Butilin, conquered Sicily as well as Italy, but this seems patently false, as well as being chronologically out of place, for Butilin's campaigns took place five years after Theudebert's death, under Theudebald. Butilin and Leuthari were two Alamannic leaders who came into Italy under Theudebald, and according to the Greek historian Agathias did indeed manage to penetrate into southern Italy, before suffering a disastrous defeat in 554 on the river Volturno, at the hands of the great Byzantine general Narses. Agathias claimed that only five men out of the 30000-strong Franco-Alamannic army survived the slaughter. Frankish involvement with Italy continued however, as did payments of imperial gold, although after 568 this was in the hope of Frankish intervention against a new enemy.

In 568 the newly-reconquered imperial province of Italy was invaded from present-day Hungary by the Lombards, under their king Alboin. While Alboin himself was besieging Pavia, groups of Lombards crossed the Alps into south-eastern Gaul and began attacking the territories of the Frankish king Guntram. The first raid was a great success; the Lombards killed many and brought back a large booty. But the second raid, which penetrated as far as Embrun, encountered one of the most successful of the generals who fought for the Frankish kings in the sixth century: Eunius Mummolus, son of the Gallo-Roman count of Auxerre. Mummolus defeated the Lombards, and also a group of Saxons who had come into south-eastern Gaul with them. The Saxons who survived this battle seem to have made some kind of arrangement with Guntram's brother King Sigibert to settle in the north of Francia after their expedition; the suspicion must exist that Sigibert had bribed those Saxons to attack his brother's kingdom, just as shortly afterwards he was to enlist 'the savagery of the tribes who live beyond the Rhine' (LH IV. 49) against his other brother Chilperic.

The last major Lombard attack came in 574, when three Lombard dukes attacked southern Gaul, devastating areas as far west as the Rhône; again they were defeated by Mummolus and driven out of Gaul. It was perhaps on this occasion that the Lombards came across the hermit Hospicius, who, according to Gregory, had prophesied the coming of the Lombards as God's punishment for the wicked Gauls. Hospicius lived in a tower, wearing a hair-shirt and heavy iron chains as a penance. The Lombards, logically enough, took him for a criminal, which was confirmed by Hospicius, who admitted to being a great sinner. Only a miracle prevented the Lombards from killing him.

Despite the Franks' well-earned reputation for faithlessness, the Emperor Maurice had little choice but to try to buy their help against the Lombards in Italy. The exact story of how he did this is difficult or impossible to disentangle; it is part of the complex web of intrigues woven by the aristocrats who ruled Austrasia in the name of the young Childebert II, son of Sigibert (who had been assassinated in 575). One of their number, Guntram Boso, went to Constantinople in 582 to meet the exiled Gundovald, who claimed to be half-brother to King Guntram. Gundovald came to Gaul, and had himself proclaimed king: the large treasure he had with him may have been the money with which the Emperor hoped to buy Frankish support. Gundovald's revolt (see below pp. 175–178), which was to win the support of many southern Gallic bishops and aristocrats, including Mummolus, came to nothing; it was crushed by Guntram in 585, the year after Chilperic's assassination had left King Guntram as the major force in Gaul. But even before Chilperic's death, his young nephew Childebert, or his generals, had set off for Italy, winning, according to Gregory, the submission of the Lombards. 'Some years before', Gregory said (VI. 42), 'Childebert had received 50,000 pieces of gold from the Emperor Maurice to rid Italy of the Lombards'.

Whether this is the money brought over from Constantinople by Childebert's magnate Guntram Boso is not clear; perhaps we should instead associate it with the 30,000 gold pieces sent to Francia by Tiberius II in 577, reported by the Byzantine chronicler Menander. It has been argued that one of the reasons why Gundovald was able to win the support of men such as Mummolus in his revolt against Guntram was that Guntram refused to submit to the widespread desire of those in Burgundy to attack the Lombards. Certainly in 588 Gregory of Tours was himself sent by Childebert on an embassy to Guntram, in part to get his help in an invasion of Italy; Guntram refused, ostensibly because of the plague raging in Italy at the time. Childebert's army attacked on its own, and met with disaster, as a result of Lombard resistance rather than plague: 'the slaughter of the Frankish army was such that nothing like it could be remembered' (LH IX. 25). Further negotiation with the Emperor Maurice resulted in another invasion in 590, when Childebert II sent 20 dukes against the Lombards: 'for nearly three months the troops wandered about in Italy, but they achieved nothing and inflicted no losses on the enemy, who had shut themselves up in strongly fortified places' (LH X. 3). However, before they returned home they 'subjected to King Childebert's authority those parts which his father (Sigibert) had held before him': this is the sole reference to Sigibert's one-time authority in Italy. It may be that Sigibert, who had inherited the kingdom of his cousin Theudebert, had inherited also the gains that Theudebert had made in the north of Italy in the 540s and 550s. It is possible that the Lombards remained tributaries of the Franks into the next century; when the Franks attacked the Slavs in the 620s, they had with them an army of Alamans, who were certainly tributaries of theirs, and an army of Lombards.

The Conquests in the North

While the campaigns of the Franks in the south across the Pyrenees and the Alps were attracting the attention of historians, the Franks were fighting other, more obscure, campaigns in the north. The most obscure, and perhaps among the least successful, were those conducted against the Bretons. The north-western peninsula of Gaul, rocked by rebellion in the early fifth century, was settled by emigrants from Britain during the fifth and sixth centuries. Whether these were simply refugees, or whether they had initially come across to help Romans against rebels, or vice versa, is unclear. And the nature of the political structure which emerged in north-west Gaul is equally problematical. Writing about events which occurred in the 540s Gregory of Tours said 'from the death of King Clovis onwards the Bretons remained under the domination of the Franks, and their rulers were called counts and not kings' (LH IV. 4). Yet he had just written about a Breton leader taking over 'the whole kingdom' (of Brittany), and his very words suggest that Breton leaders did indeed call themselves kings, and did not regard themselves as counts, that is, as officials of the Frankish kings. Gregory tells us nothing else about Clovis's conquest of Brittany, but it does emerge from his narrative that afterwards the Bretons still enjoyed almost complete independence. In 587 King Guntram sent envoys to them, as if they were a foreign power, and they agreed to stop attacking the *civitates* of Nantes and Rennes, which they conceded to be in Merovingian territory; everything to the west was tacitly admitted to be beyond Frankish control. Even after this agreement the attacks continued; the Bretons, said Gregory, would always break their word. And the Bretons almost invariably got away with it. Even in 635, when Judicael, *rex Brittanorum*, came to King Dagobert at Clichy to promise that the *regnum Brittaniae* would always remain under Frankish lordship, he had the last word; he refused to sit down to dine with Dagobert because of the king's loose morals, and he dined instead at the house of the king's referendary, the future St Audoen, 'whom he knew to lead a religious life' (Fredegar 78).

At one point in the struggle against Breton incursions, in 590, Gregory of Tours claimed that the widowed Queen Fredegund took the opportunity to strike a blow against an old enemy, the Frankish duke Beppolen. She ordered the Saxons who lived around Bayeux to dress themselves in Breton clothes and cut their hair in Breton style, and fight with the Bretons against Beppolen and his Franks. It is a reminder that the Franks, presumably under Clovis if not earlier, had brought the Saxons in Gaul under their authority: the term as used in Gaul always

Plate 18 *A gilt silver brooch of Anglo-Saxon type found in a rich woman's grave at Tournai.*

includes Angles and others from north Germany. Anglo-Saxons lived not only in the Bayeux area but also perhaps in the region of Angers (where Childeric encountered them) and in the Pas-de-Calais (where many characteristic Anglo-Saxon place-names still survive). There are archaeological traces of their presence, in the form of Anglo-Saxon metal-work, in many cemeteries near the Channel coast (see plate 18). Perhaps some of these Anglo-Saxons had not come directly from Germany, but from Britain: it may be this that lies behind some of what Procopius said about Britain, which according to him was inhabited by three nations, the Angles, Frisians and Britons:

And so great appears to be the population of these nations that every year they emigrate thence in large companies with their women and children and go to the land of the Franks. And the Franks allow them to settle in the part of their land which appears to be the more deserted, and by this means they say they are winning over the island. Thus it actually happened that not long ago the king of the Franks, in sending over some of his intimates on an embassy to the Emperor Justinian in Byzantium, sent with them some of the Angles, thus seeking to establish his claim that this island was ruled by him. (*Gothic War* VIII. xx. 8–10)

The embassy to which Procopius refers could have been sent in the early 550s, perhaps by Childebert; and the implication that the Franks were claiming to rule over not only the Anglo-Saxons in Gaul but also those in Britain, cannot be lightly dismissed. It can be viewed in conjunction with other evidence, recently assessed by Ian Wood: the *Pactus Legis Salicae*, of Clovis's time, which laid down what procedure should be followed in courts of law overseas to help Franks retrieve runaway slaves; the similarities between Frankish and Kentish law; and the letter of Pope Gregory the Great to the Merovingian kings, which implied that southern England was under Merovingian domination.

Merovingians in the sixth century, like Roman rulers in the first, would certainly have had an interest in extending their authority north of the Channel, if only to protect their own possessions in northern Gaul. Their efforts were not totally successful. During the reign of Chilperic there were at least two raids on northern Gaul by seaborne pirates. The most famous raid of all, however, was that carried out earlier in the sixth century by King Hygelac of Denmark, who raided Theuderic's territory; it is the episode mentioned in the Old English poem *Beowulf*. Theuderic sent his son Theudebert to deal with the problem; Hygelac was killed and the Franks defeated the Danes in a naval battle. It is the only suggestion we have in the sixth century – but a crucial one – that the Franks might still be the maritime power that they were in the third century. It could be, of course, that the Franks were using their Saxon or Frisian allies or subjects to help them. It is likely that the Frisians, those great sea-farers of the early Middle Ages who inhabited the coastal regions of the Low Countries, fell under Frankish domination at an early date.

The Franks had taken over the whole of Roman Gaul by 536, with the exception of Brittany and Septimania, the strip of territory which remained Visigothic. They took over what remained of the Roman administration, and they took over, to some extent, Roman attitudes. Thus, although they were much more successful in extending their rule into Germany east of the Rhine than the Romans had ever been, the Rhine nevertheless remained as a cultural and perhaps mental barrier. The Gallic church made no more efforts to send missionaries beyond it in the sixth century than they had in the fourth. No monasteries were founded across the Rhine. Coins were minted all over Merovingian Gaul, but not beyond the Rhine. Merovingian kings resided in numerous places along the Rhine, but never on its far side. Both Gregory and Fredegar spoke of Thuringians, Saxons and others as 'peoples beyond the Rhine', as if the Rhine were still a political barrier. Yet it was not – neither the lower and middle Rhine, straddled by the Franks themselves, nor the upper Rhine, which was settled on both sides (in Alsace and Swabia) by the Alamans. (The boundary between the Franks and the Alamans ran between Mainz and Worms.)

One of the most important groups of Germans beyond the Rhine was known as the Thuringians. Clovis had subjected them to his rule, said Gregory (see p. 84). After his death Theuderic aided the Thuringian king Hermanfrid against his brother, but the victor did not subsequently carry out his promise to share the kingdom with Theuderic. In Gregory's story Theuderic incited the Franks to anger by telling them stories of Thuringian atrocities; he invaded, together with

Chlothar, and Thuringia was subjected to Frankish rule once more. Chlothar took home the Thuringian princess Radegund, his future wife and a future saint, as part of the booty. Hermanfrid was last seen chatting to Theuderic on the walls of Zülpich. He fell to his death; Gregory commented, tongue firmly in cheek, 'many people have suggested that Theuderic may have had something to do with it' (LH III. 8). Thereafter the Thuringians seem to have been subject to Theuderic and his descendants, as, after the early 530s, were their eastern neighbours, the continental Saxons. It is only after the extinction of Theuderic's line, with the death of Theudebald in 555, that the Saxons, together with the Thuringians, revolted against the Franks. The subsequent war seems to have been a bloody one for both sides, and although our two sources, Marius of Avenches and Gregory, do not agree, both Saxons and Thuringians seem to have become subject once more to Frankish rule, although they retained their own rulers. In 631 the Saxons appealed against the yearly tribute of 500 cows which they had to pay to the Franks, which suggests that they were still under Frankish domination, although perhaps that tribute had had to be enforced by occasional campaigns.

These Germanic dependencies served the Franks as buffer states, protecting their eastern frontiers. In 561 the Avars, oriental successors to the Huns as rulers of the Hungarian plain, attacked the Frankish lands, and it was in Thuringia, on the Elbe, that they were defeated, by Sigibert. Five years later, however, Sigibert was captured by the Avars and had to be ransomed. Frankish protection could clearly be useful to the more loosely organized Germanic peoples in the east. Fredegar tells us that those who lived in the eastern territories of Germany begged Dagobert to come and conquer the Slavs and the Avars. Thus in 630 he sent an expedition against the Wends (a Slavic people) and their king Samo. The episode gives a fascinating glimpse into the more pioneering aspect of the Frankish experience. Samo was himself a Frankish merchant, who had aided the Wends against the Avars, and so impressed them that they had made him their king: he ruled them, his 12 Wendish wives and 37 children, for 35 years. Dagobert quarrelled with him because the Wends had robbed and killed 'a great multitude' of Frankish merchants. According to Fredegar,

Samo admitted that his territory was under Dagobert's authority, but insisted that Dagobert had to maintain his friendship.
An intemperate envoy upset relations, and Dagobert organized
an invasion. His Alamannic and Lombard allies were successful
against the Wends, but his own Austrasians were defeated, not,
according to Fredegar, because of the strength of the Slavs, but
rather through the demoralization of the Austrasians: they
apparently felt that Dagobert had deserted them by going to live
in Neustria. Samo's Wends were encouraged by this victory,
and by an alliance with the Sorbs, another Slavic people, and
began raiding in Frankish territories like Thuringia. The Saxons
offered to help Dagobert against the Wends, if he remitted the
500 cows they had paid yearly – to the Austrasians – since the
time of Chlothar I; Dagobert agreed, but to little effect, said
Fredegar, for in 632, the following year, the Wends were
attacking again. After Dagobert's death his son Sigibert III was
defeated by the Thuringians, and a Thuringian called Radulf
began calling himself 'king'. Frankish hegemony in the north
seems to have started to crumble.

Our written sources are less informative about the extension
of Frankish influence elsewhere in Germany, in the area east of
Mainz which was later called Hesse, or in the south. Alamannia
ceased to be an independent kingdom after Clovis's victory, but
the exact relationship between the Alamans and the Frankish
kingdom is unclear. Alamannic dukes like Leuthari and Butilin
fought in Italy in the Ostrogothic wars (see above, p. 98),
ostensibly in the name of the Frankish kings, but clearly with
considerable freedom of action. In 588 Childebert II was able to
replace one *dux Alamannorum*, who displeased him, by
another, Uncelenus. The latter duke encouraged the spread of
Christianity in his region, but it was also under him, probably,
that in 610 the Alamans attacked that part of the Frankish
kingdom which is now northern Switzerland. This should not
necessarily be interpreted as disloyalty to the Franks; he could
have been acting in the name of Chlothar II, who was at that
time trying to win the Frankish kingdom from his cousins. It
was Chlothar II, after he united Francia in 613, who prom-
ulgated the earliest written version of the Alamannic law-code.

Frankish rule was even more nominal over the people to the
east of the Alamans, the Bavarians. Garibald, the earliest known

Bavarian ruler of the dynasty of Agilolfings, may have tried to escape Frankish dominance by seeking Lombard protection; he married his daughter to a Lombard king in 589. In response Childebert II ordained and installed Tassilo as the Bavarian ruler, bringing Bavaria into the Frankish sphere of influence. In 631 we find Dagobert in a position to give orders to the Bavarians. The political development of Bavaria and its introduction to Christianity may have occurred under the Frankish aegis, but we may suspect that the Bavarian dukes, as the Franks called them, or kings as they appear in Lombard sources, were normally perfectly free to follow their own policies. It was only under the Carolingians that Bavaria was drawn fully into the Frankish world.

We have seen in general terms how and when the Franks extended their domination over much of western Europe. The Frankish kings made no attempt to impose a unified system of government over the territories which they conquered, nor were they at all averse to appointing local aristocrats to rule in their name. Over most of Gaul there was the same basic structure of rule; it was Roman in origin and, to a large extent, Roman in personnel. It was territorial in nature, preserving the administrative units of the Roman Empire in most cases, and making no attempt to extend them beyond the Rhine. As we shall see in chapter 5, counts and dukes were the main agents of royal rule; a high proportion of them seem to have been local aristocrats.

Inevitably, therefore, most local officials in southern Gaul were members of the Gallo-Roman aristocracy: indeed, some of these were brought north by Frankish kings to help in the royal administration. Their literacy and training, and their familiarity with the ways of Roman administration and taxation, made them invaluable. The best known of them was Parthenius, son of Bishop Ruricius of Limoges and grandson of the Gallic Emperor Avitus. As a young man he had been an envoy to the Ostrogothic court in Ravenna, and had made a good impression with his learning and eloquence. He held several official positions thereafter, finally achieving the rank of *patricius*, or governor of Provence, although it is not clear whether that was before or after 536, when the province was handed over by the Ostrogoths to the Franks. In 544 he is referred to as *magister officiorum atque patricius*, serving under a king of 'Germania' who ruled over both the Rhine and the Rhône. This can only be King Theudebert, who had brought Parthenius north to head his bureaucracy. On Theudebert's death in 548 Parthenius was pursued by a mob into a church at Trier, and there stoned to death. The anger of the mob had not been aroused by his habit of breaking wind in public (which Gregory refers to), but by the zeal with which he operated the Roman tax-collecting machine for Theudebert (see below pp. 191–193).

Frankish Colonization

Because of the willingness of the Frankish kings to work within existing structures, the Frankish conquests did not depend for their success upon Frankish colonization and settlement within the conquered areas. Some such colonization occurred seems likely, however, even if it is very difficult now to assess its extent. We are reliant to a large extent upon names and graves, and both types of evidence are not easy to use (see pp. 22–30). It is hard to establish chronology, and it is very difficult to establish ethnicity. When we meet what appear to be Frankish names in southern Gaul, can we assume that they are Franks? There is Count Leudast, for instance, Count of Tours and opponent of Gregory of Tours, the very epitome of barbaric cruelty and oppression, who bears what seems to be a Frankish name. Gregory does not reveal his nationality, but he does say that he was born on an island off the coast of Poitou, son of a slave called Leucadius, who worked in the vineyards. If we can trust Gregory's account of the origins of a man he hated, Leudast was not an example of a Frank from north-east Gaul implanted in the south as part of the process of conquest and control. Yet he may have dressed like a Frank, and thought of himself as a Frank. . . We are back to the problems raised at the beginning of this book (esp. p. 8).

From the same part of the world as Leudast survives (perhaps in its original state) the will of St Perpetuus of Tours; the names of many of his slaves are mentioned, and most of the names are Germanic in type. This might demonstrate the Germanic origin of many slaves in Gaul, captured during the wars of earlier centuries, or it might show how Romans at all levels, perhaps particularly in less privileged classes, were prepared to adopt the fashions of the ruling élite. There are certainly examples of Gallo-Romans bearing Germanic names, even within the Roman aristocracy, such as Gregory of Tours's great-uncle Gundulf. Except where a source specifically names parents or mentions the nationality, it would be dangerous to use personal names as evidence for the presence of Franks. The place-names containing Frankish personal names are equally problematical: they need not represent Franks, and place-names with Frankish names or suffixes need not relate to the period of the Merovingian conquests.

The archaeological evidence is potentially more useful. The primary evidence is that of the skeletons themselves, which have been discovered in their tens of thousands, although only recently have careful analyses of whole cemetery populations been attempted, using much more sophisticated techniques than were once thought necessary. Fifty or a hundred years ago it used to be accepted that a long-headed (dolichocephalic) skull was that of an invading German and a round-headed (brachycephalic) skull that of a Celt or Gallo-Roman (see below, p. 240, for the influence of nineteenth-century racial thought on the study of the Franks). A small group of dolichocephalic skeletons found within a largely brachycephalic population, as in the Merovingian cemetery of Fleury-sur-Orne (Calvados) *may* indicate the presence of a group of incoming Germans (though not necessarily Franks), but one cannot be sure. It has similarly been argued that 'foreigners' can be isolated in the cemetery of Vron (Somme), one of those few cemeteries which continued from the fourth to the seventh centuries and included those graves regarded as 'Germanic' by Böhme (see p. 46). The study of the physical anthropology of the Franks is in fact particularly difficult. Frankish skeletal material cannot be analyzed for the period during which they were outside the Roman Empire (they practised cremation), and when inside the Empire they cannot with certainty be distinguished. Cemeteries in Belgium (such as Braives) and the Lower Rhineland, where Franks had mingled with Romans for several generations before the Merovingian period, show a great diversity of types, which cannot be distinguished 'racially'. Investigations at Maule (Yvelines), another cemetery which

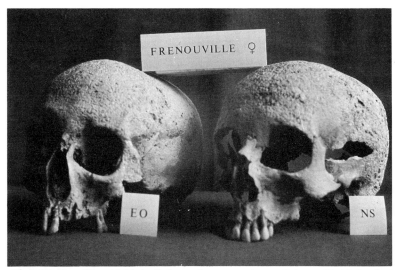

Plate 19 Two 'Frankish' skulls from the excavation at Frénouville (Calvados).

continued from the late Roman through into the Merovingian period, seem to show that although the sixth century sees the arrival of new burial customs and 'Frankish' styles of dress and jewellery, the skeletons show no change. Investigation of skeletons from two cemeteries in Calvados – Hérouvillette and Verson – suggest that basic characteristics such as occasional dolichocephaly are to be found in the population of that region from the Neolithic onwards. Either Frankish skeletons are indistinguishable from Gallo-Roman ones, or else the arrival of new 'Frankish' customs must be explained not by movement of peoples but by the adoption of new customs through 'fashion'. Traditional Merovingian archaeologists would find it hard to accept either of these, very different, explanations.

One possible way forward has been suggested by the work of the physical anthropologist L. Buchet, who has studied the 800 skeletons of the late Roman and Merovingian cemetery of Frénouville (Calvados), excavated by C. Pilet (see plate 19). Buchet has looked at the 'micro-evolution' of several anatomical features over the four centuries of the cemetery's existence, and has suggested that an incoming population can perhaps be detected. For instance, he argues that metopism (the persistence among adults of a cranial suture which normally

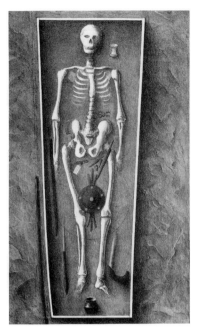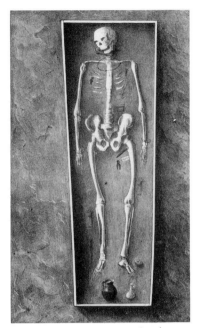

*Plate 20 Nineteenth-century illustration of the typical gravegoods of a
Frankish man (left) and woman (right) of the sixth century.*

closes in childhood) declined from 16 per cent to 9 per cent, and
that dolichocephaly increased in the community from *c.* 500.
The sixth-century graves at Frénouville are very 'Frankish' in
look; the community whole-heartedly adopted the new custom
of burying their dead with grave-goods and personal adornments. But the genetic changes, Buchet argues, could have been
wrought by the arrival of just a few individuals, perhaps just
one family, from outside the formerly tightly knit and inbred
community.

Despite the obvious problems, some archaeologists persist in
calling certain graves 'Germanic'. This is usually because they
demonstrate some supposedly 'Germanic' burial custom, such
as burial with weapons, or else contain 'Germanic' brooches or
other objects. Graves which contain no objects or which contain
such 'Roman' features as sarcophagi are regarded as 'Roman'.
In fact, of course, grave-goodless graves could be a feature of
chronology (either earlier or later than the Merovingian period)
or of poverty, while the use of a sarcophagus might depend on

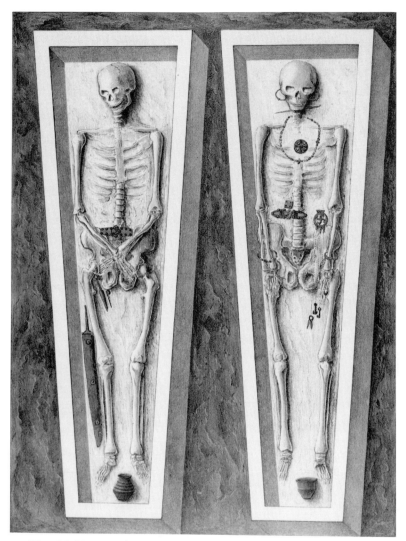

*Plate 21 Nineteenth-century illustration of the typical gravegoods of a
Frankish man (left) and woman (right) of the seventh century.*

wealth, on custom, on the availability of stone, or the existence
of a quarrying industry. Objects themselves, of course, do not
have ethnicity. An object *may* reflect the ethnicity of its makers
or of its user or wearer. But individual items can move from one
part of Europe to another by means of trade, exchange, theft or

capture in war. We might however be justified in arguing that if an assemblage of objects from a grave – on a woman, a pair of brooches, perhaps buckles, beads and other items; on a man, weapons, buckles, and so on – appears to be a set similar to those found in other graves in a particular area, then when similar sets are found outside that area they belong to emigrants of some kind. This is based on the reasonable assumption that particular styles of dress and jewellery, for either men or women, were associated with particular peoples or regions (like the Saxons who dressed up as Bretons, p. 101). In other words, a Frankish woman might wear one imported Thuringian brooch, but would not, so to speak, be seen dead wearing a complete Thuringian costume. It might follow also that if the burial customs revealed by a grave are very unlike those found in other cemeteries of that area, but are very like those found in cemeteries in another area, then we are probably dealing with more than one immigrant (on the assumption that it is the surviving friends and relatives who determine the details of funeral and burial, and not the deceased). There is a typical style of dress and accoutrement for men and women in north-east Gaul which we might call 'Frankish' (see plates 20 and 21), and these styles are indeed occasionally encountered in other parts of Europe.

Saintonge, in south-west France, may be taken as an example. In France south of the Loire the few traces of the kind of burial customs and grave-goods known in the north perhaps indicate a minimal degree of Frankish settlement. Burials with grave-goods (the grave-goods themselves usually being of local manufacture), are found over the whole region, but they are by no means numerous. They could indicate Frankish influence, and perhaps even Frankish settlement. However, it is only in the Saintonge that we find a handful of cemeteries which look very much like the row-grave cemeteries of the north. There are no sarcophagi; the dead are buried in rows, either in coffins or in the open ground, in the same style and with the same kind of objects as in the north: weapons, vessels, brooches, buckles. All these cemeteries, regrettably, were excavated in the late nineteenth century. The best known of them, Herpes (Charente-Maritime), had its finer pieces published by Philippe Delamain in 1893; some of the objects have ended up in the British

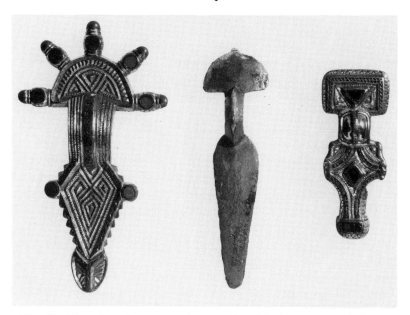

Plate 22 Three brooches among the many found in the cemetery of Herpes (Charente). They are, left to right, of Frankish, Visigothic and Jutish origin.

Museum, Cologne and elsewhere. Enough is known for it to be clear that Herpes is no ordinary settlement of Frankish conquerors. Objects like those from Visigothic Spain are also found on this site and others identical to those found in Anglo-Saxon England (or, to be more precise, those found in Jutish areas like Kent and the Isle of Wight) (see plate 22). The nearby cemetery of Biron appears to have been very similar. Whatever these cemeteries represent in historical terms, they must surely contain the remains of people from outside south-west France. The eighth-century *Liber Historiae Francorum* suggests that Clovis left garrisons of Frankish soldiers in the area of Bordeaux and Saintes to protect his new conquests; perhaps these cemeteries are evidence for the existence of these garrisons. Certainly there are more burials with weapons and more Germanic place-names in Saintonge than elsewhere in the south-west.

Beaucaire-sur-Baïse, excavated by the late Mary Larrieu, is from further south, in Gers, but also suggests a community containing a number of Franks or people closely associated with

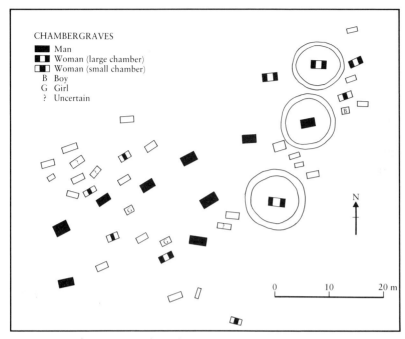

CHAMBERGRAVES
■ Man
■□ Woman (large chamber)
□■□ Woman (small chamber)
B Boy
G Girl
? Uncertain

N

0   10   20 m

Figure 13 The cemetery of Basel-Bernerring, with the aristocratic chamber-graves and the three barrows marked.

Franks. This is so far almost the only fully published Meroving-ian excavation from south-west Gaul. Things are slightly better in other areas. In Burgundy, for instance, the excavations at Saint-Vit (Doubs), discussed by Gaillard de Sémainville, may be significant. In 1971 M. Odouze excavated 130 graves, of the period *c.* 450 to *c.* 550, few of them containing much in the way of grave-goods, with no weapons and no pottery. Nine years later M. Urlacher investigated 13 graves in another cemetery, only a few hundred metres from the first. These included more elaborate graves, most of which had grave-goods, which included weapons, and pottery of Frankish type. The cemetery seemed to date to the second half of the sixth century. As at Frénouville (above p. 110) one might be tempted to argue for a change of customs in that area, resulting from the Frankish conquest; but a more plausible hypothesis may well be that the second cemetery represents a settlement of warrior Franks and their families, made after the conquest in 534.

A second and better known example from Burgundian territory is the cemetery of Basel-Bernerring, discovered by Laur-Belart in 1931 and more recently studied by Max Martin. It was a very small cemetery: 17 men, 17 women, 3 boys, 2 girls (not forgetting the horse and the deer) (see figure 13). Ten of the graves were large wooden chamber graves, like that at Morken (see below p. 138), and three were surrounded by circular ditches some 8 to 10 metres in diameter. The men in these three graves were buried with their horse harness, bronze bowl, bucket, and drinking glasses, as well as weapons; the other six chamber tombs which were men's graves also contained weapons, including long-swords. Martin's interpretation is as follows: around 540 four or five upper-class couples settled near Basel, together with their servants, some young and some in their 40s. Both their style of burial and their grave-goods show that they were not native to the region. Martin suggests that they were Franks from north of the Main and east of the Rhine, given land in the newly conquered Basel region by Theuderic I or one of is successors as king of eastern Francia.

A more controversial problem is that of the extent of Frankish settlement in south-east England. Twenty years ago Professor Vera Evison argued strongly that Franks played a leading role in the fifth-century invasions of that area. Her conclusions were the result of the study of particular metal objects inlaid with decorative wires or sheeting. These are found in graves in England, but the technique originated in northern Gaul in the fifth century, and is thus labelled 'Frankish' by Evison (see plate 23) Even if this is a 'Frankish' technique, its appearance in England does not prove the presence of Franks. And indeed Professor Evison now recognizes that Frankish items found in English cemeteries – swords and buckles made in the Meuse valley, glass goblets made in the Cologne area, purse-mounts, as well as metal-inlaid buckles – all of these could just as well be the result of trade rather than invasion and settlement. There are also a number of graves in southern England whose contents and style of burial correspond closely to those known from the Frankish mainland: tomb 21 from Petersfinger, for instance, or tomb 979 from Mucking (Essex). Graves such as these may well be evidence for the contribution the Franks have made to the settlement of England, which seems

Plate 23 Numerous 'Frankish' objects, made in northern Gaul, have been found in Kentish cemeteries, including this fine fifth-century buckle with two long-haired busts and a Latin inscription reading 'Long Life to Him who Made This'.

to be confirmed by the Venerable Bede himself, who wrote in his *History* (V. 9) that many *Boructuari* (the Frankish *Bructeri*) came to England. It helps to explain the close relations that, in the mid-sixth century, led to Frankish claims of overlordship over the southern English (see p. 103) and, in the late sixth century, were continued by the marriage of the pagan Aethelberht of Kent to Bertha, a Christian Frankish princess.

The Linguistic Frontier

The one area where Franks are known to have settled in large numbers is, of course, north-east Gaul itself. Yet here we come

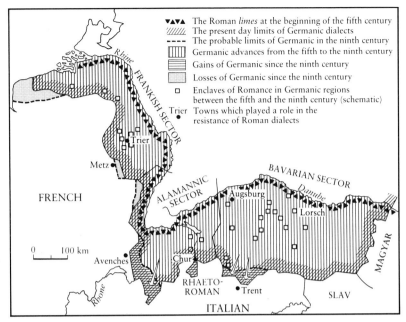

Figure 14 The new linguistic frontier between Germanic and Romance.

to another controversy that has divided scholars in a very different discipline, that of philology. There is one very obvious fact: the shift of the linguistic frontier between the Romance (Latin, French) and Germanic (Frankish, Flemish, Dutch, German) languages from the Rhine frontier of the Roman Empire to its present position (see figure 14). As André Joris (whose very useful discussion I follow) remarks 'it follows, on its entire run, no political border whatever, old or modern. Neither does it correspond to a natural geographical limit'. The problems are as follows: does the modern linguistic frontier mark the westernmost limit of the settlement of the majority of the Frankish people in the course of the fourth to sixth centuries, or is it the result of another historical process? And secondly, why did that frontier stop where it did?

At first it was thought that the linguistic frontier could be accounted for by two barriers, one artificial and one natural, which stopped the advance of Frankish colonization. The first was the Roman road which ran from Boulogne, via Bavay, to Cologne. This road was fortified along its line by fortresses and garrisons; it was a main line of Roman defence in the Lower Rhine area, where the marshy estuary region of the Rhine itself prevented the establishment of a fortified frontier, and above all in the fourth century, it was argued, when the Roman authorities allowed Franks to settle in the area to the north. The second barrier, it was argued, was the *Silva Carbonaria* (*le forêt Charbonnière*), the forest which, as we have seen (p. 89) marked the *northern* extension of the area covered by Frankish Salic law. There was forceful criticism of the idea that either of these barriers, if they existed at all (and the exact location of the *Silva Carbonaria* remains uncertain), could have played an important role. A much more ambitious argument came from the German linguist F. Petri (significantly, perhaps, in 1937), who argued that the present linguistic frontier did not represent the line reached by Frankish settlement in the sixth century, but rather represented the line reached by a slow reconquest by Romance languages which happened between the eighth and fifteenth centuries; originally Frankish had been dominant very much further westwards.

Many uncertainties still remain. Place-name experts, for instance, do not agree on whether the existence of Germanic place-names (which occur far west of the present linguistic frontier, in much of Picardy, for instance) implies a population in which Germanic-speakers were dominant numerically or simply socially. In general there seems agreement that the simple linear linguistic frontier today was much more complex in the early Middle Ages. The modern linguistic frontier is in part a result of the polarization of languages and nationalities that has arisen since the nineteenth-century – while the debate over its origins has been largely fuelled by the conflicts between Fleming and Walloon in modern Belgium: there has been much less academic work and debate over the equally significant shift of the linguistic frontier further south, which made the territory of present West Germany, west of the Rhine, a Germanic-speaking territory. In the early Middle Ages the 'frontier' between the two linguistic groups was largely invisible and undetectable because of the existence of widespread bilingualism and of large numbers of enclaves of one language within the area of another. There were enclaves of Romance around Aachen, Prüm, Trier and St-Trond, which had disappeared by the eleventh century;

there were probably enclaves of predominantly Germanic-speakers in areas which are now French-speaking. The 'recon-quests' of Romance may have occurred for political reasons, but the influence of Latin-speaking missionaries and of new bishoprics and monasteries may have played an important role. By the sixth century the Frankish kings had firmly established their main residences within Romance-speaking areas, and had begun to accept what they were taught by Gallo-Roman clergymen: that the basic divide within their kingdom was not a linguistic or ethnic one, between Germanic and Romance or between Frank and Roman, but between pagan and Christian.

4

Conversion to Christianity

The Conversion of Clovis

The story of the conversion of the Franks to Christianity traditionally starts with the conversion of an individual: Clovis. This means, once again, starting the narrative with Gregory of Tours. Gregory's story, despite its oddities, has the merit of suggesting the complexity of issues – psychological, intellectual, socio-political – which are likely to lie behind the conversion of any individual, but above all of one who is an important person in his or her society. For Gregory the process started with a nagging wife. Clovis's Burgundian wife Clotild wanted him to agree to baptise their first son, Ingomer (whose name seems to join together the Merovingian family-name with that of the Germanic god Yngvi). Gregory devises a little sermon for her to preach to her husband, which made the same points that early medieval preachers tended to make to pagans: your gods are bits of stone or wood; they were men, not gods; they set examples of immorality, like Juno, 'at once sister and wife of Jupiter' (quoting Virgil, and giving Roman names to Frankish gods, as Merovingian preachers always did). The child was baptised, and promptly died. Undaunted, Clotild had her second son baptised, and when he too fell ill she prayed and the child recovered: a sign from Heaven. Later, as we have seen, Clovis fought against the Alamanni (in *c.* 496, says Gregory). He prayed to the Christian god on the battlefield, and was granted victory, a story which suspiciously parallels the conversion of Constantine, the first Christian Emperor. Clotild ordered Bishop Remigius of Rheims to come in secret to tell Clovis of the word of God; Clovis informed him that the only obstacle to conversion was the Franks under his command.

He arranged a meeting with his people, but God in His power had preceded him, and before he could say a word all those present shouted in unison: 'We will give up worshipping our mortal gods, pious king, and we are prepared to follow the immortal God about whom Remigius preaches'. . . . The public squares were draped with coloured [or painted] cloths, the churches were adorned with white hangings, the baptistery was prepared, sticks of incense gave off clouds of perfume, sweet-smelling candles gleamed bright and the holy place of baptism was filled with divine fragrance. . .Like some new Constantine he stepped forward to the baptismal pool. . .(and) the holy man of God addressed him in these pregnant words: 'Bow your head in meekness, Sicamber. Worship what you have burnt, burn what you have been wont to worship'. (LH II. 31)

All this clearly comes from the *Life of St Remigius*, a copy of which Gregory owned, even the nicely classical Latin word 'Sicamber' in place of the barbarous 'Frank'. The *Life* may also be the source for the additional details: that three thousand of Clovis's army were baptised at the same time, as well as his sisters Albofled and Lantechild. It is the letter written in *c.* 565 by Nicetius of Trier to Clovis's grand-daughter, as she was about to marry an Arian king of the Lombards, which adds another detail: that Clovis had been very impressed by the miracles which took place by the tomb of St Martin in Tours. 'Do these things happen in Arian churches? They do not.'[13] Even more interesting is the only piece of contemporary evidence: the letter written by Bishop Avitus of Vienne to congratulate Clovis on his baptism. He says how the Emperor would rejoice at the news, and remarks how 'the adherents of all sorts of schismatic sects have been seen to blind with obfuscation the sharpness of your intelligence through their opinions, which are various in conjecture, diverse in number and empty of the truth of Christ's name'.[14] Experts in late Roman rhetoric such as Avitus are not noted for clarity, but what Avitus may have been saying is that Clovis had been a heretic before he converted, and not a pagan. Even Gregory admits that Arianism existed among the Franks, and very close

[13] Translated in J. N. Hillgarth, *Christianity and Paganism*, p. 80.
[14] Avitus, Ep. 46: translated by I. N. Wood in his 1985 article, p. 267.

to Clovis: his sister Lantechild was baptised at the same time as Clovis, but she had converted to Catholicism from Arianism, not from paganism. Gregory, with his oft-repeated detestation of Arianism, was of course not going to admit that his hero Clovis had ever been an Arian. Nor could he admit, even to himself perhaps, that many of his hero's military successes had occurred before Clovis's conversion to Catholicism. Avitus's letter, which mentions how Clovis had shown mercy to a formerly captive people, suggests that the baptism came after Clovis had liberated the Gallo-Romans of south-west Gaul from the Arian captivity, and probably after his alliance with the Emperor, in 508 at the earliest.

A date of 508 for Clovis's baptism (rather than the traditional 496), as recently argued by Ian Wood, does not mean that Clovis's *conversion* was similarly near the end of his reign. Gregory of Tours's account of the conversion makes clear one aspect which modern historians have not always remembered in their discussions of the conversion of kings. There may be at least three stages in the process: first of all, intellectual acceptance of Christ's message, the 'conversion' proper; secondly, the decision to announce this publicly, to followers who may be hostile to the change; thirdly, the ceremony of baptism and membership of the community of Christians. The Emperor Constantine reached the first stage in 312, never seems to have grasped the nettle of the second stage, and reached the third only on his death-bed in 337. The Burgundian king Gundobad, according to Gregory of Tours, reached the first stage of conversion from Arianism to Catholicism, but did not dare to progress to the second stage for fear of his followers. Avitus himself struggled to convert Gundobad, and so was very aware of the problems. In his letter to Clovis he remarked that many could not bring themselves to convert because of the traditions of their people and respect for their ancestors' worship, and praised Clovis for having had the courage to overcome these obstacles. Clovis progressed through all three stages, even if he may have taken ten or more years to do so. Gregory of Tours, for various reasons, because of what his sources told him, or because of his desire to tell a good, effective story, describes these three stages, but collapses the scale and presents them as happening in a relatively short space of time.

The Conversion of the Frankish People

In Gregory's account Clovis was the first Frank to be converted to Christianity (unless we count Clovis's Arian sister). This is almost certainly not so, even though he may have been the first Frankish Catholic king. We have seen in chapter 2 how Franks had been living within the Roman Empire since the late third century, some as captives, some as troops and federates, some as Roman generals and consuls. The Rhineland Franks came into the highly Romanized area of Cologne and Trier in the fifth century; Clovis's own Salians had been ceded land within the Roman Empire in the mid-fourth century. Some of these Franks may well have become Christians in the course of the fourth and fifth centuries, perhaps, like all other Germans, Arian Christians; all Franks must have known something about Christianity.

This surely made the task of the Frankish kings and their bishops in the conversion of the majority of the Franks somewhat easier. But in the almost complete absence of unambiguous evidence, it is very difficult for the historian to find out about the process and progress of conversion. Surviving legislation against paganism is minimal. The only mention of religion in Clovis's *Pactus Legis Salicae* is a penalty attached to the theft of a sacrificial pig; this is indeed the only neutral mention of a pagan practice in any written law-code of the early Middle Ages. The only legislation against a pagan practice in the canons of the first great Frankish church council, presided over by Clovis at Orleans in 511, is a canon forbidding the clergy to indulge in divination or auguries; but these clergy must have been Gallo-Romans, not Franks (and probably they themselves did not regard these practices as pagan). Other legislation banning pagan practices, such as that issued by the synod of Auxerre in the later sixth century, mentioning such customs as dressing up as a stag on the Kalends of January, again almost certainly refers to the paganism of the Gallo-Romans. The only surviving royal legislation, aimed probably at Franks as well as Romans, is an edict issued by Childebert I,

since it is necessary that the people, which does not keep the precepts of bishops as it should, should be corrected also by Our rule. . . We order that any men who, once admonished, shall not at once cast out images and idols, dedicated to the devil, made by men, from their fields, or shall prevent bishops from destroying them, shall not be free, once they have given sureties, until they appear in Our Presence... From (many sacrileges) God is injured and the people through sin go down to death, passing nights in drunkenness and scurrilous songs, even on the holy days of Easter, of the Lord's nativity and the other (church) feasts, or dancing on the Lord's Day through towns.[15]

The problem of persuading people that drunkenness and dancing were sins against God and the king was never satisfactorily resolved. A century later the Aquitanian Eligius was preaching to Franks in the countryside of his diocese of Noyon against these and similar practices: the annoyance of the locals was such that he nearly achieved martyrdom. 'Roman that you are', said the crowd's spokesperson, 'although you are always bothering us, you will never uproot our customs, but we will go on with our rites as we have always done, and we will go on doing so always and forever. There will never exist the man who will be able to stop us holding our time-honoured and beloved games.'[16]

The difficulty for the Church, and for us, is that of separating those customs which were genuinely non-Christian from those which were simply deep-rooted social habits or communal activities. Gregory reported that the Franks of his day referred to *dies dominicus*, the Lord's Day, dimanche, as *dies solis*, Sunday: he and many churchmen of his time regarded this as a shameful survival of pagan worship. And yet *Mercurii dies*, mercredi, Woden's day, and *Jovis dies*, jeudi, Thor's day, are still with us. The fanatical suspicion of the clergy could even lead to a cauldron of beer at a party being seen as dangerously pagan. St Vedast of Arras went to a party given by one of Chlothar I's courtiers, and although Christians and pagans were present he sabotaged the occasion by making the sign of the cross over the cauldron, which split it open; when St Columbanus did the same thing in Alamannia, the devil was spilt out as well as the beer.

---

[15] Translated by J. N. Hillgarth, *Christianity and Paganism*, p. 108.
[16] *Vita S. Eligii* II, 20: translated by P. Fouracre, 'The Work of Audoenus of Rouen and Eligius of Noyon in Extending Episcopal Influence...', *Studies in Church History*, **16** (1979), p. 82.

Plate 24 This buckle from Criel (Seine-Maritime) seems to show a man's head menaced by two monsters; this iconography may have pagan religious significance.

Our narrative sources, apart from rare anecdotes such as these, are singularly unenlightening about Frankish paganism and the progress of the bulk of the people towards Christianization. Gregory does provide us with a brief, much-quoted and unhelpful description of paganism: 'this people seem always to have followed idolatrous practices, for they did not recognise the true God. They fashioned idols for themselves out of the creatures of the woodlands and the waters, out of birds and beasts: these they worshipped in the place of God, and to these they made their sacrifices' (LH II. 10). But the only time we see pagans in action in his works is in the *Life of the Fathers* (VI. 2) when he tells of the visit of his uncle Gallus to Cologne, around 530. 'There was a temple there filled with various adornments, where the barbarians of the area used to make offerings and gorge themselves with meat and wine until they vomited [part of the ritual, perhaps?]; they adored idols there as if they were gods and placed there wooden models of parts of the human body whenever some part of their body was touched by pain.' Gallus set fire to the temple, and narrowly escaped with his life. Cologne had been a Frankish centre for several generations, but it is possible that the temple was an old Roman building; the custom of placing ex votos in a sacred place was a Gallic and a Roman one, and survives to this day in the Mediterranean Church (though now the models are plastic, wax or metal rather than wood). So even here we do not necessarily meet pure Frankish paganism, though we do meet the most direct of the various methods used by Gallic missionaries.

The conversion of Franks always went hand in hand with the conversion of Gallo-Romans. Roman Gaul may have been nominally Christian by the mid-fifth century, but the amount of contact which the average Gallo-Roman had had with church-men, particularly in the large dioceses of the north, must have been very limited. Adults or children had to go to the cathedral church – often a long way away – to be baptised, for there were no parish fonts. Receiving instruction afterwards also probably meant a long journey, or a long wait for a visiting preacher. The process of conversion, then, leading through baptism to some awareness of the Biblical teachings, was a very long one, which could hardly be completed as far as the rural population was concerned until after the strengthening of parochial organiza-tion and clerical education in the Carolingian period. But Merovingian churchmen do not seem to have thought in terms of theological or moral instruction for laymen. As far as they were concerned, or so it seems, conversion meant acceptance of baptism and the outward observance of Christian forms; knowledge of these, rather than of any inner change in the soul, is at least available to the historian in principle (if only he had the evidence).

In the absence of such evidence we may presume that the conversion of the Franks was a very gradual process, which progressed at different speeds in different parts of the Frankish world. In the territory to the west and south of the Somme, where in the sixth and seventh centuries the Franks were in a minority within a society in which the Church maintained and increased its cultural dominance, conversion in the sense of persuasion to baptism may have been fairly swift. Near the Rhine, in those parts where the diocesan structure largely survived (although the Church was no doubt much diminished in personnel) the process took longer. And in north-east Gaul, modern Belgium, where a large proportion of the Frankish people were living, and where the process of migration and settlement had totally disrupted the diocesan structure, the conversion of Franks and the reconversion, or conversion, of Gallo-Romans was still being actively pursued in the late seventh century.

We do know of some Gallo-Roman ecclesiastics who worked in what is now Belgium, as reorganisers and perhaps as missionaries. The earliest were probably those installed as bishops by Remigius of Rheims: Vedastus (an Aquitanian) at Arras and Eleutherius at Tournai. At the same time a bishop called Falco held the bishopric of Tongres. But this attempt at a diocesan reorganization in the early sixth century clearly had its problems; later in the century we find that the see of Arras had moved to Cambrai, Tournai had moved to Noyon and Tongres had shifted to Maastricht; later still, around 700, the bishop of Maastricht moved to Liège, where the missionary bishop Lambert was buried. Further east, in what became Austrasia, where there was more continuity of sees, as at Cologne, there was more activity in the sixth century: the local clergy was strengthened by deliberate imports of Aquitanian clergymen, such as Nicetius, who became bishop of Trier, and Sidonius of Mainz. By the end of the sixth century some of these sees were occupied by bishops with Frankish names, who may indeed have been Frankish: Magneric of Trier, Ebergisel of Cologne, Sigismund of Mainz and, further south in Alsace, Arbogast of Strasbourg, whose name recalls famous Franks of the past (see

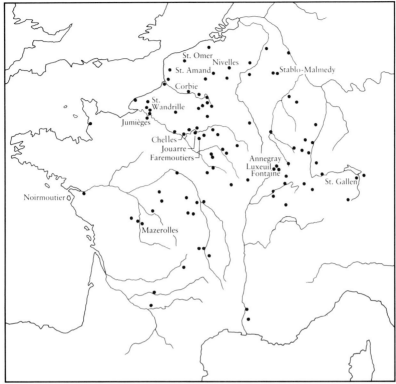

Figure 15 The distribution of monasteries founded from or influenced by Luxeuil up to c. 730 shows that the main influence was on the Frankish north-east.

pp. 43 and 73). But we hear little of missionary bishops until the seventh century; then most of those we hear of seem to be associated with the monastic movement begun by St Columbanus.

St Columbanus and Frankish Monasticism

Columba, or Columbanus as historians call him to distinguish him from the famous apostle to the Picts, was a nobleman from the Irish province of Leinster, who went first to take up a monastic life in Bangor, in Ulster, and then, desiring to impose an even greater penance on himself, left Ireland altogether, with 12 companions, and came to Gaul. He arrived, it seems, around

590. King Childebert II was impressed by his preaching and his asceticism, and encouraged him to take up residence in the Vosges mountains. He founded one monastery, Annegray, which attracted so many monks that he was forced to found another, at Luxeuil. It was Luxeuil which was to prove one of the most influential of all monasteries in Francia, and particularly so for the Franks themselves (see figure 15). Seventh-century monks influenced by Luxeuil were in no doubt as to the reason: Columbanus brought a new Christian devotion and a new monastic enthusiasm to a tired and corrupt Gallic church. Some modern historians have accepted this judgement on the Gallic church, picking out the more lurid episcopal or monastic careers from Gregory of Tours's works as corroborative evidence. This is unfair. There may have been corruption – the church in Gaul was extremely wealthy – but there was also a good deal of asceticism and genuine devotion to Christian ideals. It may be that Columbanus did bring a different style of Christianity: Wallace-Hadrill has noted the gulf between the piety of the Gallic church, 'centred upon relics and the patronage of local holy men, and the piety of Columbanus, focused upon God and the relationship of God with man. It was indeed a gust of fresh air.'[17] Certainly this exotic figure must have seemed a living reminder of the days of the apostles or the Old Testament prophets. What Columbanus also brought, however, was a somewhat different brand of monasticism, and one which was arguably very well suited to conditions in Gaul, above all northern Gaul.

Columbanus was brought up in the Irish monastic tradition, which was different in some important respects from the Gallic tradition. Irish monasteries were rural; there were no towns in Ireland. They could be large and wealthy, with considerable amounts of land, and hence their abbots were frequently more powerful than the impoverished bishops. Irish monasteries had perforce to be educational establishments; in the sixth century, Irish men and women were the only Christians in western Europe who would, before entering a monastery, be ignorant of Latin, the language of the Church. And Irish monasteries did not on the whole cut themselves off from the lay population in

---

[17] J. M. Wallace-Hadrill, *The Frankish Church*, p. 63.

the region: they acted as religious and educational centres for laymen as well. Gallic monasteries, on the other hand, were often urban, were kept very firmly under the thumb of the local bishop, and had few intellectual pretensions. Clerical education went on in episcopal schools, and the monasteries did not cater for those not brought up to speak Latin from birth (although often a Latin which had developed a long way from classical Latin). Most Gallic monasteries were in central and southern Gaul; there were very few in the more Frankicized and less urbanized north. Irish monasticism, the first type of monasticism developed for a non-urban and non-Roman society, seemed ideally suited for the Franks. In particular, perhaps, Luxeuil presented Frankish aristocrats with the model of a rural monastery founded effectively outside episcopal jurisdiction; no aristocrat would want to give large amounts of property to a monastery, if he knew that the bishop might be able to use that property as he wished, or drain it of its profits. As in Ireland, the great Frankish families who founded monasteries in northern Gaul were often able to treat these monasteries as 'family monasteries', sending their own surplus children there, having their relations appointed as abbots, and 'borrowing' monastic land to give its profits to their retainers. In addition, of course, they had the spiritual satisfaction of knowing they had done a pious deed, and that, because of this, monks would pray in perpetuity for the salvation of their souls.

Such things were hardly uppermost in the minds of those inspired to follow the life of Christ by Columbanus himself, or caught up in the enthusiasm of Luxovian monasticism. It is noticeable, however, that many of these enthusiasts were Franks, mostly of aristocratic families, who had perhaps not found what they wanted within the traditional Gallic church. The latter had begun to receive Franks as clergymen; indeed Frankish bishops (if one regards them as Franks on the ambiguous evidence of their personal names: see pp. 29, 128), do begin to appear in the sources in the late sixth century. Frankish queens had founded nunneries, and others had entered them; the scandals which took place in the royal and aristocratic nunnery of the Holy Cross in Poitiers, as reported in detail by Gregory of Tours, suggest that their inmates were not necessarily motivated by any great ascetic zeal. There is in fact little evidence of lay piety among the Franks until the coming of Columbanus, and few signs of monastic or missionary enthusiasm.

Columbanus sometimes had a direct personal effect on the lives of individual Frankish families, most famously in the case of Chagneric's family. Chagneric's son Chagnoald had himself been attracted to Luxeuil at an early date. In 610 Columbanus stayed with Chagneric, near Meaux (east of Paris), and there he blessed Chagneric's young daughter Burgundofara. She took this as a sign that she should enter the monastic life herself. A monastery was founded on the family estate of Eboriacum under the supervision of her brother and another monk from Luxeuil; Burgundofara, St Fare, eventually became its abbess, and is commemorated in its later name of Faremoutiers. It was a so-called 'double monastery': another Irish innovation, it seems. Traditional Gallic nunneries were in towns, and imported priests for saying mass from the urban clergy; a rural nunnery, however, needed resident males, for manual labour as well as liturgical purposes, and hence abbesses like Burgundofara ruled a house containing both men and women: 'rural nunnery' would be a better name than 'double monastery'. Her will survives: a fascinating document, giving some insight into how this minor aristocratic family had accumulated its estates, by donation, purchase and inheritance, and also showing the willingness with which the family contemplated the alienation of many of those estates by Burgundofara to the church. It was not only Burgundofara who followed her brother Chagnoald into the church: her monastery housed several other members of her family. Chagnoald himself became bishop of Laon and another brother, Burgundofaro, bishop of Meaux.

Columbanus met another family on this trip, themselves related in some way to Chagneric. The couple were Authar and Aiga. Columbanus blessed their sons: Ado, Dado and, according to a later source, Rado. Ado was to found a nunnery at Jouarre, whose famous funerary crypt with its decorated sarcophagi can still be seen, including the sarcophagus with an inscription to Theudechild, the first abbess and Ado's cousin (see plate 25). (Theodechild had a brother whose career is a

Plate 25 Sarcophagus of the first abbess of Jouarre, Theodechild, in the monastery's crypt.

fascinating example of the new Frankish piety. Agilbert went to Ireland to study, and then became bishop of the West Saxons in southern England. In the end the West Saxon king became frustrated at their communication problems – Agilbert did not speak English – and dismissed him. In 664 Agilbert was at the Synod of Whitby, and got his priest Wilfrid, later St Wilfrid of York, to speak on his behalf against the schismatic ways of the northern Irish. Agilbert ended his days as Bishop of Paris, and was buried next to Theodechild at Jouarre, in a sarcophagus (see plate 26) whose closest artistic parallels are in Northumbria.) Authar and Aiga's second son was Dado, better known in English as St Audoen and in French as St Ouen, who went to the royal court, founded the monastery of Rebais in Brie, on land given by King Dagobert, and eventually became bishop of Rouen. At the court of Dagobert he met others of like mind, notably Eligius, and the king himself was keenly interested in supporting the new monasticism. Another major royal monastic patron was the wife of Dagobert's son Clovis II: Balthild, who founded Chelles, which became the most prestigious nunnery in Francia. Balthild and Chelles are pieces of English history as well as of Frankish. Balthild herself had been an Anglo-Saxon slave, given by the Neustrian mayor of the palace Erchinoald (whose daughter married a king of Kent) to Clovis II. Chelles and other nunneries like Faremoutiers attracted a number of Englishwomen from royal families in the mid-seventh century, when there were still few nunneries in England. The most notable of these stayed only a year at Chelles: the Northumbrian princess Hilda, who returned home to found nunneries at Hartlepool and Whitby.

Contact with these other newly-converted barbarians, Irish and English, may have interested Franks in the work of conversion; a number of those connected with the new monasticism at the courts of Dagobert and Clovis II were also involved in missionary work. Columbanus himself served as an active missionary among the Alamans. His monasteries became centres of a permanent mission, on the pattern of monastic houses in Ireland, attracting lay people there for religious

Plate 26 Sarcophagus of Bishop Agilbert of Paris, which stands near that of Theodechild at Jouarre.

instruction, education and penance. (The custom of private penance, with the nature of the penance for a particular sin being laid down in a penitential, was developed by the Irish and spread through Gaul thanks to Luxeuil and other Irish houses.) The Irish church, itself still a missionary church among a very recently converted barbarian people – the Irish were the first barbarians outside the Roman Empire to be converted – was convinced of the importance of missionary work. It is not surprising, therefore, that most of the missionaries who worked among the Franks in north-east Gaul in the seventh century seem to have been under the influence of Luxeuil. One of the earliest of them was Walaric, who worked in the dioceses of Rouen and Amiens at the time of Chlothar II; his successor Blitmund founded the monastery named after Walaric: St-Valéry-sur-Somme. In the time of Dagobert, Richarius worked in the diocese of Amiens, and founded the abbey of Centula (St-Riquier), while Dagobert himself reestablished the diocese of Thérouanne: its first bishop was Audomar, trained in the Luxeuil school.

The most famous of all was Amandus, another Aquitanian, who did missionary work among Basques and Slavs as well as Franks. The *Vita Amandi*, written not too long after his death, tells of a quarrel he had with King Dagobert over his right to carry out his missionary work wherever he wished, following Christ's precept to 'teach all nations'. Dagobert felt that missionary work should go together with the extension of Frankish power and influence, and the king won: Amandus went to the northern Franks and the southern Frisians, and there worked for nearly 40 years in the region of Tournai, Ghent and Antwerp, earning himself the title of the 'Apostle of Belgium'. He died in 675 at his own monastery of Elnone, now St-Amand, founded in part on land given by Dagobert. Following his advice, one of the most important nunneries in the area was founded, by Itta, the widow of Pippin I, Dagobert's Mayor of the Palace. The nunnery was Nivelles, and its first abbess was St Gertrude, the first saint belonging to the family which later, as the Carolingians, was to take the Frankish throne from the Merovingians. One of Amandus's companions was Bavo, who gave his name to an important monastery in Ghent. Other missionaries in the area at the time include St

Eligius, bishop of Noyon, who worked in the area of Courtrai, Bruges and Ghent; Audomar (St Omer), bishop of Thérouanne, who founded the monastery of Sithiu for his fellow monk from Luxeuil, Bertin (the monastery was later known as St Bertin), and who founded a nearby chapel which eventually grew into the town of St-Omer; and, a generation later, St Lambert, who worked in Toxandria, the first home within the Roman Empire of the Salian Franks, and Hubert, who worked also in the Ardennes and in Brabant. All the monasteries founded by these men became the foci of religious life for the Low Countries, and some of them began the work of conversion among the neighbouring Frisians which was to be continued by Englishmen like Wilfrid and Willibrord.

The precise means used by these missionary bishops and monks in working for conversion is not known. Only the *Vita Amandi* gives some details. It is clear that it was not without its dangers, and that it was not a question simply of preaching. Amandus started by buying slaves and baptising them, to serve as a core of converts in the region. Slaves and tenants would naturally tend to follow the religion of their lord; the extension of Christianity in the countryside was very directly bound up with the extension of Church property. And the *Vita Amandi* suggests also that it was the reputation of miracle-working which convinced the average rural pagan of the power of the Christian God: the raising of a dead man by St Amandus seems to have been a significant stage in his conversion of the region of Ghent.

Christianity in Frankish Cemeteries

As in the question of Frankish settlement one can turn to archaeology to fill out the shadowy picture provided by the historical sources. We can, clearly, look at the evidence provided by churches themselves. Much of the evidence, is, however, again provided by cemeteries. Is it in fact possible to see a transition in burial customs from pagan to Christian?[18]

[18] In much of this I follow Bailey Young: his Philadelphia doctoral dissertation of 1975 and his article in *Archéologie Médiévale* 7 1977.

Plate 27 A reconstruction of the rich Frankish warrior grave from c. 600 at Morken in the Rhineland, showing the distribution of the weapons, helmet, horse-bit, vessels, animal bones and other objects in the coffin and burial chamber.

The most obvious feature of Merovingian burial customs, a custom which spans almost the whole of the Merovingian period, from c. 500 to c. 700, is the burial of grave-goods with the dead. Grave-goods are of two types, those which formed part of the personal attire of the person (including weapons, perhaps) and those which were additional (notably containers of various materials, pottery, glass, metal and, probably the most common although it very seldom survives in the soil, wood). The two are clearly distinguished in a grave such as the 'chieftain's grave' at Morken, where the one set of grave-goods, those which formed part of the chieftain's equipment, are inside the wooden coffin within the burial chamber, and the rest are outside it. Placing containers in the grave had been common in Roman cemeteries; burying the dead fully dressed was not. In very general terms we find both customs together in graves of the sixth century in Gaul (above all Gaul north-east of the Seine); in the seventh century we find the dead still buried with items of personal apparel, but without containers; in the eighth century we find, on the whole, no grave-goods at all.

Many have seen the whole custom of deposition of grave-goods as 'pagan'. But we might legitimately ask whether grave-goods such as weapons, or vessels containing items of food or drink, actually were intended as things which the dead person might need on a journey to a pagan afterlife. Were they perhaps part of a social ceremony which may have involved, for instance, the ritual sharing of the funeral meal with the dead, or a display of conspicuous expenditure by the bereaved family? That richly endowed burials had anything especially pagan about them is made unlikely by two facts in particular. The Franks, from the kings downwards, adopted such customs enthusiastically in the very generation in which Clovis and his followers were converted to Christianity. Secondly, such customs have been found in their most elaborate form within churches themselves. The wealthy graves under Cologne Cathedral, from the first half of the sixth century, or the grave of Arnegundis under St Denis (see below p. 155), must belong to the very highest ranks of Frankish society, and these people were surely buried with the approval of the resident clergy.

The church, so ready to denounce what it perceived as pagan customs (even apparently harmless ones, such as the wearing of amulets), never issued a decree condemning burial fully dressed or with grave-goods. It did condemn some aspects of burial practice, however, and primarily not those which it regarded as pagan, but those which were seen as sacriligious within a Christian context. Thus the Church condemned burying a corpse wrapped in an altar cloth, or with a consecrated host in the mouth. St Caesarius, Bishop of Arles in the early sixth century, also denounced the 'pernicious error which has developed among Christians, not to say among pagans as well, of bringing food and drink to the tombs of the dead, as if the

Plate 28 Vessels buried with the dead ranged from simple parts to expensive bronze bowls imported from Mediterranean areas, such as this example from Cologne.

souls which had left the body had need of material nourishment' (Sermon 190). There is indeed archaeological evidence for this custom, above all in graves of the fourth and fifth century, and even in an ecclesiastical context. Two tombs under the church of St Severinus at Cologne contain our best evidence of fifth-century cuisine: one contained two eggs in a bowl, a pot with cooked chicken, and a glass vessel with a bird cooked in honey; the other had a bowl with meat cooked in fat, flavoured with mustard and sage, a pot containing porridge sweetened with honey, together with a jug of beer and a glass of wine. At the feet of the 'princess' under Cologne Cathedral, of the mid-sixth century, there was a bottle still one-third full of wine, and a box containing nuts and dates. On the whole, however, evidence for food offerings in the sixth and seventh centuries is slim; it is not nearly as common as it had been in the Roman period. Perhaps the disappearance of this practice can indeed be regarded as one of the successes of Christian preaching.

There are other aspects of burial behaviour which have been regarded as significant. Later medieval Christians would interpret the placing of a grave so that the head was at the west and the feet to the east in a specifically religious way: when the general bodily resurrection comes on the Last Day, Christians will sit up in their graves to face the rising sun and their Judge. In more practical terms, perhaps, later medieval graves were placed parallel to the church, which itself faced east. In the third and fourth centuries Roman graves in Gaul were frequently aligned west-east, that is, with the heads to the east, or else north-south or south-north; by the Merovingian period there had been a definite change to an east-west orientation. However, the beginnings of that change, like the change from cremation to inhumation itself, are to be found in late Roman rural cemeteries of north-east Gaul, too early, it seems, to be ascribed to the direct impact of Christianity. Cremation is in fact the one burial custom which the Church *did* attack ferociously in the early Middle Ages, but this is a custom which had largely died out among the Roman population before the spread of Christianity, and it seems largely to have been abandoned by the Franks west of the Rhine as well. Some of the Germanic burials in northern Gaul in the Roman period are cremations: three out of 85 at Abbeville-Homblières, for

Plate 29 One side of the grave-stone from Niederdollendorf, perhaps
portraying the dead warrior.

instance. It rapidly died out. At Vron (Somme) there were nine cremations out of 110 burials for the late Roman period, but in the Merovingian period there was only one out of 225.

Archaeologists have made attempts to categorize individual graves according to the religion of their occupant. Cremation might indeed be a certain indicator of the paganism of a particular individual (or the paganism of those who cremated him). Other rituals – placing the body on a layer of burnt material, for instance, or decapitating or otherwise mutilating the corpse before burial – are much less certain. Some have looked instead at the objects actually placed within the grave, objects of Christian significance indicating Christian burials, and objects that seem to be non-Christian signifying pagan burials. There are some obvious absurdities with this argument:

Plate 30 Another side of the Niederdollendorf stone, depicting Christ (?).

objects themselves do not have religious allegiances, and it would be difficult indeed to determine precisely what an individual object might have meant to the person in whose grave it was found – someone who, after all, was not responsible for placing it there. Even if we find gold-foil crosses carefully placed on the chest of the dead person, as we do in Alamannic graves, we cannot assume that this sacred symbol necessarily denotes the presence of a baptised Christian. Only if a grave is found in clear association with a Christian epitaph, or if a grave is found in association with a church, can we be really sure of religious affiliation.

Some of the problems of determining religious affiliation in other cases emerge when we look at iconography, funerary and otherwise. We can start with the most famous problem piece:

the stone of Niederdollendorf. It is of limestone, 42 cm. high, and decorated on five of its six sides. On one broad side a warrior grips his sword in its riveted leather scabbard, while raising his right arm, in prayer or perhaps in combing action. At his feet appears to be a bag or flask. A two-headed serpent attacks (?) him from above, and a single-headed serpent bites at his sword-grip (see plate 29). On the reverse, stands a figure holding a spear, a circle on his chest and rays (?) coming from his head; the figure stands on interlaced bands, and the rest of the field is filled by chevron patterns (see plate 30). The first figure has been interpreted, by Jean Hubert for instance, as representing the dead man, being threatened in death by evil spirits, while the second has been seen as Christ in glory. A Christ bearing a spear is perhaps not such a strange image, given the role of the spear as a symbol of power or rule among the Franks (cf. p. 178): no stranger than the image of Christ dressed in purple and sitting on an imperial throne, as in the apse-mosics of Byzantine churches. Professor Wallace-Hadrill, on the other hand, sees the whole thing as 'thoroughly pagan': it is not Christ, but Woden, a ring on his chest ('as it might be, the ring Draupnir of the Eddas') and a snake or dragon beneath his feet.[19] Do we have to assume that the ambiguity presented by these images to the twentieth century was necessarily absent in the sixth or seventh? It is surprising how rare totally unambiguous religious images are. The man menaced by beasts is a common motif in both Germanic and late Roman art; in one context it must be interpreted as pagan, and in the other as Christian, as a representation of Daniel in the lions' den. The average Frank probably lived in a mental world in which that image could represent either of those ideas, or both. The missionary and the historian who reads the missionary writings tend to assume that Christian and pagan are two diametrically opposed systems of belief. Any tinge of something which does not look like what the twentieth century regards as Christian will be denounced as 'paganism'. Yet Christianity in the fifth- or sixth-century Roman Empire had resonances that were very different from modern Christianity. Most Franks probably accepted Christianity initially as a welcome addition to the

[19] J. M. Wallace-Hadrill, *The Frankish Church*, p. 20.

already complex mythology and ritual of their ancestors; they would naturally adapt their iconography to suit the new cult, and interpret Mediterranean Christian iconography in their own way.

Church burials

Archaeology can provide us with some information, however: there are indeed changes in burial practice in this period which we can plausibly relate to the conversion and Christianization of the Franks. The most important of these changes is the growing frequency of burial in or near churches. Clovis himself was buried in a church, as were all subsequent Merovingian kings; and the earliest discovered aristocratic graves in churches are in the generation immediately following Clovis's death. It was a custom which in fact proved rather too popular as far as clergymen were concerned: there is surviving ecclesiastical legislation which attempts to exclude lay corpses from churches, and to restrict church burial to worthy ecclesiastics only. It is doubtful if this was very effective, particularly in the case of those churches which had been built by aristocrats, where there is often evidence of a so-called 'founder-grave', a grave placed in a central position or close to the altar in an apparently privileged position, or showing its priority simply by the size of the grave and the dating of its gravegoods.

Arlon may stand as an example of the type. In 1936 21 graves were found at Arlon, an important Roman *castrum*, inside a small stone building (18 m. X 10 m.). Initially this building was interpreted as a room of a ruined Roman villa, with a cemetery installed inside it, but it is now generally thought to be a church. The oldest grave was no. 10, a large wooden chamber grave in the corner of the church, with weapons and other objects decorated in a cloisonné style which places them in the second quarter of the sixth century. The other graves, a good proportion of them with rich grave-goods, range from the second half of the sixth century to the late seventh: we may interpret the site as a church built by a Frankish aristocrat converted at the time of Clovis, which continued to be used as a family mausoleum for about a century and a half.

*Plate 31 A model of the cemetery excavated by Demolon at Hordain,
showing the small church and its burials.*

Another intriguing site, excavated in 1974 by P. Demolon, is
that of Hordain (Nord). It is a cemetery of 430 graves. The
earliest are in the north of the site, dating from the late fifth
century, and are aligned north-east/south-west. They include
three cremation graves and two horse graves, which would all
indicate the presence of pagans. In the middle of the sixth
century a new core to the cemetery was created, to the south,
where the graves were oriented east-west. Around the year 600
a small church (13 m. X 8 m.) was built in the southern area,
with stone foundations and, perhaps, a wooden superstructure
(see plate 31). Remains of the altar were found, making its
function clear, and fragments of greenish window glass. At the
same time a ditch was dug around all the previous burials,
making a cemetery enclosure. Some, but not all, of the
subsequent graves organized themselves around this church.
The church itself contained two types of burial: large graves
containing rich grave-goods (two men with shield, spear, and
other weapons; women with their jewellery), and smaller tombs
near the altar, now empty. The latter were perhaps the graves of
priests, whose bodies were removed when the church was
abandoned. More intriguing, however, was the discovery of a
cremation grave, placed originally under a barrow, which could
be dated to the end of the sixth century – contemporary, that is,
with the church. Burials continued in both parts of the
cemetery, each with their own orientations, until the end of the
seventh century (when the chapel fell into disuse), and beyond.
Burials were soon transferred to the parish church, which was
constructed (in the eighth century?) some 300 metres away.

The excavations conducted in 1974 at the former monastery of Saint-Evre at Toul (Meurthe-et-Moselle) may serve as the final example. Thirteen sarcophagi were found here, and a few more simple burials. Two of the sarcophagi contained exceptionally rich burials: no. 1 had a gold disc brooch, a gilt silver finger-ring, with a monogram which can be read as ENDVLVS, a silver damascened spur, a knife and other objects from the seventh century; no. 2 contained a silver ear-ring, a heavy bronze bracelet, a gold seal-ring with a monogram which can be read PRETORIA, and silver shoe-buckles, all probably from the early seventh century. We thus have two important people, a man and a woman, buried near the altar of this church: if the readings of the monograms are correct, then they would appear to be Endulus (also appearing in the sources as Eudulanus and Eudila), bishop of Toul from *c.* 600 to *c.* 622, and Praetoria, who is referred to in the later *Deeds of the Bishops of Toul* as an aristocratic lady who was a great builder of churches in the diocese of Toul. One of the rewards for service to the church seems to have been burial in a consecrated building.

Burial in church was for privileged people only. Second-best was burial immediately outside a church, *sub stillicidio*, under the eavesdrip, so that rain-water sanctified by its contact with the holy building might fall onto the tomb. Third-best was burial in the area around the church, the *atrium*. By the eighth century most cemeteries were probably church-yard cemeteries. It is difficult to know precisely when this custom began in Frankish areas. Most sixth- and seventh-century rural cemeteries do not seem to have been near churches at all. Sometimes this may have been more the result of modern excavation policy, which has mostly concentrated on the graves themselves, not giving sufficient attention to traces in the soil between them. In some well-excavated cemeteries, such as Grobbendonk and Sézegnin, post-holes have been found within the cemetery which probably indicate the presence of a wooden church.

In some cases, it might be possible to assume the presence of a church simply from the way in which the graves lie. Mazerny in the Ardennes, for instance, is a fairly typical row-grave cemetery (see figure 3 p. 27). It developed on a spur facing north-east, and looking over the plain where the modern village (and, perhaps, the Merovingian village) lies. Some 270 graves were excavated between 1963 and 1967, 155 of which contained grave-goods. The cemetery began towards the middle of the sixth century, and ceased to be used around 700. Most of the graves were aligned towards the north-east, following the lie of the land. At the east of the site there was a small group of graves dated to the second half of the seventh century and aligned east-west. The graves seem to have been of a fairly high social level: there was a bronze spur in one male grave, and gold and silver jewellery in a neighbouring female grave. A plausible interpretation of the cemetery would be that it belonged to a small rural community, of about 30 people, and that it was largely untouched by Christianity until the second half of the seventh century. At that time the more important people of the community had a wooden church built to one side of the cemetery, and had themselves buried in it. At the beginning of the eighth century a church was built in the village itself, and a churchyard cemetery was established next to it. There it remained until the municipal cemetery was created on the outskirts of the settlement in the nineteenth century. This migration of cemetery from one site to another can be found across much of Europe, and may well be related to changing attitudes towards the dead. In the Roman and Merovingian periods the dead were unclean, and were to be kept away from human habitations; burial in or near a church sanctified and cleansed the dead, and so, from the Carolingian period onwards, the dead could be brought within the community; in the nineteenth century the dead again came to be seen as polluting, though for very different reasons.

Frankish Churches

The final type of archaeological evidence which survives to tell us something about Frankish Christianity consists of the ecclesiastical buildings themselves. Certainly few of these were actually built by Franks, and there are no architectural innovations which can be regarded as strictly Frankish. Yet some of the most important churches in sixth- and seventh-century Gaul were built at the behest of Frankish kings, queens and aristocrats; and summoning up an image of the physical environment in which Franks learnt about Christianity and worshipped the Christian god is relevant to our purpose. Yet it is very difficult. We can enter the churches and monasteries of the twelfth or thirteenth century, and learn much about Church life and about the artistic achievements of the age, but this is impossible for the Frankish Church. Surviving Merovingian buildings are so scarce that the cautious scholar might be advised to ignore them. The baptistery at Poitiers *might* be partially Merovingian in construction, but could be largely late Roman. The Hypogeum of Abbot Mellebaudis, also at Poitiers, constructed as his funerary chapel, *c.* 700, is a rather ramshackle semi-basement building, which may give us very false ideas about the incompetence of Merovingian architects if we imagine it to be a typical example of church architecture. The crypts of Jouarre are now generally thought to be early Carolingian. There are no pictorial representations of churches, such as help or mislead the Carolingian archaeologist. We have to rely on plans of buildings demolished before or during the French Revolution, on plans recovered by nineteenth- or early twentieth-century excavations, and on the very occasional modern excavation (many of which are never published properly). Most churches are known from old excavations, where the identification of Merovingian remains beneath a later church may be faulty dating or faulty identification. The plans, the masonry, the building techniques proclaimed as Merovingian are in almost all cases dated by analogy, by recourse to historical sources, by prejudice or by wishful thinking. One eminent and despairing French scholar suggested that we should look at Anglo-Saxon churches (at least one of which, Jarrow, was built in the seventh century by Gallic masons) if we want to learn about Frankish ones. Anglo-Saxon churches survive, often in poor or more remote areas; no area in Francia escaped well-intentioned and well-heeled modernizers and rebuilders, who have been at their work of demolition and reconstruction since the eighth century.

It is clear that at the time of the Frankish conquest of Gaul there were many churches, and that during the sixth and seventh centuries many more were built. Gregory of Tours mentions 38 places with churches in the Touraine, and several of these places had more than one church: he mentions 13 in Tours itself. Using a very basic calculation, if every Gallic diocese had a minimum of 38 places with churches, then one might reckon on a minimum of 4000 places with churches around the year 600. Gregory himself mentions 400 of them. Many of these churches would not, of course, be Merovingian in construction. Late Roman churches were probably still standing in large numbers; some stand to this day. Some Merovingian churches were Roman secular buildings adapted for ecclesiastical use in the Frankish period: two well-known examples are the church of St-Pierre-aux-Nonnains in Metz and the monastery of Oeren (Trier), built in and named after a Roman grain-warehouse or *horrea*.

We may have very little archaeological evidence for these churches, but there is quite a lot of historical evidence. There are even Michelin-guide descriptions of two churches by Gregory of Tours: one, the cathedral church of Clermont, clearly 'mérite le détour'. It is

150 feet long and 60 feet wide across the nave and 50 feet high to the ceiling. It has a rounded apse, and on either side are elegantly made wings; the whole building is in the shape of a cross. There are 42 windows, 70 columns and eight doors. In it one is conscious of the fear of God and of a great brightness, and those at prayer are often aware of a most sweet and aromatic odour which is being wafted towards them. Round the sanctuary it has walls which are decorated with mosaics made of many varieties of marble. (LH II. 16)

Light and brightness are the major aesthetic features of churches, as in contemporary Byzantium. Indeed many Gallic churches of the fifth and sixth centuries, with their marble and their mosaics, may have closely resembled the magnificent churches of the East, or those of Byzantine Ravenna. The best known (or most regretted) is probably Notre-Dame-la-Daurade in Toulouse, whose elaborate iconographic programme in mosaics is known from a seventeenth-century description, but which was destroyed, apart from a few carved marble columns and gold tesserae, in 1761. Such churches were probably being built in northern Gaul too, by Frankish monarchs. There is Clovis's Church of the Holy Apostles in Paris (see below p. 158) or St Martin's in Autun, built with the help of Queen Brunhild in the 590s, which was, according to an eleventh-century description, decorated with marble columns, fine beams of pine and admirable mosaics. Some of the mosaics could still be seen in the apse in 1724; it was demolished in 1741. Another was the Church of the Holy Cross and St Vincent, built by Childebert I in Paris after he had acquired a relic of St Vincent on his Spanish expedition. It was later dedicated to St Germanus, and is now St-Germain-des-Prés. Around 1000 it was described in some detail:

> It seems superfluous to describe the clever arrangement of windows, the precious marbles which support it, the gilded panels of the vault, the splendour of the walls which were covered with a sparkling gold colour and the beauty of the mosaic-covered pavements. The roof of the the building is covered with gilded bronze and reflects the rays of the sun, shining so brightly that onlookers are dazzled, and call the church St Germanus the Golden.[20]

Also attributed to Childebert I in Paris was St Stephen. It is under and in front of the present Notre-Dame. Recent excavations have shown it to have a width of 36 metres and a probable length of 50–60 metres, and there seems to have been a tower at the west end: bell-towers, it has been suggested, are a Gallic introduction to western church architecture. As was not uncommon in Gallic cities, there was not just one cathedral church, but a whole group: to the east of St Stephen was the church dedicated to Mary (under the choir of the present cathedral) and nearby was the baptistery. What astonishes us today is the great number of churches in Merovingian towns, few of which are thought to have had more than a few thousand inhabitants: as many as 35 churches are known or suspected from Paris, for instance. Most of these urban churches were small, of course, like rural ones, and decorated at most with paintings, such as are described for several churches of the period. But the sixth and seventh centuries were clearly a great age of Gallic church-building; as far as the Frankish north-east was concerned, that process accelerated with the foundation of monasteries.

[20] Quoted from the *Vita S. Droctovei* by Jean Hubert in *L'Art Préroman* (Paris, 1938), p. 9.

It was often felt that for a monastery, as for the seat of a bishopric, more than one church was appropriate; counting the monasteries on the map, therefore, hardly gives an idea of the number of churches that were constructed. Filibert's monastery of Jumièges, near Rouen, according to one interpretation of the description, had five churches within the monastic enclosure; Itta's nunnery at Nivelles had four, according to a Carolingian description. Excavations there discovered only three: St Mary's, 28 m. X 14 m., with two aisles; St Paul's, 9.5 m. X 7 m.; and St Gertrude's, 23 m. X 7 m., where the first abbess was buried. It was decorated like the other churches, quite simply, apparently, as befitted a monastery, with a floor of red-painted mortar and walls of white plaster. In the south-east corner six grave-cuts were found which had clearly been made at the same time as the church was built; the stone walls of each grave were covered with the same red-painted mortar. Elsewhere in the church graves had been cut into the floor at a later date. This is the clearest example in Merovingian archaeology of a church designed and built specifically as a funerary church.

Royal Burials

Royal funerary churches and the burials they contain are especially interesting as evidence of Frankish Christianity. All Frankish kings and their relatives after the time of Clovis, as far we know, were buried in churches: it was a public expression of their trust in the god they had chosen. Royal burials also introduce one way in which kings used the Church to further their power; Frankish kings, like kings in the rest of early medieval Europe, were well aware of the political advantages to be gained through Christianity and the Church.

The most spectacular 'royal' graves found since the discovery of Childeric's grave in 1653 (see above pp. 59–64), were, by a strange coincidence, found within a matter of weeks of one another, in 1959: two under Cologne Cathedral and one under Saint-Denis. They were all inserted below the floors of major Christian churches. The two Cologne graves date from the second quarter of the sixth century, and therefore from one or two generations after the conversion of King Clovis and many

Plate 32 The crystal ball from the Cologne 'princess's' grave with its gold mount. These balls are known from numerous Frankish women's graves; they were suspended from the belt, and are thought to have been fertility talismans.

of the Franks: the choice of burial site and burial rite must have been made by Christians. At one end of the chamber containing the princess's grave was a coffin, in which was the body together with her items of apparel: her head-band woven with gold thread, her dress fasteners, her crystal ball (plate 32) and her amulet container. Outside the coffin lay the other objects: the vessels of pottery, glass, and bronze, perhaps containing, as in other contemporary graves, offerings of food and drink. The second grave from Cologne is even more remarkable: it contained the body of a six-year old boy, laid out upon a wooden bed, and at the foot of the bed stood a chair – our only two surviving pieces of Frankish furniture (figure 16). The traces of wood have enabled archaeologists to date this grave to *c.* 537, using tree-ring dating. A child-sized helmet hung on the back of the chair; by the bed were laid adult-sized weapons, including a long-sword, a battle-axe, a bow with some arrows, and a shield. By the boy's left side was placed a lathe-turned wooden stick. It has often been assumed that it was a sceptre, and this together with the fact that these two were buried with

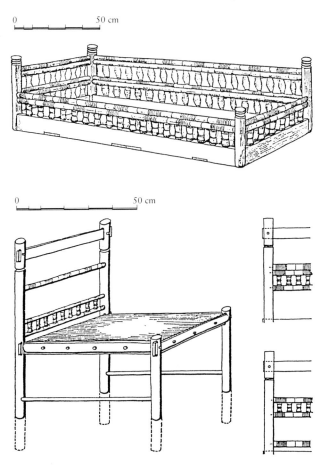

*Figure 16 Reconstruction of the bed and the chair from the grave of the boy
'prince' in Cologne Cathedral.*

their luxury grave-goods within the cathedral of Cologne has,
for some, been sufficient proof that the pair were royal. There is
obviously plenty of room for doubt. Certainly these burials are
richer than other early sixth-century Frankish burials in
churches, but we know enough about the wealth of sixth-
century Frankish non-royal aristocrats to know that they could
be very wealthy indeed. Nor is it clear who these royals could
be, buried in Cologne rather than further west in Gaul like all of
Clovis's descendants who are known to us. But perhaps they

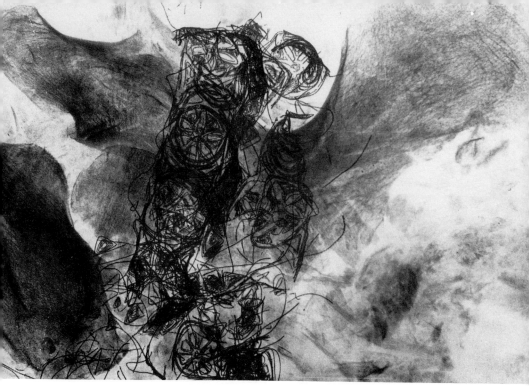

*Plate 33   An X-ray taken of the sleeve of Arnegund, showing the pattern of the
gold-thread embroidery.*

were relatives or descendants of the royal dynasty of Cologne
whose last representative, Chloderic, had been killed by Clovis.
If so, the significance of the wooden staff is even more
important. If it represents royal power, then it might suggest
that the Cologne dynasty continued to have some recognized
status. However, if royal at all, perhaps they are unknown
members of the family of Clovis's son Theuderic, who ruled that
area.

'Not proven' should probably also be the verdict on the third
burial found in 1959: the grave of Arnegund from St-Denis.[21] It
was a fascinating find. Sufficient fragments of clothing survived
to enable a reconstruction of her clothing to be made. X-rays
were used to help this reconstruction (see plate 33): even traces
of her hair and body tissue survived – fragments of lung
preserved by the embalming fluids that were forced down her
throat after death. It was her ring – not a seal-ring, but
nevertheless inscribed with a name – which identified her as

[21] The most useful publication so far is the special issue of the popular magazine
Dossiers de l'Archéologie, **32** (1979).

*Plate 34 The two gold-and-garnet disc brooches from Arnegund's grave in
Saint-Denis together with her ring inscribed ARNEGUNDIS.*

Arnegund, and the monogram in the centre was almost
immediately deciphered as REGINA, queen, which allowed the
identification of the body as that of Queen Aregund, the third
wife of King Chlothar I, who probably died in the late 560s.
Gregory of Tours described how Queen Ingund had asked her
husband Chlothar to find a suitable husband for her sister
Aregund, and Chlothar saw her, 'in amore Aregundis incedit',
and announced to Ingund that the most suitable man available
was himself.

The only dissenting voice at this identification of Arnegund
with Aregund then was Dr, now Sir, David Wilson, who
suggested common-sensically that the monogram read ARNE-
GUNDIS, not REGINA: all similar early medieval monograms are
those of personal names, not titles. Indeed, the archaeological
evidence now seems against the idea that this grave of Arnegund
can be that of the sixth-century Aregund. The burial with
personal adornments only and no grave-goods proper belongs
more to the seventh century than to the sixth, and many of the
objects – the large buckle and plate, the smaller buckles and

strap-ends, the pins and earrings, and the disc-brooches – would all fit better in the seventh century. Patrick Périn has pointed out how one disc-brooch seems to be a maladroit copy of the other, and suggests that the woman may have been a south German, used to wearing one such brooch on her cloak, who had come to the Paris region, to find that current fashions there required two such brooches, one on each shoulder.

Our most famous royal burial from the period after Childeric may thus not be royal at all. But there may be one or two others. Burial no. 16 at St-Denis had been robbed, but still contained traces of a fine war-harness, rich embroidery, and three gold rings, including one ring with a sapphire. This has been interpreted by Edouard Salin, with grudging acceptance by Professor Wallace-Hadrill, as the possible burial of Chlothar III, who died in 673. Another possible royal burial was found in the same decade as Childeric I's tomb: Childeric II's tomb. This is surrounded by very much more uncertainty, since descriptions date only from 1724. It seems that in 1645 several tombs were discovered under the floor of St-Germain-des-Prés in Paris; they were re-opened, or others were discovered, in 1656, three years after the discovery of Childeric I's grave had given an impetus to such investigations. One body had a gold head-band and clothes with gold thread, and belt- and shoe-buckles of silver: it appears to have been associated with a sarcophagus that had CHILDR. REX inscribed on it. Nearby was a grave also with gold robes, which was identified as that of Belechildis, the young queen who had been assassinated in 675 together with Childeric II. One wonders whether the gold head-band does not denote the grave of another woman: such finds have been made in numerous women's graves. And there was a description of another grave, or even of the same grave, which may be much more appropriate as that of a king. It had a large hazel-wood staff in it, as long as the tomb itself, a sword, gold belt-fittings and other metal objects. Only one of these apparently survived into the eighteenth-century to be illustrated: a small bronze plaque with a double-headed serpent, which in 1980 Périn dated to the later seventh century and accepted as being from Childeric II's burial. Montfaucon in 1724 wrote that a monk of St-Germain had confessed on his death-bed that he had sold everything else that had been found, and thereby raised 13000 livres for the

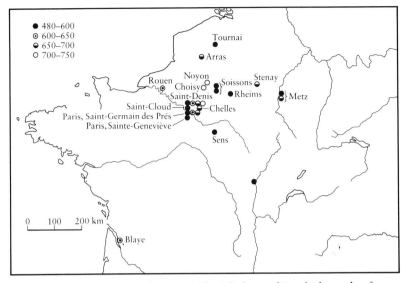

Figure 17 The known and suspected burial places of Frankish royalty, from historical and archaeological evidence.

building of a new organ. Rich graves they certainly were, but whether they were royal, let alone those of Childeric II and Belechildis (whom later traditions claim to have been buried in St-Ouen in Rouen and not St-Germain-des-Prés at all), must remain very much an open question.

The burial places of a number of ruling Merovingian kings are however known from historical sources. A map drawn from this data (figure 17) shows clearly how concentrated they are in the Paris area. The first was the church of the Holy Apostles in Paris, built by Clovis. St Genevieve was buried here as well as Clovis, and the church later on acquired her name. Her *Life* said that it had a triple portico in front – perhaps a three-sided columned arcade, with the fourth side formed by the west front of the church – and that its walls were decorated with scenes from the lives of patriarchs, prophets, martyrs and confessors. It was largely destroyed by the Vikings in the ninth century, but a twelfth-century writer said that mosaics could still be distinguished on the ruins both inside and outside. To this church were brought, from a considerable distance, not only the body of Clovis's widow Clotild, but also that of their daughter, also called Chrotechildis or Clotild, who died on her way back home from a disastrous marriage in Spain. But if Clovis had intended to found a dynastic mausoleum here, the division of the kingdom among his four sons after his death frustrated any such ambition. Of his sons, only Childebert I was buried in Paris. Childebert returned from an expedition to Spain in the early 530s with the cloak of St Vincent, and built a church in Paris to shelter the relic and to serve as his burial place. He died in Paris in 558 and was duly buried in St Vincent's. When his nephew King Chilperic was assassinated, the bishop of Senlis brought him to Paris for burial in this same church, and there too were buried his wife and three if not four of their children, including Chlothar II, the king who reunited the Frankish kingdom in 613. Two of them were those sons murdered by Chilperic or his wife (see p. 175); their bodies were brought to St Vincent's after Chilperic's death by his brother Guntram. Later still, as we have seen, Childeric II and his wife may have been brought there after their assassination in 675. Sadly none of these early graves was found in the excavations of 1807, when a number of late Merovingian sarcophagi were discovered: it is possible that the royal graves had all been disturbed in the explorations of 1644 and 1656.

Again, if this was an attempt to found a royal mausoleum, it was frustrated by political chance and the appeals of a rival church. Chlothar II was buried in St Vincent's. His son Dagobert's favourite estate was Clichy, near the church containing the relics of the martyr St Denis. In addition to proximity, the antiquity of St Denis himself gave him an obvious claim to be a major patron saint of Gaul, and of the dynasty which ruled it. Dagobert enlarged the church after he moved westwards to Paris in 629; Arnegund was apparently buried within his extension, which again argues against her identification with Aregund. However, only two Merovingian kings were buried in St-Denis: Dagobert himself, who fell ill near Epernay, and was brought to St Denis to die, and his son Clovis II. Clovis II's widow Balthild preferred burial in the monastery which she had founded at Chelles. Only much later, long after St-Denis had received the burials of a number of Carolingian rulers, including Charles Martel and Pippin I, did it become the almost undisputed burial place of the French kings.

In the Merovingian period itself, the political geography was too changing and unstable for a dynastic mausoleum to emerge. There could be no equivalent to Canterbury, the burial place of Kentish kings for two centuries: the kingdom was too large, and too often divided among different branches of the dynasty. But it could also be argued that the Merovingian dynasty was so strong and unchallenged that it did not need the support of such a centre; it was in Kent, where dynasties were more fragile, that kings needed to celebrate their adherence to royal traditions. Even when Frankish kings seem deliberately to have built burial-churches for themselves, these churches served no more than one or two generations. St-Médard at Soissons, for instance, was built by Chlothar I, and his body was brought there from Compiègne in 561; 15 years later his son Sigibert I was brought there 100 kilometres from where he had been assassinated, and thereafter Soissons received no more royal burials. Guntram was buried in his own church of St Marcel at Chalon-sur-Saône, founded, he proclaimed, 'for the safety of the king and the salvation of his soul'; his wife and two sons, who all pre-deceased him, had already been buried there. *Laus perennis*, perpetual unceasing prayer for, above all, king and kingdom, was established there as, later, at St-Denis and St-Médard. But again St-Marcel was never used again for royal burials.

The evidence suggests that it did matter to kings and queens where they were buried, and suggests also that particular kings (Childebert I, Guntram, Dagobert) may have tried to establish mausolea at least for their own immediate family. Kings do seem to have done what they could to build up the importance of their own burial-churches. It is surely significant that when the *Vita Balthildis* in the late seventh century names the six greatest churches of the kingdom, all but two – St Martin of Tours and St Anianus of Orleans – were royal burial-churches (St-Germain-des-Prés, St-Médard, St-Denis and St Peter's – Holy Apostles, Paris). The inclusion of churches dedicated to Germanus and Medard, both sixth-century bishops, suggests that it was the prestige of the *king's* bodies and not the bishops' bodies which made these churches important: neither of them would seem to be saints of exceptional importance in their own right. It is perhaps significant that kings did not choose to be buried near the holiest relics or in the most venerated churches; St-Denis is the possible exception to this, although here it may have been royal patronage which raised a formerly obscure figure to prominence. Kings were able to use the church to show themselves, in death as in life, superior to all their subjects.

5

Frankish Kings and Their Subjects

Frankish kingship

Gregory of Tours was at a loss to understand the origin of kingship among the Franks: the origin, that is, of an institution that would correspond to the Latin *rex*. Centuries earlier Tacitus had just the same problems trying to reconcile Latin vocabulary with German practice. He had claimed that German kings, *reges*, were selected because of their birth, and warleaders, *duces*, on account of their valour or ability. Tribal kings were not ideally suited to leading a group of tribes in warfare; a war-leader would be chosen when the need arose. It may have been this custom among the Franks that confused Gregory. The earliest leaders of the Franks he names are called *duces* in his sources, not *reges*; the tribal kings were not directly involved in dealings with the Romans. Gregory's Roman sources also talk of 'royal leaders' (*regales*) and 'kinglets' (*reguli*). We cannot know what the Frankish equivalents might have been, or how misleading these Latin translations are. However, we can perhaps have more faith in Gregory when he is following these contemporary Roman historians, such as Sulpicius Alexander or Renatus Profuturus Frigeridus, than in what he says when written sources fail him. Gregory is our sole source for a number of traditions, most notably one saying that the Franks crossed the Rhine and 'set up in each district (*pagus*) and each *civitas* long-haired kings chosen from the foremost and most noble family of their people'. He named Chlogio who captured Cambrai, and added that 'some say' Merovech, the father of

Childeric, was descended from him. He does not mention the later tradition that Merovech was the off-spring of a sea-monster (a classicizing feature which some historians have strangely used as evidence of Germanic pagan beliefs). With Merovech, Childeric and their Merovingian descendants, we are on firmer ground. We may question, however, whether most other Frankish kings were related to this Merovingian dynasty. Gregory's account of Clovis's assassination of rival kings, some of whom, he says, were his own relations, does confirm Gregory's claim that Frankish kings in the fifth century came from 'the foremost and most noble family of their people', but it is hardly independent evidence. Gregory has an interest in presenting the Merovingians as natural rulers of the Franks. In reality the Merovingians were probably descended not from any family of tribal kings of the Franks, but from the most powerful and successful of their war-leaders, who appropriated for themselves the Roman title of *rex*.

If that is so, then we are unlikely to find very much in the way of 'traditional Germanic characteristics' in Merovingian kingship. The institution grew up within the Roman Empire, partly in response to the need of the Romans themselves to manipulate and organize military support. The ceremonial of Merovingian rule probably owes more to Roman military and imperial ceremonial than anything else. A nice example is the custom of kings being raised on a shield carried by their followers. This may well go back to ancient Celtic and Germanic roots, but because of the number of Germans within the imperial army in the fourth century, it became a recognized way by which a Roman army could elevate a man to imperial position. The only time it happens in the sixth century, it happens to a would-be Merovingian king in southern Gaul; it is the *Roman* precedent which is all-important. However, trying to separate 'Roman' from 'Germanic' in Merovingian culture may be a time-honoured procedure for early medieval historians and archaeologists alike, but ultimately it is a misconceived and futile one. From the time of Clovis if not earlier, Frankish kings ruled with the help of Roman advisors, both lay and clerical, using what remained of the old Roman machinery for administration and taxation, and behaving as what, in constitutional terms, they were: rulers, in the absence of the Roman Emperor, of a portion of the Roman Empire. For the bulk of his subjects, who were Roman by birth and tradition, the Merovingian king held a position not unlike a Roman Emperor: war-leader, judge, a potential source of patronage, and an object of awe and fear.

Like Roman Emperors since Constantine, Frankish kings also had a special relationship with the Church. This was demonstrated very early on by Clovis himself. A letter from Bishop Remigius shows us that Clovis was in a position to order the uncanonical consecration of an unworthy priest – and to have his action defended by Remigius. It was Clovis too who summoned the bishops of his whole kingdom in 511, at Orleans, and pointed out to them the areas where decisions were needed. Later in the sixth century we see kings appointing bishops, and using churchmen as royal agents. The Church on the whole benefited from the arrangement; the Merovingian kings gave it protection as well as many donations and privileges. Like Byzantine Emperors, but unlike the Carolingian kings of the Franks, the Merovingians never made the mistake of letting the Church think that royal power came from God via the Church; kings were above the Church, and serious displeasure, exile or death awaited those, like Bishops Nicetius of Trier and Desiderius of Vienne or the Irishman Columbanus, who dared to question that position.

It is, again, through Gregory of Tours that we have our best hope of understanding how Frankish kings ruled their kingdom. He presents us with a vivid picture of individual Frankish kings, particularly of the two he knew personally and whose actions affected him, as bishop of Tours, most directly: two of the sons of Chlothar I, Chilperic (king from 561–84) and Guntram (561–93). Some idea of the factors affecting the political actions of Frankish kings may be gained by looking at Gregory's picture of these brothers and at the political events of these years. It is inevitably a partial picture: Gregory was not interested in details about the day-to-day running of the kingdoms (nor, perhaps, were the kings themselves), and he viewed politics from the particular viewpoint of a Gallo-Roman aristocrat and a senior churchman. Nevertheless, reading between Gregory's lines we can still piece together an interesting picture of life at the top end of Frankish society.

Chilperic

A useful starting place for understanding these kings, and Gregory's attitude to them, is the obituary he wrote for King Chilperic:

The evil which Chilperic did has been set out in this book. Many a district did he ravage and burn, not once but many times. He showed no remorse at what he did, but rather rejoiced in it, like Nero of old who recited tragedies while his palace was burning. He frequently brought unjust charges against his subjects with the sole object of confiscating their property. In his day churchmen were rarely elected to bishoprics. He was extremely gluttonous, and his god was in his belly. He used to maintain that no one was more clever than he. He wrote two books, taking Sedulius as his model, but the verses were feeble and had no feet to stand on: he put short syllables for long ones, and long syllables for short ones, not understanding what he was doing. He composed some other short pieces, hymns and sequences for the Mass, but it was impossible to use them. He hated the poor and all that they stood for. He never ceased his attacks on those who served our Lord and, when he was among his intimate friends, the bishops were the constant butt of his ridicule and facetiousness. One he would accuse of levity, another of pride, a third of excess, and a fourth of lust. . . There was nothing that he hated so much as he hated the churches. He was perpetually heard to say: 'My treasury is always empty. All our wealth has fallen into the hands of the Church. There is no one with any power left except the bishops. Nobody respects me as king: all respect has passed to the bishops in their cities.' With this in mind he made a practice of tearing up wills in which property had been bequeathed to the bishops. He trampled underfoot the royal decrees of his own father. . . It is impossible to imagine any vice or debauchery which this man did not practise. He was always on the look-out for some new way of torturing his subjects. Whenever any were judged guilty of some crime or other, he would have their eyes torn out of their heads. . . When his time came to die, he died deserted by all. (LH VI. 49)

The closest literary parallel to this passage is the attack on the Emperor Justinian in Procopius's *Secret History*, written just over a generation earlier. There is the same wilful exaggeration, the same twisting of facts to fit the worst possible interpretation. We can no more trust it at face value than we can trust the other literary set-piece relating to Chilperic, the panegyric pronounced at his court by the Italian poet Venantius Fortunatus. It is preserved for us in Fortunatus's book of poetry, dedicated to his friend Gregory of Tours. (We may wonder what Gregory made of it.)

King, illustrious by arms and by descent from great kings. . . When you were born a new light was brought into the world, and your name shines fresh rays into all parts. . . Your name, powerful Chilperic, translated from the barbarian tongue into Latin, means 'strong aid', and that name indeed belongs to you. . . Suddenly fate, jealous of so many merits, troubled the tranquillity of your realm. It shook the emotions of whole peoples, and the alliance which united the brothers. . . (But) when enemies plotted against you with blameworthy wars, Faith took up arms and fought valiantly for you. Your cause was won, and Paris returned to its legitimate master. . . The hard trials which you endured so long have been succeeded by happiness. . . In letting you, the terror of nations, live, the Creator has considered the interest of your house, of the country and of the people. The name of victorious which is yours will prevent armed rebels from attacking the Gallic countryside. You protect vast lands. The Goth and the Basque tremble, as does the Dane; the Euthian [Jute?] trembles too, and the Saxon and Breton. . . You are the terror of the Sueves and the Frisians, who are confined to the sea. . . and admit your domination. . . Not one of your subjects surpasses you in intelligence and eloquence. You understand their different languages without interpreter, and translate them all into your own. . . You shine as a warrior and as a legislator. . . You are the equal of kings, but you are above them by your talent in poetry. . . In your understanding of theology you surpass your father. . . May you enjoy the throne peacefully, with your wife the honour of the kingdom by her manners, who governs it while sharing authority with you. . . The illustrious Fredegund. . . is filled with love for you and is a great support to you. Under her direction, which confuses itself with yours, palaces become more numerous, and if the royal house is flourishing and honoured it is because of her. (Carm. IX. 1)

There is no doubt that if Venantius's poem had survived and Gregory's *Histories* had been lost, we would have a very different image of Chilperic, and of sixth-century Merovingian kings as a whole. What can the historian make of this apparently contradictory evidence? First of all, we have to recognize that neither panegyrics nor invectives were intended to be taken at face value. Both of them were designed, in part at least, to fulfil the same function: to present the reader or listener with a view of an ideal king, either by presenting that ideal (in the presence, perhaps, of a king perfectly aware of the implicit criticism in the panegyric, but unable to respond to it publicly) or else presenting its reverse, as Gregory did. By taking the facts as presented in Gregory's obituary and elsewhere in the *Histories* one can draw a much more realistic picture of the king. It does seem that he was a representative of that class of barbarian kings whom modern historians are usually willing to admire: he was learned, and keen on imitating the Roman past and keeping up Roman traditions. Both Venantius and Gregory show that he was a literate and indeed educated man; he used to write Latin verse and compose Masses. One of his poems, in honour of St Medard of Soissons, survives: not a remarkable piece of poetry, but the medieval monarchs who could even have attempted Latin verse are few indeed. Elsewhere Gregory shows him as someone interested in theology, writing a little book on the Trinity: Gregory, with the disdain of the professional towards the layman, makes fun of his incompetence. His interest in preserving Latin traditions is displayed by his action in 'building' (presumably restoring) amphitheatres in Paris and Soissons, 'for he was keen to offer spectacles to the citizens' (LH V. 17), and even, one could argue, in his practice of blinding criminals – in imitation of the very latest civilized ways of the Eastern Roman Empire. Chilperic's 'hatred of the poor' is illustrated elsewhere by Gregory, in Chilperic's attempts to raise taxes and in the suffering of ordinary people in the civil wars: neither, presumably, actually directly inspired by this hatred of Chilperic's.

Chilperic's supposed hatred of the Church is a more crucial factor, because of its relevance to Bishop Gregory himself. Chilperic's dislike for proud, avaricious or lustful bishops, which Gregory affects to regard with loathing, is, of course, a sign of a concerned and pious layman, and elsewhere Gregory shares Chilperic's concern. Indeed, through Gregory we can easily see the problems which incompetent or unsuitable bishops created for the kingdom, since their independence from outside authority made their removal extremely difficult. It is hardly surprising that Chilperic should bemoan the power and influence of bishops in their towns; Gregory shows us the extent of their power and influence in his narrative, and shows us also how, when gathered together in councils, they can influence the policy of the kingdom as well. Chilperic's practice of tearing up wills bequeathing property to bishops is a fine example of Gregory's twisting of the evidence. In sixth-century Frankish law it was forbidden to make wills, because the inheritance laws demanded that property be divided up among all the legal heirs: leaving property to an individual, or to the Church, meant that legal heirs would be disinherited. The Roman practice of drawing up wills was undoubtedly spreading among the Frankish aristocracy in Chilperic's day, to the great benefit of the Church, but Chilperic was clearly within his rights in his attempt to uphold traditional Frankish law.

Gregory's attitude to Chilperic was undoubtedly in part a result of his own personal experience. The *civitas* of Tours suffered much from Chilperic's attacks, and when Tours was finally captured by Chilperic it was exploited, as conquered territory, by his tax-collectors. Moreover, on more than one occasion Gregory himself came up against the king, either because he found himself having to give sanctuary in Tours to Chilperic's enemies, or because he was himself perceived as one of the king's enemies. Gregory was appointed to his bishopric in 573 by Sigibert, and consecrated in Rheims, contrary to canon law, and regardless of the wishes of the Tours clergy or the other bishops of Gregory's province. Shortly afterwards Tours was taken from Sigibert by Chilperic. Gregory was Sigibert's man, and always showed some loyalty to the Austrasian kingdom. Gregory's distrust of Chilperic's queen, Fredegund, is almost as great as his dislike of Chilperic; he seems always willing, for instance, to believe any rumour about the queen's complicity in plots and assassinations. It is perhaps not surprising that in 580 Gregory was brought before a council of bishops to answer charges of slandering Fredegund and Bishop Bertram of Bordeaux (himself related to the Merovingians); perhaps it is more surprising that, according to Gregory, 'all present marvelled at the king's wisdom and restraint' when he allowed the bishops to accept Gregory's word that he was innocent. Gregory also portrays himself in 577 as standing up before his terrified fellow-bishops and speaking of Chilperic's sins and the way God had struck down sinful kings in the past; on another occasion the king had to put up with Gregory telling him to his face that those who followed Chilperic's (rather original) ideas about the Trinity were fools. Chilperic seems indeed to have shown 'wisdom and restraint'.

The Frankish kingdoms after 561

We can understand the problems of Chilperic, and hence of other Frankish kings, rather better if we look at the narrative provided by Gregory in the *Histories*. Chilperic's father was Chlothar I, the youngest and last surviving son of Clovis, who had ruled a united Frankish kingdom between his brother Childebert I's death, without heirs, in 558 and his own death in 561. Chlothar had had seven sons by various wives: Gunthar, Childeric, Charibert, Guntram and Sigibert by Ingund; Chilperic by Ingund's sister Aregund; and Chramn by Chunsina. Gunthar and Childeric died before their father, and Chramn, who rebelled against him, was burnt alive, together with his wife and children, on Chlothar's orders. Chlothar himself died on the anniversary of Chramn's death, said Gregory, implying perhaps the hand of God's justice. By coincidence Chlothar left four surviving sons, just as his father Clovis had done, and the the kingdom was divided into four just as it had been 50 years before in 511 (see figure 19). Indeed Gregory (LH IV. 22) presents it as an exact repeat of the 511 partition: Sigibert took Theuderic's kingdom, with Rheims as his residence; Charibert took Childebert's kingdom, with Paris; Guntram had Chlodomer's kingdom, with Orleans; and Chilperic received Chlothar's kingdom, with Soissons. The tiny size of Chilperic's kingdom may have been an inverse product of the size of his ambition. As soon as he had heard of Chlothar's death Chilperic seized his father's treasure at Berny, used it to try and win the support of leading Franks, and entered Paris, which had been since the time of Clovis a symbol of rule over a united Francia. He seems to have been trying to take over Chlothar's kingdom wholesale. But perhaps he merely feared that his half-brothers, all three sons of Ingund (Chilperic's aunt – see family tree figure 18) would exclude him from any inheritance. His brothers drove him from Paris, and in the subsequent partition forced him to accept the smallest of the four kingdoms.

That action may have contributed to the violent and ambitious character of Chilperic's subsequent career (as Gregory portrays it), but a glance at figure 19 suggests other reasons for Chilperic's determination to extend his kingdom. A king could only prosper with the support and assistance of warriors,

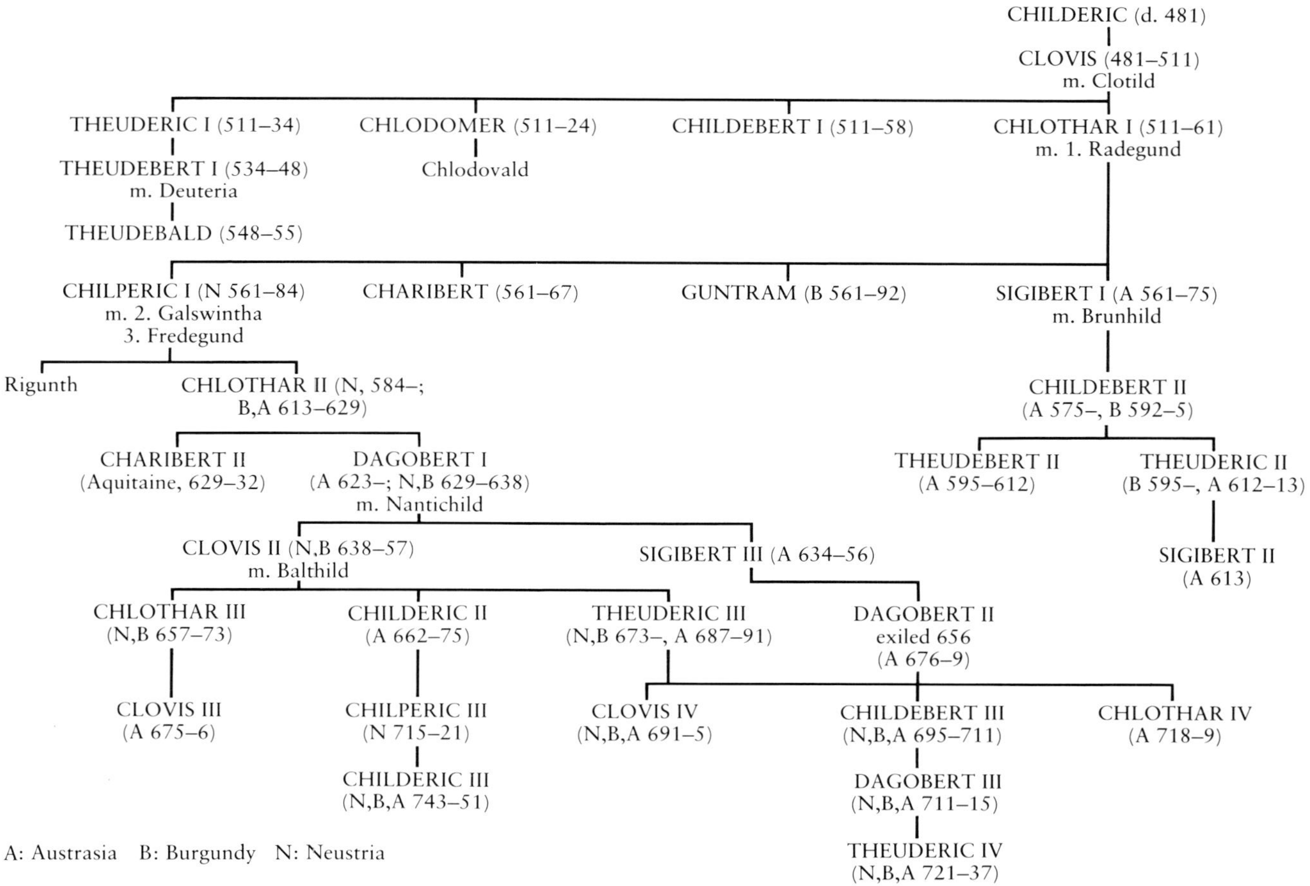

Figure 18 A simplified genealogy of the Merovingians

A: Austrasia   B: Burgundy   N: Neustria

CHILDERIC (d. 481)

CLOVIS (481–511)
m. Clotild

CHLOTHAR I (511–61)
m. 1. Radegund

THEUDERIC I (511–34)

THEUDEBERT I (534–48)
m. Deuteria

THEUDEBALD (548–55)

CHLODOMER (511–24)

Chlodovald

CHILDEBERT I (511–58)

SIGIBERT I (A 561–75)
m. Brunhild

GUNTRAM (B 561–92)

CHARIBERT (561–67)

CHILPERIC I (N 561–84)
m. 2. Galswintha
3. Fredegund

Rigunth

CHLOTHAR II (N, 584–;
B,A 613–629)

CHILDEBERT II
(A 575–, B 592–5)

THEUDEBERT II
(A 595–612)

THEUDERIC II
(B 595–, A 612–13)

SIGIBERT II
(A 613)

DAGOBERT I
(A 623–; N,B 629–638)
m. Nantichild

CHARIBERT II
(Aquitaine, 629–32)

SIGIBERT III (A 634–56)

CLOVIS II (N,B 638–57)
m. Balthild

DAGOBERT II
exiled 656
(A 676–9)

CHILDERIC II
(A 662–75)

THEUDERIC III
(N,B 673–, A 687–91)

CHLOTHAR III
(N,B 657–73)

CHILDEBERT III
(N,B,A 695–711)

CLOVIS IV
(N,B,A 691–5)

CHILPERIC II
(N 715–21)

CHLOTHAR IV
(A 718–9)

DAGOBERT III
(N,B,A 711–15)

CLOVIS III
(A 675–6)

CHILDERIC III
(N,B,A 743–51)

THEUDERIC IV
(N,B,A 721–37)

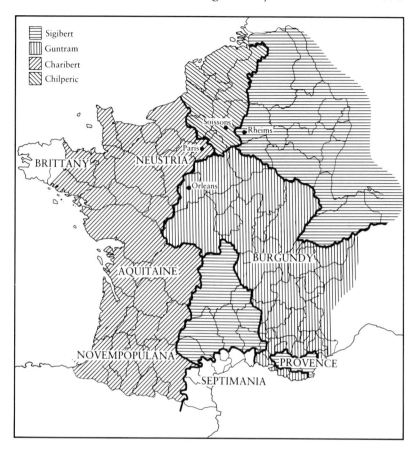

Figure 19   The partition of Francia on the death of the Chlothar I in 561; the towns marked are the main residences of four kings

and these had to be rewarded, with land or with gold and other luxuries. Both types of wealth could most easily be won through warfare; frequent warfare may also have been necessary in order to satisfy those who had been brought up to regard it as their main pursuit. Chilperic's brothers were able to raid the territories of foreign powers, across the frontiers of Septimania, the Alps or the Rhine; Chilperic alone was forced, if he started a war, to attack his brothers. (Although admittedly Fortunatus's panegyric presents him as dominant over sea-powers like the Frisians: however, we know almost nothing of the extent of Frankish sea-power.) Civil war, an inevitable result of the

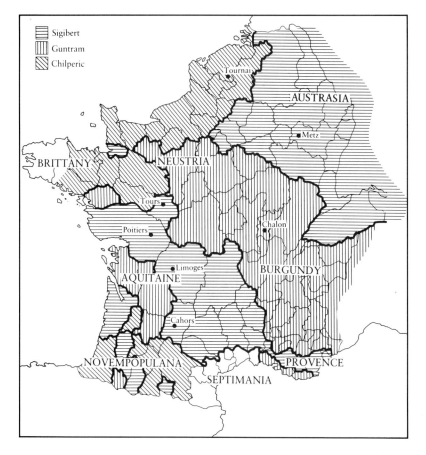

*Figure 20   The Frankish kingdoms in 571 showing the partition made after
the death of Charibert in 567.*

pressure of political or economic necessity, also resulted from
the social pressure to avenge any wrongs done to the royal sense
of honour. Civil war, which Gregory saw as the great political
evil of his day, was thus hardly the result of the moral failure of
his generation. The idea of feud, the duty that members of a
family had to act together against any threat to their honour,
was one of the most powerful moral imperatives acting for law
and order in Frankish society. The tragedy for the Merovingian
dynasty was that feud took place within the family; instead of
strengthening family bonds, it shattered them.

The wars began soon after Chlothar's death. Sigibert led his army east against the invading Avars, and Chilperic, in his brother's absence, attacked Rheims and other cities. In response Sigibert captured Soissons, and held Chilperic's son Theudebert as hostage for one year. Gregory is silent on the affairs of the next few years; the next major political event was the death of King Charibert in 567 and the partition of his kingdom among the three surviving brothers (see figure 20); Chilperic extended his territory, but his kingdom remained surrounded by those of his brothers. One of Charibert's wives, Theudechild, went over to Guntram with her treasure, deceived into thinking that he would marry her; instead he took the treasure and packed her off into a nunnery.

Like Chlothar I, Chilperic and Guntram both had several wives, although it is not known whether they practiced polygamy or 'serial monogamy'. Guntram's first wife was the servant of one of his subjects; his son by her, given the good Burgundian name of Gundobad, was poisoned 'so they say' by his second wife, who was subsequently dismissed to make way for the third. (In 580 the latter died, but not before having made Guntram promise to kill her two doctors if they failed in their duty to keep her alive.)

Chilperic himself married Fredegund, whom Gregory implies had been his servant, as his second wife. Sigibert, on the other hand, king of the eastern kingdom and heir to the grand ambitions of Theudebert, determined to increase his prestige by marrying a social equal, and he successfully negotiated for the hand of Brunhild, the daughter of the Visigothic king of Spain. Not to be outdone, Chilperic set Fredegund aside and married Brunhild's elder sister Galswinth. But the newly-weds quarrelled over Fredegund, and one morning Galswinth was found strangled in bed. Venantius Fortunatus had one of his more difficult commissions when he had to compose her obituary. He wrote in detail of her journey through Gaul, but carefully avoided any comment on the manner of her death:

I myself, recently arrived in Poitiers, saw Galswinth pass, quietly sitting in a silver tower carried on wheels. . . The Loire then received her, and finally she arrived at the mouth of the fishy Seine, and went upstream to Rouen. It was in this town that the young girl married the king. . . Hardly married, Galswinth, entering into life, was taken by death. Surprised by the speed of the blow, she fell, her eyes closed, she died. (Carm. VI. 5)

Soon afterwards Chilperic took Fredegund as his wife once more. Gregory had no doubt that Chilperic had ordered the assassination, and neither, apparently had Chilperic's brothers. There were no immediate repercussions, however. Gregory reports that Chilperic sent his son Theudebert to ravage Sigibert's territories south of the Loire – Touraine, Poitou, Limousin and Quercy – killing clergy, raping nuns and causing great devastation. In 574 Sigibert sent an army of pagan Germans from beyond the Rhine to attack Chilperic; Guntram was cowed into withdrawing support from Chilperic, and Chilperic was forced to submit. In the following year Chilperic again tried to negotiate an alliance with Guntram; again Guntram deserted him, and Sigibert recovered his territories, killing Chilperic's son Theudebert, and forcing Chilperic to take refuge in Tournai. Sigibert heard from some of Chilperic's Franks that they would welcome Sigibert as their king, and Sigibert advanced towards Tournai, intending to get rid of his brother once and for all. On the way, at Vitry, he was assassinated by two men with poisoned scramasaxes. Gregory claimed that they were in the pay of Queen Fredegund.

This assassination was a crucial event, which helps to explain many of the political events of the next generation. Sigibert's kingdom was not partitioned. Sigibert's Austrasian followers clearly wanted to preserve their independence as a kingdom, and, perhaps, to increase their own political influence; they, or at least one faction among them, installed Sigibert's five-year-old son Childebert II as king in 575. Chilperic took immediate advantage of the situation, invading Childebert's territories, notably the front-line *civitas* of Tours. But he had his problems too. His son Merovech secretly married his uncle Sigibert's widow, Brunhild, presumably to better his own political chances, although it is possible that Brunhild herself – later to emerge as one of the most forceful leaders in Merovingian history – saw the marriage as her chance to regain the political authority she had lost with the death of her husband and her removal, by Chilperic, from her son's side. Chilperic acted quickly, capturing Merovech and forcibly tonsuring him. When he escaped from the monastery to which he had been entrusted, Chilperic pursued him into sanctuary at St Martin's in Tours, and from there into hiding in Childebert's kingdom. There, in

577, Merovech was discovered; he ordered his own servant to kill him.

Chilperic's attempts to annex portions of the young Childebert's kingdom soon forced Guntram to intervene, sending Mummolus, the hero of the Lombard wars (see above p. 98), against Chilperic's Gallo-Roman duke Desiderius in the Limousin, and cementing an alliance with Childebert and his advisors. Guntram's own two sons had died of dysentery, and he made Childebert his son and heir. Not long afterwards, in another epidemic, the two surviving sons of Chilperic and Fredegund also died: a punishment, Fredegund thought (according to Gregory), for being greedy and extorting too much in taxation from their subjects. The royal couple burnt the tax-assessments, 'and from this time onwards King Chilperic was lavish in giving alms to cathedrals and churches, and to the poor too' (LH V. 34). Chilperic had only one son now, his son by his first wife Audovera, Clovis: a plot led by Fredegund discredited Clovis, and in 580 he was put to death. His mother Audovera was murdered, and his sister Basina forced to enter the convent of the Holy Cross at Poitiers. (Given the circumstances, it is perhaps not surprising that a few years later Basina should lead the nuns' revolt described so graphically by Gregory of Tours.)

Another important stage in Merovingian history was thus reached. There were now three kings: a ten-year-old boy and his two childless uncles. This potentially unstable situation led, in 581, to a dramatic change of alliances. There was a palace coup in Childebert's kingdom, and the boy king's new advisers broke the treaty that had been made with Guntram and formed an alliance with Chilperic, in which Childebert was recognized as Chilperic's heir. Shortly afterwards a quarrel arose between Childebert and Guntram over the revenues from Marseilles, and Chilperic started to move south from Tours and Poitiers, which he had taken from Childebert's kingdom, to attack Guntram's cities in Aquitaine: a full-scale attack on his brother's kingdom was narrowly averted.

At this point a ship arrived at Marseilles from Constantinople, and the usurper Gundovald disembarked. Thirty years earlier his mother had claimed him as a son of Chlothar I: Childebert and then Charibert had both accepted him as such, but Chlothar and Sigibert had denied his claims, and each forced him to cut the long hair that was the distinguishing mark of the Merovingian dynasty. In the end he had fled to Italy and thence to Constantinople. Now he returned, at the invitation of some of those engaged in the tortuous political manoeuvrings of the time. There were fears that he was the emissary of the Roman Emperor in Constantinople, paving the way for the return of Roman rule. In fact he seems to have been invited by some of Childebert's Austrasian advisors – Gregory accused in particular Egidius, bishop of Rheims, and Guntram Boso – with Chilperic's blessing perhaps, as a further lever in the struggle against Guntram. The enterprise did not get far: Gundovald's treasure was seized, and he withdrew to an island in the Mediterranean. Chilperic's support may have been withdrawn at a crucial moment; Chilperic's own political position had altered once more, with the birth of another son.

On Easter Day 583 Chilperic entered Paris, to celebrate the baptism of his son Theuderic: he ordered relics to be carried in front of him, to avoid the curse which, in the pact between himself and his two brothers in 567, had been promised to any of them who entered this city without the permission of the others. (It was a curse which, Guntram later warned Childebert, had cost the deaths of both Sigibert and Chilperic.) Later that year, encouraged by Childebert's advisors, Chilperic joined Childebert in attacking Guntram's kingdom. The campaign is notable in Gregory's account for revealing the splits in Childebert's camp. Ordinary Franks in the army protested against the way in which the young king's advisors were betraying the king's best interests, and chased them out of the camp: the chief of them, Bishop Egidius of Rheims, narrowly escaped with his life. Chilperic, on the other hand, seemed at the height of his power and influence (see figure 21). He began arranging a marriage between his daughter and Reccared, the son of the Visigothic king. Things soon went wrong. The marriage was postponed when Chilperic's young son Theuderic died, leaving him heirless once more. Even his alliance with Childebert began to crumble, for Guntram and Childebert patched up the old quarrel over Marseilles and, it were rumoured, was preparing a joint attack on Chilperic. Chilperic did send his daughter off to Spain with an enormous treasure,

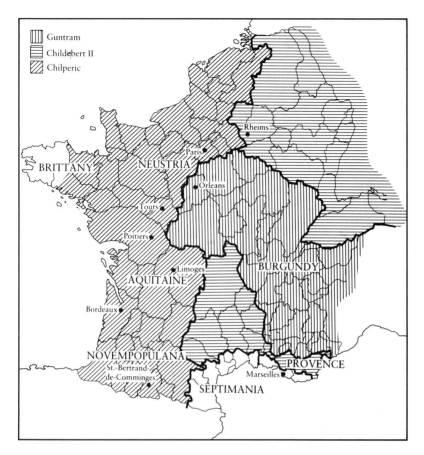

Figure 21 The Frankish kingdoms in 583 before Chilperic's assassination.

some of which was purloined by her entourage when only a few miles outside Paris, and none of which was ever to reach Spain. He himself went off to Chelles, near Paris, for some hunting. A man stepped forward as he was dismounting, and stabbed him: thus died 'the Nero and Herod of our times', as Gregory called him.

Guntram

Chilperic's death in 584 left Guntram the sole surviving adult king. Guntram was well aware of the fragility of the Merovingian position; Gregory reports how he begged a congregation in Paris not to assassinate him: to give him three years, at least, to bring up his two nephews, his adopted sons, that is, the fourteen-year-old Childebert and the four-month-old son of Chilperic and Fredegund, Chlothar II. Fredegund had announced that she was pregnant again very shortly after Chilperic's death, which caused Guntram, and Gregory of Tours, to wonder whether Chlothar was indeed Chilperic's son. Later Guntram forced Fredegund to assemble three bishops and 300 leading Franks to swear that Chlothar was indeed Chilperic's heir. Guntram did, however, act as Fredegund's protector, refusing to hand her over to Childebert, who wanted her seized as the murderer of his father, uncle, and two cousins.

Guntram proclaimed himself as the elder statesman and peacemaker, but his ambitions were perhaps not wholly selfless. He forced the inhabitants of Tours and Poitiers to transfer their allegiance to him, rather than to Childebert, representing himself as ruling all Francia in trust for his nephews. This hardly went down well with Childebert's advisers, who were still the same men who had favoured the alliance with Chilperic: Bishop Egidius of Rheims, Guntram Boso and others. It was Guntram Boso, according to Gregory, who had gone a few years before to Constantinople, to bring back the pretender Gundovald. Now Gundovald returned again to lay claim to a portion of the Frankish kingdom, and began gathering together an army of supporters in south-west Gaul, led by numbers of disaffected dukes, counts and bishops, including Bertram of Bordeaux.

As before, in 582, Gundovald was probably invited by Childebert's advisers, who saw him as a useful means of distracting King Guntram. The year 585 was particularly crucial: it was the year in which Childebert reached the age of 15 and his majority, and could thus rule without his advisers. Guntram's action was a sensible one in the circumstances: he summoned Childebert to listen to the confessions (under torture) of Gundovald's ambassadors, who implicated Childebert's leading advisors, then he handed Childebert a spear as a symbol of rule, and declared him his sole heir, restoring to him everything that had been Sigibert's. An army was sent against Gundovald, who was penned into the fortress of St-Bertrand-de-Comminges and eventually killed, together with most of his supporters.

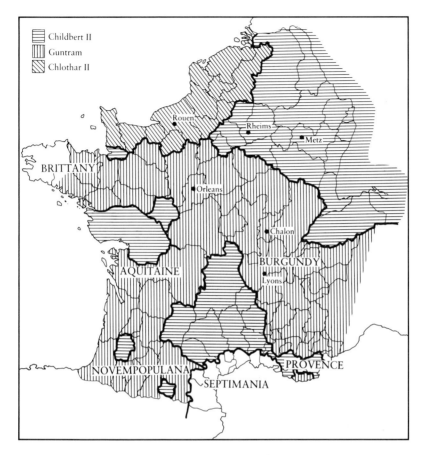

Figure 22 The Frankish kingdoms in 587 as described in the terms of the Treaty of Andelot.

Later that year, in July, King Guntram came to Orleans; Gregory of Tours was there, and we get our closest glimpse of the king in action. We can see why Gregory saw in him such a contrast to his brother Chilperic. At his triumphal entry into the town he was acclaimed by crowds of Romans, Syrians (Greeks?) and Jews, carrying banners and singing songs of praise, each in their own language. Chilperic had been on familiar terms with at least one Jew, but Guntram had no love for them. 'One cannot fail to wonder at the wisdom of this famous king: he saw through the cunning of the unbelievers' (LH VIII. 1), and refused to let their flattery persuade him to rebuild a synagogue destroyed by the Christians. To his own Christian subjects

Guntram was much more affable, having meals in the houses of the townsfolk of Orleans, and dropping in on Gregory at his lodgings for a quick drink. Guntram showed his clemency in Orleans by merely berating the bishops who had cast in their lot with Gundovald (although later he plotted to send them into exile). At the end of one pleasant meal with his bishops Guntram revealed that he had had a vision of his brother Chilperic: three saints argued about how the dead king should be punished for his sins, and eventually decided to break his limbs and throw him into a cauldron of boiling water. 'He was dissolved away and quite melted in the steaming water, and soon no trace at all of him remained.' The bishops were all much astonished, Gregory said, as well they might be, and soon made their excuses and left the party.

Plots continued after Chilperic's death – many of them, according to Gregory, fomented by his widow Fredegund, who tried to assassinate Childebert, Brunhild and Guntram on several occasions. One attempt that was successful was that against Chilperic's old enemy Bishop Praetextatus of Rouen (who had presided at the marriage of Merovech and Brunhild); he was assassinated in the middle of a church service. The accusation that Fredegund was behind such plots comes from a combination of rumour and word received of confessions made under torture; we cannot take them all literally, although we can believe that Fredegund needed to work hard to maintain herself and her young son Chlothar II in the tiny kingdom he had inherited, the kingdom which had belonged before him to Chlothar I and then to Chilperic. Childebert had to work almost as hard. As he became more used to ruling his kingdom himself, he and his mother Brunhild, with Guntram's backing, began to move against those advisors who had invited Gundovald into the kingdom and excluded Queen Mother Brunhild from any role in the government of the kingdom. One after the other these rich and powerful Austrasian aristocrats were removed from the scene: Rauching was killed by Childebert's men after an interview with the king; Guntram Boso was killed by a mob urged on by King Guntram; other unnamed people were deprived of their title of duke, or forced to flee from Childebert's kingdom. However, it was not until 590 that moves were made against one of the chief conspirators, Bishop

Egidius of Rheims. The trial took place in Metz, in the presence of a council of bishops. One of the main accusations made against him concerned his close relations with Chilperic. Letters between the two were produced in court, letters which contained veiled references to plots against Childebert and Brunhild; Egidius, of course, claimed that these were forgeries, but one of his servants, who kept shorthand copies of letters for the episcopal archives, testified against him. Other incriminating letters had been found in Chilperic's own archives, discovered at Chelles after his death. (The whole story gives quite a favourable impression of the efficiency of the Merovingian bureaucracy.) Eventually Egidius was convicted, and confessed himself worthy of death for high treason; the bishops exiled him to Strasbourg.

We are sadly deprived of obituaries for the main characters in this drama: Guntram, Childebert, Fredegund or Brunhild. Gregory's *Histories* came to an end in 591: Guntram died in 592, Childebert in 596, Fredegund in 597, and Brunhild in 613 – tortured to death at the orders of Fredegund's son Chlothar II, who in that year united the whole kingdom for the first time since his grandfather Chlothar I. We can well imagine what Gregory's obituary for Fredegund might have been, a fit widow for 'the Nero and Herod of our times'. Guntram would undoubtedly have served Gregory well as the exact antithesis of Chilperic. Despite his occasional acts of ruthlessness (which, in an obituary, Gregory would no doubt omit, as he did the occasional kindnesses of Chilperic), Gregory gives hints that Guntram was the nearest approach to an ideal king. He loved peace, but he was ready to go to war for the sake of justice. He had a strong sense of responsibility for his family. He treated the Church well and took the advice of bishops. One chapter in Gregory's *Histories* contains the most favourable comment that Gregory wrote on any Frankish king:

King Guntram was well known for his charity, and much given to vigils and fasting. At this time [588] it was reported that the people of Marseilles were suffering from a severe epidemic of swelling in the groin [bubonic plague] and that this disease had quickly spread to St-Symphorien-d'Ozon, a village near Lyons. Like some good bishop providing remedies by which the wounds of a common sinner might be healed, King Guntram ordered the entire people to assemble in church, and to celebrate the service of Rogations with great devotion. He then commanded that they should eat and drink nothing else but barley bread and pure water, and that all should be regular in keeping the vigils. His orders were obeyed, and he seemed so anxious about all his people that he might well have been taken for one of Our Lord's bishops, rather than for a king. . ... The faithful had a story which they used to tell about Guntram. There was a woman whose son was seriously ill of a quartan ague. As the boy lay tossing on his bed, his mother pushed her way through the vast crowds and came up behind the King. Without his noticing she cut a few threads from his cloak. She steeped these threads in water and then gave the infusion to her son to drink. The fever left him immediately and he became well again. I accept this as true, for I have often heard men possessed of a devil call upon Guntram's name when the evil spirit was in them, and through his miraculous powers confess their crimes. (LH IX. 22)

It is an extraordinary passage, made even more so when we realize that Guntram is the only western European king before the eleventh century to be reported as working miracles while still alive; until the eleventh century, and the spread of the belief in the king's power to cure scrofula, the only miracle-working kings apart from Guntram were those who died martyr's deaths. Gregory seems to be implying that Guntram could work miracles because he acted more like 'one of our Lord's bishops than a king'. Perhaps, for Gregory, the king ought to model his rule over his kingdom upon the bishop's rule over his diocese, and share in the bishop's sense of responsibility, charity, and trust in God. It is an idea that was to be elaborated in Gaul later, by the Carolingian church, but it is otherwise unknown in the Merovingian period.

Royal Administration

The narrative of Gregory, like any political narrative, concentrates on the high points – the personal drama, the scandals and the disasters. What we can know about the day-to-day rule of the Frankish kingdom must come from elsewhere. But we can certainly learn from Gregory some of the perennial problems faced by Frankish kings in controlling their kingdom. Most of these stem ultimately from the problems of communication in a kingdom in which travel was slow and uncomfortable, and reliable information was difficult to come by, either for the king or for his subjects.

Roman Emperors and later medieval monarchs solved the problem of communication in part by making constant progresses around their territories, moving from palace to royal villa to monastery over their kingdom. This had, of course, the advantage that it helped solve the problems of transporting huge quantities of food and drink across the kingdom; it could be consumed where it was produced, and supplemented by hunting, a traditional pursuit of monarchs (even now). Merovingian kingship was itinerant too, but on a surprisingly limited scale. Chilperic is seldom found far from the triangle made by Rouen, Soissons and Paris; Guntram moved rather more, as befitted the greater size of his kingdom, but never too far from his favourite residence of Chalon-sur-Saône. These kings did not lead their armies outside their own kingdoms. Neither of them, indeed very few kings at all after the initial conquest, seems to have gone into Aquitaine, which may in part explain the readiness of Aquitanians to accept the usurper·Gundovald as their king. To a large extent kings had to rely on their agents to tell them what was happening in the further flung regions of their kingdoms: the most important of these were bishops, counts and dukes.

Bishops, as we have already seen, were mostly Gallo-Roman in origin, and their main function was certainly not to act as royal agents; nevertheless they were, or could be, very useful to the Frankish kings. Sometimes they were, of course, royal appointees. Gregory of Tours was one, appointed by Sigibert without reference to the local clergy, let alone the local community; he happened to be at court when news arrived of the death of the previous bishop, his cousin Eufronius. Sometimes the men that kings appointed were career clerics, like Gregory; others were, until their appointment, laymen, often royal civil servants, given the job for their retirement. The latter does not appear to have been very popular with the Church, or, perhaps, with local congregations, since such men were often outsiders, but they may have been efficient administrators of the church, and they clearly provided kings with useful sources of information and support within their kingdom. In the early seventh century, court officials seem to have been appointed to bishoprics very deliberately: the most famous examples were Eligius, Audoen and Desiderius, appointed to Noyon, Rouen and Cahors respectively. But even those bishops, a clear majority, who were local men with no court connections – holy men, career clerics, local aristocrats, or even all three at once – could be of assistance to kings. Through Church councils, which were often attended by kings or their officials, kings could be informed about what was going on in their kingdom, and bishops could bring back the king's word to their dioceses. Bishops were powerful figures in their locality, fulfilling, in the name of the Church, some of the duties which Frankish kings might regard as their own – acting as judges or repairing town walls – and taking responsibility for other things which no Frankish king thought of as having anything to do with him – poor relief, hospital building, the ransoming of prisoners-of-war – but which could give bishops considerable local prestige and influence. It was important for a king to have these men on his side, as Chilperic recognized when he lamented how powerful they had become (see p. 165). Bishops could, for instance, inform the king about any injustices which an aristocrat or royal agent was committing in their diocese; they had a position not unlike that of a modern ombudsman, in that they were, theoretically, impartial agents for peace and justice. The theory depended for its success on the rectitude of individual bishops and their willingness to stand apart from local politics. Given that many bishops were themselves from local aristocratic families, such an ideal of impartiality was not always attained. There are a handful of flagrant examples in Gregory's *Histories* of men using their bishoprics in order to obtain their own pleasure or political advantage, and often they got away with it, for the bishops were so keen on enhancing their own prestige and independence that they were usually very reluctant to condemn or depose fellow bishops who broke the rules.

In most *civitates*, keeping his eye on the bishop on behalf of the king – and in his turn being watched closely by the bishop – was the count, the *comes*. (The Germanic word *grafio* was used in the north-east; in some intervening areas, around Paris, the *grafio* was subordinate to a count.) The count was a secular official, in charge of a law-court (which could sometimes be in collision with that of the bishop), responsible for tax collection and for assembling the local contingents for the royal army. Like the bishop he was frequently a local man; thus, in southern Gaul in particular, he was generally a Gallo-Roman. It is not clear how far kings tried through personal contact to remedy the danger of fragmentation: whether, for instance, counts were expected to travel to meet with the king each year. Sometimes kings might have attempted to extend royal control by appointing their own courtiers as counts, men who were outsiders to the territory over which they had jurisdiction. Chlothar II's legislation in 614 put an end to this, in theory at least, because in cases of corruption or malpractice it was much more difficult for such counts' estates to be confiscated and distributed to their victims in compensation. Most counts then, like most bishops, were members of a local aristocratic family; indeed, in some cases count and bishop were of the same family.

The third royal official, and in some ways the most important in the government of the kingdom, was the duke. The office of *dux* probably descended from the Roman *duces*, who were military officials in command of troops in an area including several *civitates*, although the word is also used in Latin (as it had been by Tacitus) to refer to the military leaders of bands or tribes of Germans: it could have had this dual significance for the Franks. Gregory of Tours names 41 dukes, as opposed to only 25 counts; most of the aristocrats who appear to be politically important are dukes. Another possibly significant distinction is in their ethnic origin. While most counts whom Gregory mentions were Romans, most dukes (judging by their names) seem to be Franks. As in the Roman period, dukes seem to have been primarily military officials; since the Franks achieved their predominance in Gaul through their military power, they may have attempted to retain that predominance by reserving the major military positions for themselves. Some of these dukes had clearly territorial jurisdictions, such as Lupus who under Childebert II held the *ducatus Campaniae* (the duchy of Champagne, made up of the *civitates* of Rheims, Laon and Châlon), or Berulf who, at the same time, controlled a western district made up of Tours, Poitiers, Nantes and Angers. Other dukes, however, seem to have been attached to the royal household.

The most prominent of these Frankish dukes in Gregory's

account were those who emerged as the effective controllers of the young Childebert II's kingdom after 581. They were, in Gregory's eyes, a boorish and thuggish crowd, ever ready, like Duke Rauching, to torture their own slaves for fun, or, like Duke Guntram Boso, to order their servants to steal the gold ornaments from the grave of a woman who had been buried in the church the day before. None of them seems to have had any respect for the Church; they were avaricious, and amassed great treasures of gold, silver and precious objects. These were men to whom Gregory was opposed politically, of course, and we must place this stereotype of the barbarian aristocrat against the image of other Frankish aristocrats of the period. Another paradigm, for instance, is Gogo, whom these dukes displaced from his position as governor to Childebert. Gogo wrote Latin verse and had been trained in rhetoric, and was hence compared by Fortunatus to Orpheus and Cicero. His four surviving letters suggest that his level of literary attainment was at least equal to that of his Gallo-Roman contemporaries.

Gregory's dukes and counts are seen committing criminal acts, scheming, or leading royal armies; we rarely see them in their day-to-day work. We can get a better picture of that, even if only on an abstract level, from a fascinating text from *c.* 700 known as Marculf's *Formulary*. Marculf was a monk, possibly a former civil servant, who was asked by Bishop Landeric of Paris to write down two books of form letters, which could be used (filling in the blanks as appropriate) in many different legal or administrative circumstances. This he did, 'although I have fulfilled seventy or more years of my life, and my trembling hand can no longer write, my obscured eyes can no longer see, and my troubled brain is no longer able to imagine anything'. Marculf's formulas give a remarkable insight into the different ways in which the written word was used in Merovingian Gaul. The first book of the *Formulary* for the most part contains letters appropriate for the public administration of Gaul; the second book contains models of private deeds, such as a letter of reciprocal donation between husband and wife, or an act of sale concerning a male or female slave.

One of the earliest formulas concerns the appointment of a royal official:

Before all things one praises a clement king, if he finds from among the people good and vigilant men, and if he does not give the dignity of official to the first comer... Consequently, as we have already had experience of your loyalty and ability, we entrust you with the office of count (or duke or *patricius*) of the province of . . . . . ., that your predecessor . . . . . . has occupied up until now, to be occupied and governed by you in such a way that you always observe an unshakeable loyalty towards our government, and that all the peoples who dwell there, Franks, Romans, Burgundians, and those of other nations, live and be moderate under your leadership and your government, and that you maintain them in the right path according to their law and their custom; that you become an ardent defender of widows and orphans; that the crimes of brigands and wicked men be severely punished by you, so that people may live well under your rule and may be happy and remain in peace. And all that the fisc expects each year from this province must be delivered to our treasury at your instigation. (I. 8)

It is interesting that this purports to apply to a duke as well as a count, that, in other words, dukes as well as counts had civil and not just military powers over a territory. A *patricius* certainly had: this title is most often used of the governor of Provence, who wielded both civil and military powers. (In Gregory's time the *patricius* Mummolus was one of the most successful of royal generals, and, after he threw in his lot with Guntram Boso and his cronies (see p. 175), one of the most dangerous royal enemies. For several years after 581 he operated quite independently of the king, from his stronghold in Avignon.) In the sixth century a duchy seems in most cases to have comprised several counties, each of which also had their count (although there were exceptions: there may have been no counts within the duchy of Champagne). By the seventh century, however, there may have been more duchies that were both civil and military in nature: by then, perhaps, count, duke and *patricius* were titles signifying offices which were basically the same. It is also interesting to note in this passage the stress laid on the judicial role of the count (or duke or *patricius*). And the final sentence, underlining his duty to transmit the taxes to the king, reminds us of those aspects of the count's duties which may have been of overriding interest to the Merovingians themselves. A king could probably forgive a good deal in a count who managed to keep up the supply of revenue to the royal treasury.

Other formulas preserved in Marculf's collection are useful illustrations of the way in which kings might encourage obedience and loyalty among their subjects. One (I. 26) is a formula for admonishing a bishop who transgresses the law. Another (I. 24) offers a monastery or bishop the personal *mundeburdium*, or protection, of the king and his count. Such protection was also offered to those who came personally to the palace to swear trust and fidelity to the king: 'because of that we decide and order by this precept that the said . . . . . . shall be counted in the numbers of *antrustions*, and if anyone should kill him, he should know that he must pay six hundred solidi as wergild' (I. 18). This figure of 600 solidi is confirmed by the earliest Frankish law-code, which specifies that 'if anyone kills a man who is *in truste dominica* (in the royal following), he shall pay 600 solidi' – three times that due for the killing of an ordinary Frank (see below, p. 216). We may presume that dukes and counts were sworn followers of the king – *antrustions* (or *leudes*, the term Gregory uses) – but it is not possible to know how many other Franks (or Romans) had this personal bond of loyalty. One of Marculf's formulas illustrates the attempt under the Merovingians (as later under the Carolingians) to extend the oath of loyalty to all subjects:

King . . . . . . greets Count . . . . . . Since with the consent of our magnates we have commanded that our glorious son . . . . . . shall govern the kingdom of . . . . . ., we order you to assemble all the citizens of your province, Franks, Romans and other peoples, and to make them come together in suitable places, in towns, villages and fortifications, so that, in front of our illustrious envoy . . . . . . that we have deputed to you for this purpose, they may promise and swear fidelity and *leudesamium* to our excellent son and to us, by the holy places and the relics which we have sent with the same person. (I. 40)

Other formulas relate in other ways to the government of the kingdom. One is a letter from a king granting immunity to a church or named individual, a 'privilege, that no public agent shall ever enter, to hear trials or to receive fines, in whatever manner, into the rural properties of the church of St . . . . . .'; effectively the king concedes that such a property is ruled by the owner rather than by the king. There are formulas whereby a king can ask a count to intervene on behalf of a wronged individual, and whereby a province can appeal to the king for remission of taxes after devastation caused by armies, or an individual can appeal for redress when his legal documents have been burnt in the course of a military campaign. Further, a reminder that kings had to think about foreign diplomacy as well, there is a letter to all royal officials on behalf of his ambassadors, two individuals with the titles 'apostolic' and 'illustrious', hence, a bishop and a count or duke. It tells them to provide specified quantities of

post-horses or relief horses, measures of fine bread, measures of ordinary bread, measures of wine, measures of beer, pounds of lard, pounds of meat, so many pigs, piglets, sheep, lambs, geese, pheasants, chickens, eggs, pounds of oil, pounds of dish sauce, honey, vinegar, pounds of cummin, pepper, preserving spices, cloves, nard, cinnamon, dates, pistachios, almonds, candles weighing one pound each, pounds of cheese, salt, cartloads of vegetables and wood, torches; and likewise, as fodder for their horses, so many cartloads of hay and measures of bran. Each of you must transport that and measure it for them, each day and at the usual places, both on their outward and, if it pleases God, return journeys, so that they may not be delayed or troubled, if you wish to have our good favours. (I. II)

There are few other documents that remind us of the logistical problems of Merovingian government, and of the complex bureaucracy that must have lain behind the apparently haphazard structure. We cannot, of course, know how effective such official letters actually were. Almost certainly the problems of supplying large armies were not susceptible to similar methods; Gregory of Tours shows us that friendly armies foraging for food and supplies could have just as devastating an effect on the population as enemy armies pillaging for booty. But this was no doubt something that could have happened in Roman times too, and the formulas in Marculf show that, like the Romans, indeed borrowing from them, the Merovingians did at least try to look after the interests of their subjects.

Many of the formulas in Marculf's collection in fact show the extent to which, by the seventh century, the Franks and their kings had absorbed Roman customs and traditions. The idea of swearing personal oaths of loyalty is a Roman one, as is the idea of freeing slaves to celebrate a monarch's birthday (Marculf I. 39). More interesting is a document by which a father can ensure that a daughter shares equally with the son in the inheritance:

. . .Among us there is an old and wicked custom according to which sisters cannot obtain any part of the lands of the father, as their brothers do; but

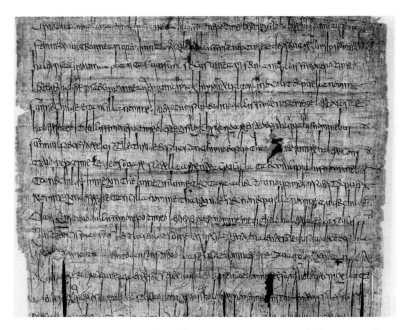

Plate 35 *Detail of an early will, written on papyrus in the later seventh century, by which Ermintrude leaves land, serfs, gold and silver to various Parisian churches.*

in considering this injustice, I think that just as God has given you to me as equal children, so I ought to love you equally, and after my death you ought to enter equally into the possession of my goods... (II. 12)

'Us' clearly means 'Franks', for this formula must stem from a misunderstanding of the oldest Frankish law-code, which included a clause forbidding a daughter to inherit 'Salic' land. By the seventh century this was probably understood as meaning all land held by Salian Franks, even though that was not its original meaning; indeed the original text of the Frankish law makes it fairly clear that daughters were in fact expected to share in the inheritance. What is most interesting, however, is that this formula shows that it is possible to write a document or a will which specifies who shall inherit, even, as this formula admits, 'to the great loss of (one's) brothers'. The idea of a will, whereby property can be given to any individual, or to the Church – and one's legitimate heirs, as reckoned by Frankish law, disinherited – was a Roman one. A further formula in the collection explains this; it refers to a will written by a notary, 'so that, the legal day after our death having arrived, the seals being recognised, the linen thread being cut, as prescribes the authority of Roman law, it may be placed in the archives of the town. . .' (II. 17). In the sixth and seventh centuries Frankish aristocrats seem to have been happy enough to take over these Roman legal habits; the Church, who had the most to gain from donations by will, naturally encouraged them wholeheartedly. A number of the formulas preserved by Marculf relate to the gift of property to the Church, as do all the actual legal documents which survive from the Merovingian period, either in originals or copies.

It was in this way that, insensibly, Franks came to take over the ways of Romans, which in turn eased that equally intangible process by which those Romans ruled most closely by Frankish kings – those in northern Gaul – came to think of themselves as Franks. Frankish kings did try to preserve the structure of Roman rule. Yet they did so only imperfectly. To see this we shall look at two important ways in which rulers impinged on their subjects' lives: the imposition of taxes and the minting of coins.

Taxation

The Roman taxation system was so complex, and the responsibility of so many different individuals and departments, that it is hardly surprising that it did not survive intact; almost certainly it atrophied in the fifth century, before the Franks came to power in Gaul. Few Romans would have mourned its passing; many, indeed, apparently saw the arrival of the barbarians as a liberation from an oppressive burden of taxation. The Franks themselves saw any taxation as an oppression from which they, as Franks, were exempt; the *Pactus Legis Salicae* refers dismissively to 'Roman *tributarii*': tax-payers.

The attitudes revealed by Gregory of Tours are interesting in this light. Taxation for him (as for Merovingian hagiographers) is invariably a result of unpardonable royal greed. Gregory tells of Queen Fredegund's reaction to the illness of her two sons in

579. After confessing to her greed and her oppression of the poor, she burnt the tax assessments belonging to the cities whose tax revenues formed her wedding gift, and asked Chilperic to follow her lead: 'We may still lose our children, but we shall at least escape eternal damnation!' So Chilperic 'tossed all the files of the tax assessments into the fire. As soon as they were burnt he sent messengers to ensure that no such assessments should ever be made again' (LH V. 34). Whether or not this scene ever took place outside Gregory's imagination is not clear. Perhaps the royal reluctance to proceed with new tax demands stemmed more from the popular reaction to them. A few chapters earlier Gregory had described Chilperic's intentions:

A great number of people emigrated from their native cities or from whatever bits of land they occupied and sought refuge elsewhere, for they preferred to go into exile rather than endure such punitive taxation. The new tax laws laid down that a landowner must pay five gallons of wine for every half-acre which he possessed. Many other taxes were levied, not only on the land, but also on the number of workmen employed. . . The people of Limoges called a meeting on 1 March and decided to kill Mark, the tax collector who had been ordered to put the new laws into effect. They would have carried out their threat too, had not Bishop Ferreolus saved Mark from the danger which threatened him. A mob gathered; the people seized the tax-collector's assessment-books and burned them to ashes. (LH V. 28)

Frankish kings had little success in establishing new taxes (unless one counts the fines which were an essential element of the legal process), and the old Roman taxes which did survive, most notably the land tax levied on free landowners, were gradually whittled away by royal grants of privilege. Immunity from taxation, along with immunity from other burdens, was frequently bestowed by kings on churches or on individuals, as a reward or mark of favour. Theudebert I, for instance, remitted all tribute – land-tax – paid by the churches of Auvergne; in 589 Gregory himself defended the city of Tours from Childebert II's attempt to impose taxes on the citizens of Tours, successfully claiming that Chlothar I had burnt all the tax-books out of respect for St Martin of Tours. Such immunities were probably granted for specific pieces of land; thus, in 590, when Childebert II again remits the tax due from the churches of

Auvergne, he was probably doing this for the tax-paying properties which the Church had acquired since the time of Theudebert I. Likewise the angry Franks who stoned the tax-collector Parthenius to death (p. 107), when his master Theudebert I died in 548, or who attacked the tax-collector Audo, on Chilperic's death in 584, were probably objecting to having to pay the land tax on properties which they had acquired from Romans. The anomaly seems to have been resolved by Chlothar II, who made immunity apply not to specific properties, but to all the properties held by the immunist. By the seventh century there are almost no references to a land tax being paid to a king. The freedom from such taxation claimed in the sixth century by Franks inevitably ate away at the foundations of the system, as more and more people in the Frankish kingdom came to regard themselves as Franks. (Indeed, that freedom from the land-tax may have been one of the major incentives for Gallo-Romans to shift their ethnic allegiance.) One of Marculf's formulas (I. 19) relates to a licence to join the clergy being given to anyone who is 'properly free (*bene ingenuus*) and not inscribed on the public polyptych': that is, not a tax payer. *Tributarii* were now equated with *coloni* or the unfree, men forced to pay rents, taxes or services to their landlord. As Walter Goffart commented in 1982, 'under these circumstances, the association of "Frank" with freedom rather than nationality could begin to take hold.'

This did not mean that Franks were free from all burdens. Rather it moved their obligation away from an impersonal payment to the State towards a more personalized display of their duties to the king, such as service at court or in the army. And they were still, presumably, liable to payment of one of the forms of taxation which did survive from the Roman Empire: tolls or customs dues.

Continuity of the customs structure can, nevertheless, only be assumed; it cannot be proven, nor, given the paucity of evidence, can the importance of this type of income. Our first mention of customs (*teloneum*, Fr. *tonlieu*) in the post-Roman period comes in the Council of Mâcon in 581–83, which prohibited Jews from being *iudices* (judges) or *telonarii* (customs officers). In 614 Chlothar II agreed to the demand that customs dues should only be raised in the same places and on the same goods as in the time of his predecessors Guntram, Chilperic and Sigibert. Grants of immunity from customs are very rare, and only relate to freedom from tolls for a limited number of ships or carts. There are only two known concessions of the right to collect the *teloneum*: one (probably under Dagobert I) to the abbey of St-Denis, which was limited to the period of the annual fair of St-Denis, and one under Sigibert III, which gave the full revenue from two customs posts on the lower Loire to the monastery of Stavelot-Malmédy. The paucity of such grants may indicate the importance of this source of income to kings (or to their officials in the provinces), as does some indirect evidence, such as the importance to kings of the control of the port of Marseilles in the late sixth century. The fact that, in addition to the customs points controlled by kings and counts, there may also have been purely private toll houses is suggested by Charlemagne's legislation, which tried to eliminate them. Privatization of customs is perfectly conceivable in a society which also seems to have seen the privatization of the money system.

Coins

Under the Roman Emperors the minting of coins was an imperial monopoly. The Frankish kings took over the imperial coinage, continuing to mint in all three metals. A few bronze coins are known with the names of the sons of Clovis on them; silver coins (*argentei*) were issued, some of them copies of imperial types, but some in the names of kings such as Theuderic I or Sigibert I. The most important coin in the sixth and early seventh century, however, was the *triens* or *tremissis*, one-third of a gold *solidus*. The *triens* became recognized as the standard gold coin, so much so that, confusingly, in the texts it is often called a *solidus*, meaning simply 'gold coin'. The most jealously guarded imperial privilege had been the appearance of the emperor's name and head on the gold coinage, and for most of the sixth century this privilege was respected by the Frankish kings. There was one notable and notorious exception: Theudebert I, who, around 538, actually issued a gold *solidus* with his own name on it, thus shocking the Byzantine Empire

Plate 36 Coin of Roman Emperor, minted in Provence.

and its historian Procopius to the core. Later Childebert I and the sons of Chlothar I seem to have minted gold coins in their own name; once the break with tradition had been made it became easier to repeat it again.

The most important series from the sixth century was the quasi-imperial gold coinage minted in Provence, in Arles, Uzès and Viviers, but above all in Marseilles, in the names of emperors from Justin II (d. 578) down to Heraclius (610–40) (see plate 36). They were imitations of imperial types, although increasingly distorted and poorly executed. A large proportion of the surviving Frankish coinage from *c.* 575 to *c.* 620 consists of coins from this series; it is thought that the gold for the coins came from Byzantine coins, arriving at the Provençal ports and being immediately reminted. The series ended when these four mints replaced Heraclius's name with that of Chlothar II: a significant step in the assertion of Frankish independence from the Empire, or from outmoded imperial privileges.

Other changes occurred in the Frankish coinage around 575. There was a temporary abandonment of coinage in silver and bronze. There was a general acceptance of a new weight in the gold coinage, with 84 *solidi* being produced to the pound of gold instead of 72. This was nothing to do with a decline of standards under the Franks; even in 458 the Emperor had been complaining about a light-weight *solidus gallicus*. The traditional Roman solidus weighed 24 siliquae (4.55 gms); the light-weight coins were often acknowledged as such by the appearance of XXI on the solidus, or VII on the triens, signifying the new weight of 21 siliqae (3.89 gms, 1.29 gms). Outside Provence, there is not only the increased number of coins with royal names on them, but the appearance in large numbers, soon to swamp the royal coins altogether, of coins without royal names at all, but simply the names of the moneyers.

This phenomenon is clearly vital to the problem of Frankish royal power and its control of the coinage. Were these moneyers private individuals, or acting on behalf of royal government? There are other linked problems. What was the function of the coinage? Was it intended for prestige payments (of tax, for instance) or was it regularly used in commerce? How far were changes in the coinage after *c.* 590 – notably the gradual debasement of the gold coinage and its eventual replacement, *c.* 660, by a silver coinage – the result of royal policy?

The moneyers' names were normally placed on the coins together with the mint-site. Over 1600 moneyers are known altogether from the known Merovingian coinage, and there are hundreds of mint-sites, above all in the north and west of the kingdom (see figure 23 p. 201). Sometimes individual moneyers are known from more than one place, minting coins of different styles, which suggests that they were not just manufacturers, but men of some importance, perhaps acting on behalf of kings or royal officials. This is certainly the case of the only moneyer about whose career anything is known at all: Eligius.

Eligius was a Gallo-Roman, born in the *civitas* of Limoges *c.* 588, and apprenticed to a gold-smith and moneyer there called Abbo. His talents as jeweller and gold-smith brought him to the attention of the court of Chlothar II; a number of the works he made under Chlothar II and Dagobert are known, at least from drawings, such as the chalice of Chelles, destroyed in 1793, and the jewelled cross he made for St-Denis (of which a small fragment survived the French Revolution: see plate 37). In 641 Clovis II made him Bishop of Noyon (see above p. 137); he remained in that office until his death in 660. If we assume that the ELIGIVS and ELEGIVS legends on coins relate to this same person, we find him minting first at Marseilles, under Chlothar II; all Dagobert's coins from Marseilles are also minted by Eligius (see plate 38). He also produced coins for both kings at Paris and at other sites, as well as many coins without the name of a king. His last coins were for Sigibert III and Clovis II; he may have stopped working as a moneyer when he became bishop.

Plate 37 The gold jewelled cross made by Eligius for the church of St-Denis was destroyed in 1794; one small fragment survives.

The large number of coins bearing Eligius's name and his close association with the palace have suggested to some that he was a major figure in developments in Chlothar and Dagobert's coinage. The coins were redesigned, and the standard of production improved. However, there was also a drastic reduction in the gold content of the coins. Up until *c*. 590 the gold content was often above 90 per cent; between 590 and 615 this fineness was maintained in Provence, but elsewhere the gold content was no more than 85 per cent. In the early years of Chlothar's reign, however, the fineness fell below 90 per cent in Provence, and was normally between 60 per cent and 70 per cent elsewhere. The coins Eligius minted for Dagobert in Marseilles preserved a fineness of 80–90 per cent, while his

Plate 38 Coin of Eligius, minted in Paris.

Parisian coins were between 60 and 80 per cent. The fineness of some coins minted by other moneyers under Dagobert fell below 50 per cent, and it seems (although most Merovingian coins are difficult to date) as if the most debased coins were those latest in his reign. Hardly any of the coins minted by Eligius in the early years of Clovis II's reign exceeded 50 per cent fineness, and in subsequent reigns the standard declined still further. By the 660s the relationship of silver to gold was such that the coinage was basically a silver one, and the inevitable change to a wholly silver coinage came soon after.

Some numismatists have argued, on the basis of accurate analyses of the coins, that such debasement was planned, and proceeded by deliberate stages, a reduction of one siliqua of gold at a time. Yet debasements apparently did not occur over the whole kingdom at the same time, so it can hardly have been centrally organized. One must imagine moneyers in different regions, working for counts, bishops and, perhaps, private individuals, responding to initiatives set, perhaps, by the king. Another such initiative, it seems, was the revival of a purely silver coinage, under Dagobert I. These coins were called *denarii* (Fr. *deniers*), although they were silver, not bronze like Roman *denarii*. Some gold coins continued to be minted in the later seventh century, but the coin-hoards of the early eighth century are made up exclusively of *denarii* (see plate 39).

The reasons for this shift are much debated. Commonest have been arguments about the decline of the Merovingian economy, a result of the drying up of Mediterranean trade and hence of the flow of gold. Historians and numismatists alike had the feeling that somehow a monetary system relying on silver rather

Plate 39 Silver coin minted in northern France.

than gold was inferior. But silver was more readily available in western Europe, from the mines near Melle in Poitou, for instance, whose name METALLO appears on many Merovingian *denarii*, and it may even denote increased rather than reduced trade. Gold coins were of very high denomination, and silver was probably of more use for normal transactions. The late seventh century saw the rapid growth of trade in the Channel and the North Sea, with the rise of trading towns like Quentovic and Dorestad in Francia, and the *wics* of England, Hamwic (Southampton), London (or Londonwic, as one source called it), Ipswich and Eoforwic (York), and the increasing domination of Frisian merchants, with their own silver coins, the *sceattas*. Henri Pirenne saw the shift of the economic heart of western Europe from the Mediterranean to the lower Rhine and northern Gaul as a crucial stage in the development of western civilization. Few historians would now agree with him that this shift was the result of the rise of the Islamic Empire in the southern Mediterranean. The shifting of the political, and hence economic, heartland of Gaul from the south to the north under the Frankish kings must have been just as important; it is another measure of the significance of the Franks and their kings in the history of Europe.

6

Economy and Society

Exchange and Production

Coins offer us a rare chance to get beyond the evidence of the law codes and the cemeteries which are, with all their problems (see pp. 13–14 and 22–28), almost the only sources to give us some idea of how ordinary Franks organized their lives. Thousands of coins have survived. Sometimes they were deliberately placed in a grave, or hidden in a pit as a hoard; occasionally they were lost accidentally. They can be studied in various ways. Their gold content can be analyzed (see above p. 197) to give us some idea of trends within the coinage as a whole. Iconography can be studied to illustrate influences between mints. Thanks to the fact that Merovingian coins often bear a legend naming the mint-site, the distribution of the coins from a particular mint can be studied, and the variation in mint organization from region to region. In the far south of Gaul, for instance, mint-sites are very largely the *civitas*-capitals; the Roman administrative structure is honoured even in the late seventh century. Elsewhere, it seems, coins could be minted in any village, by almost any constituted or self-constituted authority.

What is more difficult to tell is the precise role played by the coinage in the economy. Were coins merely a convenient way of storing bullion, in a way which enhanced the prestige of the minting authority, and were they used perhaps largely for the formal or ritual payment of, for instance, taxes, tribute and fines? Or did coins play a significant role in the economy, and

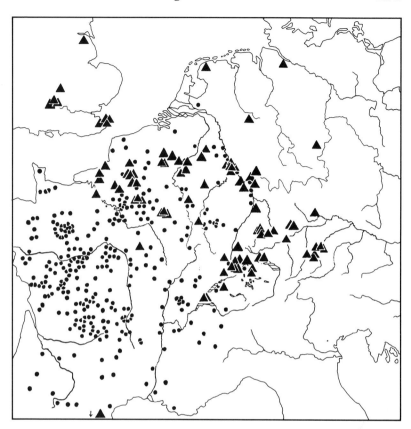

Figure 23 J. Werner's map of mint-sites (dots) and grave-finds of balances (triangles) suggests two main economic areas within Gaul: one where coins were used as coins and another where they were weighed as bullion.

function as a means of commercial exchange? One graphic way of helping to answer this problem was a map drawn up by Joachim Werner over 30 years ago (figure 23), which displays mint-sites and finds (in cemeteries) of sets of scales. While the number of both types of data has increased over 30 years, the main picture has not altered. The Frankish kingdom appears divided into three parts, roughly by the rivers Rhine and Seine. There is only one mint-site beyond the Rhine, and indeed there are very few finds of Merovingian coins; those that are found are often made into jewellery (cf. plate 41, see p. 205). Clearly Merovingian coins were not in circulation there. South and east of the Seine, however, we find numerous mint-sites and coins, and the mint-sites of coins in such hoards as Bordeaux and Plassac indicate contacts by sea and river, as one would expect if the distribution of coins was through trade. In the area in the middle, between the Seine and the Rhine, mint-sites are much fewer, and we have another element: cemeteries in which are graves of men, and occasionally women, containing a set of balances and weights, and occasionally special stones for testing the gold content of coins. Werner argued that the map suggests a 'monetary region' south of the Seine; a 'fine balance region' in north-eastern Gaul, in which coins were often not accepted at their face value, but regarded as small pieces of bullion, to be weighed and tested; and a 'natural economy' east of the Rhine. The distinctions between these three regions do not, of course, indicate three different types of economy; if anything they merely illustrate three different attitudes towards coins and the place of coins in the economy. It does not mean that the commerce of the area east of the Rhine, for instance, was not just as vigorous as the commerce in western Gaul; 'natural economy' means merely that other means of exchange were used in place of discs of metal. Indeed the Rhine, in addition to being a frontier between economic regions, was also probably the most important thoroughfare for merchants in the Frankish kingdom.

Archaeology can give us some clues about Frankish trade in this period. With luxury objects, of course, such as the Mediterranean bronze bowls found on a straight line all the way from Central Italy, across the Alps, along the Rhine and up into the Thames valley, one can never be sure that trade was the means of distribution; such prestige objects may well have reached their destination by way of war-booty, tribute or gift-exchange, rather than by trade. Rather more likely evidence of trade is that provided by objects of Frankish manufacture whose place of origin is known and which can be traced in other areas. One has to say immediately that most of these objects of 'Frankish' manufacture were in fact almost certainly made by Gallo-Romans in Francia rather than by Franks themselves – even though it may have been Frankish lords and merchants who now made the profits from them. Thus the glass industries of north-east Gaul, which flourished in the late Roman period,

Plate 40 A bottle, bowl and beaker: some typical pieces of Frankish glassware from the sixth century.

continued through the period of Frankish invasions; their products in the sixth century can be found throughout Francia, Anglo-Saxon England and Scandinavia (see plate 40). A glass-making furnace has been found at Formathot, near the source of the Oise, at a site where glass-making had been carried out in Roman times. The Frankish glass was technically of much poorer quality than the best of the Roman glass from the area, however, and only available in a fairly restricted range of types. Another product brought down the Rhine and thence into many parts of Gaul and Britain was mill-stones, made from the basalt of the Mayen region. The potteries of north-east Gaul continued to produce and to export also, although the wheel-made pottery produced by 'Frankish' potters seems generally to have had a limited distribution area. Cemeteries with a continuous history from late Roman through to Merovingian times, such as Vron, in Picardy, demonstrate clearly that 'Frankish' pottery, in the shapes and decorations used, evolved directly out of Roman pottery; there is nothing 'Germanic' about it.

Swords were certainly traded. The swords used by the Franks were often of exceptional quality – hard, durable, yet extremely flexible: one can almost believe in the swords of the heroic literature, which could be bent until the tip touched the pommel, only to snap back again, perfectly straight, or swords so sharp that they cut a human hair as it drifted down a river. The technique used in the best swords is known as 'pattern-welding': a number of bars of different qualities of iron and steel are welded, hammered and twisted together, not only producing the necessary suppleness, but also providing the surface with attractive swirling patterns. The technique is pre-Roman and Celtic in origin, but reaches its heights in the workshops of Francia; in the sixth and seventh centuries Frankish swords seem to have been exported to much of the Germanic world.

In the two generations after Childeric these swords, and their scabbards, were often decorated with gold-foil and gold-and-garnet cloisonné work: that is, thin shaped sections of garnet held in place by cells or *cloisons* of gold. This technique originated much further east and was in Childeric's day an international aristocratic fashion, but it became naturalized in the sixth century, and was used extensively in Francia, by our only named gold-smith, Eligius (see above p. 197) among many others. Birgit Arrhenius's recent work on garnet jewellery suggests that the garnets themselves came mostly from south-west Bohemia. She has also identified different workshops, partly on the basis of the different types of cements used in the construction of the pieces, and argues that Trier was a major production centre, making luxury articles itself but also exporting cut garnets and mounted garnet panels to other workshops; among its earliest products are the pendants found in the woman's grave at Cologne (see above, pp. 153). There were some 4000 individual pieces of garnet found in the royal Anglian treasure at Sutton Hoo, dated to the mid-620s, many of them exported from Trier, Arrhenius argues: she estimates that they represent a year's gem-cutting for a workshop of 17 men. A fine example of the goldsmith's work survives in the cathedral treasury at Trier: it is a Frankish disc brooch, incorporating a gold coin of the Emperor Justinian, itself incorporated into the

Plate 41 In the tenth century a shrine was made in Trier for a nail from the True Cross, some of Peter's beard and a strap from Andrew's sandal. It incorporated a Frankish disc-brooch from c. 600 (also perhaps made in Trier), which itself incorporated a gold coin of the Emperor Justinian.

shrine made by Bishop Egbert of Trier in the tenth century for the relic of St Andrew's foot (see plate 41).

A major problem of studying early medieval trade and industry archaeologically is that much of the material does not survive, or survives in such a damaged form that origins cannot be assessed. Some of these might have been extremely important trade items: one can think of grain and other agricultural products (including wine, oil and spices), salt, textiles, items in leather or wood – and slaves. To some extent our information can be filled out by the literary evidence. Gregory of Tours, again, is a major source. He mentions cargoes of oil coming to Marseilles; wine from Gaza, Ashkelon and Laodicea; papyrus, which came from Egypt and was used by the Merovingian bureaucracy until the late seventh century. He also gives us some information about merchants. He relates how a merchant called Christopher travelled from Tours to Orleans because he had heard that a large quantity of wine had been brought there; he bought it and had it put on boats; he himself travelled back by horse (and was killed by his two Saxon slaves: LH VII. 46). He introduces us to a merchant who traded in salt up the Moselle from Metz to Trier (VSM IV. 29), as well as to a number of Syrian and Jewish merchants, (although we cannot assume, as Henri Pirenne and others have done, that all Syrians and Jews in Merovingian Gaul were involved in commerce). There are intriguing and frustrating glimpses of the commercial life of Gaul, such as the story (LH III. 34) of how King Theuderic lent 7000 gold pieces to the town of Verdun so that its merchants could reorganize their business affairs: they did recover their prosperity, and were able to pay back their interest-free loan to Theuderic. There was the profitable year of 585, when famine was so widespread in Gaul that merchants made a great killing, selling measures of grain or wine for a *triens* (and forcing some of their customers to sell themselves into slavery to raise the cash: LH VII. 45).

Even less is known about the craftsmen in Frankish society. Certainly many craftsmen are mentioned in sources of the sixth and seventh centuries – bell-founders, builders, carpenters, glass-makers, gold-smiths, masons, wall-painters, smiths, tailors, weavers, wood-carvers and many others – but very little is known of their status or how their work was organized. The only craftsmen who appear in the legal sources are slaves, because of the need to state their value: smiths and some other types of craftsmen are regarded as more valuable than other slaves. Some craftsmen in the narrative sources were slaves too, and others, such as those attached to royal palaces, or the 40 weaving-girls donated by Count Eberhard to a monastery in Alsace, in 735–37, may well have been. Other craftsmen seem to have been independent, and quite mobile. Bishop Ansbert of Rouen assembled gold-smiths 'from many provinces' to construct his predecessor Audoen's shrine. Audoen's own colleague Eligius (see above p. 196) was clearly a craftsman who could work, as a goldsmith or as a moneyer, all over Gaul. It may be, of course, that gold-smiths were peculiarly mobile, since they probably worked largely on commission, and their materials would be supplied by their patrons. It has also been suggested, however, that their work was not appreciated for itself: the written sources frequently make reference to old works being melted down to make new, and in wills gold-work was valued by weight, not by quality.

Eligius was a craftsman who was much in demand (and despite his calling, was able to become Bishop of Noyon), and he was also versatile in his metal-working skills. We may perhaps compare him to the anonymous man found in tomb 10 from Hérouvillette (Calvados) (published by Decaens), which may stand as an example of the small number of known craftsmen's graves in Francia (see plate 42). The man was clearly not a slave: a lance rested on his right arm; an axe was fixed into the bedrock by his left side, his hand apparently grasping its haft; a sword and a long knife rested on his body. A purse hung from his belt, near the axe, holding 17 silver coins, mostly of the period 525–50, some minted by the Ostrogoths in Provence, others by Franks in northern Gaul; a gold coin in the name of Justinian (*c.* 535) had been placed in his mouth (like the Charon's obolus of Roman times). At his feet, in either a wooden or a leather container, was a collection of tools: hammers, tongs, gouges, chisels, files, iron bars of all shapes and sizes, a small balance, whetstones: some thirty tools, for the work of both a smith and a jeweller. Together with them were placed some raw material: broken axes, some pieces of bronze; two sets of coins, placed separately in the grave, one consisting

Plate 42 The smith from Hérouvillette; his weapons can clearly be seen, together with the parcel of tools at the foot of his grave.

of twelve large bronze coins from the early Empire, the other of seven late Roman copper coins; two pieces of glass (for setting into jewellery); and a capsule of mercury, presumably for using in the process of gilding.

Rural Life

Many Frankish craftsmen, like the Hérouvillette smith, may have lived and worked in the countryside. We may no longer believe, as some historians have done, accepting Roman prejudices, that barbarians had some innate aversion to towns, but it certainly does seem likely that the great bulk of the Frankish population lived in the countryside. Towns in late Roman Gaul were already declining in social and economic importance, and the towns of north-east Gaul more than most; the population of those towns that survived was probably to a large extent ecclesiastical, either clergy, monks and nuns, or else those who supplied the clergy and pilgrims with their necessities. Most Franks must have lived and worked among the fields.

The primacy of agriculture in the life of the Franks is usefully displayed by the *Pactus Legis Salicae*. It shows us a wholly rural world. The law code begins with livestock: 20 clauses about pigs (crimes ranging from striking a sow so that it no longer gives milk through to the theft of 50 pigs) (2);[22] 14 clauses on the theft of cattle (including the very stiff fine of 90 solidi for stealing the king's bull) (3); 14 clauses on the theft or mutilation of different types and ages of horse (38); five on the theft of sheep (4); two on goats (5); four on dogs (hunting dogs, greyhounds, sheep dogs) (6), 10 on birds (thefts of falcons, poultry, domesticated cranes, swans, ducks and geese) (7); four on the theft of swarms of bees (8); nine on damage to crops or enclosures by someone else's livestock (9). There are 28 clauses relating to miscellaneous offences such as stealing a cow-bell; breaking off a graft from an apple- or pear-tree; breaking into a locked or unlocked work-shop; and stealing items such as flax, grapes, firewood, eel nets, stake-nets or trawls (27). Other clauses relate to the burning of outhouses, granaries and pig-sties (16); the theft of boats and

---

[22] The numbers in brackets refer to titles in the *Pactus Legis Salicae*.

sailing vessels (21); stealing grain or an iron tool from someone's mill, and breaking the sluice in someone's water-mill (22); and the taking of stags or boars that another's dogs have already exhausted (33). The phraseology and scale of values in the first clause of title 10 is also revealing: 'If anyone steals another's male or female slave, horse or draught-horse, let him be liable for 35 solidi, in addition to its value and a fine for the loss of use'. *Lex Ribvaria* describes a similar society, though one that appears somewhat more complex and more Romanized (as befits a code which, conventionally at least, is dated to the 620s rather than to the early sixth century). The clause on the purchase of farms or vineyards or other properties, for instance, mentions the possibility of a written property deed or charter, although the ceremony it decrees in the absence of a charter is as concrete and colourful as anything in the Salic law:

Let him go with witnesses to the place that was sold. . . Let him pay the price in the presence of these and let him acquire the property. And let him give a box on the ear of each one of the little ones, and let him twist their ears in order that they can give testimony. (LR 63)

Memory, even in a largely oral society, sometimes needed to be reinforced. . .

Laws, particularly laws so apparently haphazardly collected and written down as those in the Frankish law-codes, can never give any precise guide as to how society operated, but they do perhaps provide an indication of those things which a particular society thought important and worth protecting. The enumeration above gives a fairly clear if generalized idea of the nature of the Frankish rural economy. *Lex Ribvaria* even gives a scale of monetary values, which is unique for the Merovingian period, as a guide to those who wish to pay fines in kind for the wergild (the amount a murderer has to pay to the victim's family, an amount dependant on the victim's social status) rather than in the enumerated *solidi*:

If anyone begins to pay a wergild, let him give a horned ox, able to see and healthy, for two solidi. Let him give a horned cow, able to see and healthy, for one solidus. Let him give a stallion, able to see and healthy, for seven solidi. Let him give a mare, able to see and healthy, for three solidi. Let him give a sword with a scabbard for seven solidi. Let him give a sword without a scabbard for three solidi. Let him give a metal tunic in good condition for

Plate 43 Part of the settlement site excavated recently at Juvincourt-et-Damary, near Soissons.

twelve solidi. Let him give a helmet in good condition for six solidi. Let him give a shield with a lance for two solidi. Let him give leggings in good condition for six solidi. Let him give an untrained hawk for three solidi. Let him give a crane-seizing hawk for six solidi. Let him give a trained hawk for twelve solidi. If he pays with silver, let a solidus be equal to twelve denarii, just as was decided long ago. (LR 40)

It is not just the rural crimes which give us some idea of the rural economy of the Franks; the structure of the law itself often implies smallish, tightly-knit rural communities. There is title 45 of the *Pactus*, for instance: *De migrantibus*.

If a man wishes to migrate to another village and one or more of those who live in the village wish to receive him, but one or more of those who live there disagree, he shall not have permission to migrate there. But if he attempts to settle in that village contrary to the objection of one or two of them, then the latter must warn him. And if he refuses to depart, he who warned him must do so with witnesses, and must say: 'Man, I inform you that you may remain here this next night, as the Salic law specifies, and I inform you that within ten nights you must leave the village.'

It is in small communities such as that law implies that the whole legal system described or inferrable from the *Pactus Legis Salicae* can best be enforced. The primary law enforcement agency among the Franks was the family or kinship group (within which an individual can be adopted, in a ceremony described in title 46, or from which he can be cast out or voluntarily separated: titles 58 and 60). Criminals were brought to the local court, the *mallus*, by the victim and/or his family; most crimes were punished by the payment of a fine, the bulk of which went to the victim and/or his family (the rest going to the king and his officials). It was the socially accepted sanction of feud – the family's right to pursue an injury done to its honour, even to death – which persuaded accused criminals to go to the law-court. As the anthropologist Max Gluckman argued many years ago, by analogy with similar systems that he had observed in operation in Africa, in a rural society in which there is much intermarriage within and between villages, kinship groups usually had considerable overlap: it was thus in everyone's interest to resolve potential feud by peaceful negotiation.

Settlement Archaeology

The picture of village life gleaned from the legal sources cannot yet be filled out to any great extent by archaeology. Few Frankish village sites have been excavated so far, and fewer published; however, this is the area where the greatest advances can be expected in the next few years. At the moment we can do little more than list a number of sites; it is impossible to know how typical they may have been.

The first Frankish village in France to be excavated was Brebières (Pas-de-Calais) (*Berbiariae*, mentioned in a document of 872, means 'sheep-folds'), near Vitry-en-Artois – the royal villa where Sigibert I was assassinated (above p. 174). It was a dismal site, on the edge of a permanent marsh, and drained by two large ditches, several hundred metres long and sometimes two metres wide, themselves served by smaller drainage ditches which came from the huts themselves. All the buildings discovered in Pierre Demolon's excavations were of the type known in France as 'fonds de cabane', in Germany (and often in England) as

Plate 44 One of the houses at Juvincourt-et-Damary, as reconstructed in Soissons.

'Grubenhäuser' (sunken huts), and perhaps more properly called 'sunken featured buildings', or SFBs. That neutral phrase avoids deciding between those SFBs which were simply squalid holes in the ground with a roof on top, and those in which the buildings may have been quite large, and the sunken areas merely storage pits below the plank floors of the house. At Brebières the only buildings discovered were 31 SFBs, ranged along 400 metres of land (the whole area of the village was not excavated). Some of these SFBs were used for storage; some, apparently, as weaving-huts; three, slightly larger (2.50 m X 4 m), could have been permanent dwellings. The settlement as a whole perhaps supplied the royal villa with provisions. Clearly there was stock-raising; the site yielded bones of pig, oxen, horses, hens, goats and geese, together with one duck, one wild boar and a few deer. Brebières seems to have been occupied from the beginning of the sixth century, and was abandoned in the course of the seventh century, maybe when the royal villa ceased to be used: 'perhaps', commented Professor Wallace-Hadrill, 'it was a relief to take their rheumatism away from all that mud'.[23]

[23] J. M. Wallace-Hadrill, *Early Medieval History* (Oxford, 1975), p. 2.

Demolon undertook a rescue excavation at Vitry itself in 1985, where more SFBs were discovered. There also appears to have been confirmation at Vitry of the doubts that had been voiced since the publication of Brebières, that Frankish houses were not all as small and as squalid as some people (like Wallace-Hadrill) assumed. The surface levels were stripped at Brebières, leaving only the deeper levels, including the pits of the SFBs. But at Vitry there were indications to suggest that the SFBs were mere out-houses. There are a number of postholes of buildings which did not have sunken features, including one 6m wide, and there are also heavy concentrations of small finds, that may indicate Mero-vingian floor-levels. There have been other excavations showing that larger rectangular houses without sunken features were usual in Frankish villages. Gladbach, near Bonn (excavated before the last war, and not yet published), a settlement site of the sixth and seventh centuries, had eight rectangular buildings, two of them as large as 12.5m. X 9m. – although these were outnum-bered by 57 SFBs. Much more recently Didier Bayard has disco-vered a Merovingian settlement site at Juvincourt-et-Damary (Aisne), with numerous SFBs, but also a number of large wooden buildings with multiple post-holes (see plate 43). The largest was 15m. X 5m.: reconstructions place it at least 5m. high. A full-scale reconstruction has in fact been made, in the gardens of the ruined abbey of St-Jean-des-Vignes, in Soissons, where some idea can be gained of what a Merovingian house may actually have been like (plate 44). The SFBs at Juvincourt-et-Damary seem to have been used as weaving-huts, pig-sties, poultry-pens and the like.

The Merovingian archaeologist's dream would be the detec-tion and excavation of a settlement (preferably with its associated cemetery) with a lifespan of several centuries, from the Roman through to the Carolingian period and beyond. A village with a more extended life (though with a cemetery only starting in the late seventh century) was excavated recently by Claude Lorren at Saint-Martin-de-Mondeville, south-east of Caen (Calvados). In the early Roman period it seems to have been a relatively prosper-ous *vicus*, whose inhabitants built in stone. Some time around 300 the stone houses were replaced by more rudimentary wooden buildings, many of the SFB type: most of them had floors dug into bedrock. They were of various sizes, from 1.60m. X 2.10m. up to 2.50m. X 4.70m., with roofs, presumably of thatch, supported by two posts at the two narrow ends. Most of these dwellings are not easy to date; there seems to have been little, if any, change in methods of construction between the fourth and seventh centuries. There was one building, datable by pottery to the sixth century, whose roof was supported by five posts; its occupants seem to have thrown their rubbish into an abandoned SFB of the late Roman period. Some metal-work of *c.* 700 dates one of the two-post SFBs, and shows that this type lasted for some four centuries. Similar objects of the same date were also associated with the first stone building to be built since the third century. Prosperity, defined in terms of small finds and of stone buildings – one as large as 5m. X 9.50m. – seems to have returned in the early eighth century. It was at that time, too, (cf. above p. 148) that the dead begin to be buried near the settlement, apparently in the midst of ruined Roman walls, although it is quite possible that a church had been built there in the early eighth century, using those Roman walls as foundations.

While waiting for more excavation and publication, we can still learn more about Frankish settlements by looking at the cemetery evidence. it is possible, after all, to get some idea of the size of a community (see above, pp. 28) and of its duration by looking at the cemetery. By examining the cemeteries of a region, some idea of overall settlement patterns may be gained. Hermann Ament, for instance, has looked at the whole region around Mayen, and tried to distinguish between different types of settlements from their cemeteries, and to suggest their social importance and their economic links with Mayen. If there is much to learn about the structure of settlements, the question of how those settlements related to each other is also an interesting one. The historical sources show us, for example, that aristocrats frequently possessed estates across the whole of Gaul, and probably deliberately set out to acquire these scattered estates; if an aristocrat (or a monastery) possessed vineyards in the Bordelais, olive-groves in Provence, salt-pans on the Atlantic coast, and arable land on the great northern plain, then his family was largely self-sufficient, and need not resort to the merchant. Much internal 'trade', indeed, may have been merely the movement of goods around Gaul from one portion of an aristocrat's estates to another. What cannot yet be seen archaeologically is the effect this had at the level of the individual estate or settlement – in terms, for instance, of economic specialization. Nor can the settlement of independent free peasants be distinguished from the settlement of tenants or slaves, although sometimes the grave-goods may provide excellent clues.

Divisions within Frankish society

Frankish society was, in the sixth century, highly stratified, in terms of the legal classes revealed by the laws, and the differing levels of material wealth displayed by the graves. The laws and the graves both appear for the first time in the reign of Clovis, of course; it is impossible to know how far back in time these divisions went. There are those historians who still believe in the myth of the democratic Germanic society of the 'good old days' – a powerful myth in the nineteenth century, when liberals in England and Germany alike took it as a foundation for their 'love of freedom'. Perhaps given the nineteenth-century view of democracy, i.e. rule by propertied males, there was something in the myth. In the first century AD there may have been relatively little social differentiation in terms of material prosperity (at least for the free-born); ownership of land by kinship groups rather than individuals may have resulted in some levelling of distinctions. But from the third century onwards the closer contacts between the Empire and the Franks – increased booty, political subsidies, employment opportunities within the Empire – must have brought about considerable changes in Frankish society. Those changes surely accelerated between *c.* 450 and *c.* 550, as Frankish kings and their followers came into possession of huge estates in Gaul and other conquered territories. The earliest laws come in the middle of this process, but reveal nothing of the dynamics.

The law-codes divide the population into a fairly clear set of legal categories, marked by different wergilds (see p. 210). In the event of murder most of this amount (probably two-thirds) is paid to the kin of the victim; the rest to the king or his representatives. In the *Pactus Legis Salicae* the average free-born Frank (or any barbarian who is living in accordance with the Salic law: 41.1) is given the wergild of two hundred *solidi* – a very high figure, as one can see by comparing it with the prices

given on p. 210. Young girls and women past child-bearing age
have the same wergild; a woman of child-bearing age ('up to the
age of sixty years old who can have children' specifies a later
addition to the *Pactus*) and a free-born boy under twelve, on the
other hand, have wergilds of 600 solidi. This high wergild is
shared by a Frank who is in the king's retinue (*trustis*), and by a
high royal official, the *grafio*. (A lesser royal official, such as a
sacebaro or an *obgrafio*, has a wergild of 300 solidi). All these
figures are tripled if someone is murdered in his own house, and
by a group of conspirators. However, 'if anyone abducts, kills,
sells or manumits another's slave' the criminal pays the set fine
of 35 solidi. The freedman is likewise not regarded as having a
wergild, or indeed a kin who can avenge him; his value is placed
at 100 solidi, payable to his lord. Some slaves are valued nearly
as highly: title 35.9 values the following categories of slave at 75
solidi: female domestics, blacksmiths, gold-smiths, swineherds,
vine-dressers and grooms.

Lex Ribvaria has almost precisely the same provisions, with
one or two minor adjustments: the child-bearing age for women
is taken (more realistically) as ending at 40; the cost of the
murder of a slave is put at 36 solidi. There are some additions
and refinements, however. Anyone killing a 'king's man', a
'church man' or a 'church girl' over forty (all of whom I take to
be royal or ecclesiastial slaves) must pay 100 solidi, or 300
solidi for a 'church girl' of child-bearing age. Ecclesiastical
grades were brought within the system, too, ranging from the
lowest rank of the clergy at 100 solidi, through a sub-deacon at
200, a deacon at 300 and a priest at 600, to a bishop at 900
solidi. The wergild of a king is not mentioned. But since *Lex
Ribvaria* 72 regards even infidelity to the king as punishable by
death and confiscation of all property, we may confidently
presume that kings do not have a wergild; no monetary
compensation was possible for crimes against them.

We thus have a society which is divided up into a number of
legal categories. Many historians have taken it that these
correspond to social classes – and some archaeologists have
even imagined that the different sets of grave-goods that are
found in Frankish cemeteries may be equated with these legal
and social classes. Thus, according to one archaeologist, those
buried with a sword were freemen; those buried with a spear

and/or arrows were half-free or freedmen; those buried with no
weapons at all were slaves. For another archaeologist, those
buried with several weapons were freemen; those buried only
with a scramasax were half-free. And so on. In addition to the
sheer arbitrariness of such equations, there are real problems
with such interpretations. For instance, the distinction between
sword-burials and scramasax burials may be chronological
rather than social; single-edged scramasaxes were replacing
double-edged swords from the later sixth century, in graves, at
least, if not in actual everyday use. The historians who have
written about the origins of the Frankish aristocracy have had
some problems with the non-appearance of a clearly defined
aristocratic class in the law-codes (as there is, for instance, in
Roman law, or in seventh-century West Saxon law). The only
candidates for legally defined aristocrats are those members of
the king's *trustis*, his retinue, who had three times the normal
freeman's wergild: hence the theories that the earliest Frankish
aristocracy was a royal nobility, which owed its social position
solely to its proximity to the king's person, or to its holding of
office on behalf of the king. There is no reason to believe that
the categories revealed in the law-codes necessarily have much
to do with social classes at all.

Some examination of the categories makes this clear. The
basic distinctions are three-fold: between the unfree; the
ordinary Frankish freeman or freewoman; and those among the
free who deserve extra protection because of their importance
for the Frankish people as a whole – those on royal business,
women of child-bearing age and boys under 12. The later *Lex
Ribvaria* shows that there was a tendency to elaborate on these
basic distinctions, by translating clerical grades within the
Church into legal equivalents, for example, or to carry the
distinctions one logical step further, as by giving an extra value
to royal slaves. But the distinctions in the law-codes reflect a
desire on the part of the legislators (whoever they were) to
categorize the worth of individuals, not to divide them up into
social classes. That social privilege and social distinctions
played a part in the actual operation of the law is highly likely,
but it played little part in the minds of the lawyers. With the
Franks, as with the Romans, social status and wealth did not
necessarily correlate with legal status: consequently, the law-

codes do not provide us with much of a guide to the social divisions among the Franks.

The law-codes may be particularly misleading at two ends of the spectrum: with the slaves and with the aristocracy. The law-codes treat slaves as property, alongside cattle and cart-horses. Yet it would seem from other sources that the condition of slaves in Frankish Gaul, under the influence either of a more mild Germanic practice, or of the Gallo-Roman church, or, perhaps more plausibly, of economic and demographic developments, was slightly improving – at the same time, perhaps, as that of the free peasantry was deteriorating. In terms of the criminal law the two categories were treated quite differently; in terms of their economic and social positions there was probably little to choose between them. Both were tied to the land and to their lord and master, yet both could work their own land and had a limited amount of personal freedom – which included, perhaps, the ability to contemplate upward social mobility. But all this is speculation. Our evidence for slaves or free peasants in the sixth or early seventh century comes mainly from Gallo-Roman sources and refers largely to Gallo-Roman conditions. Things might have been very different in a Frankish village.

The only class of Franks which is visible in the sources of the sixth and early seventh century is the aristocracy, and those aristocrats we see in the pages of Gregory of Tours and Fredegar seem to have a power-base – in land and in supporters – independent of the king and of royal office. That does not mean, of course, that the Frankish aristocrats who are active in Gregory's *Histories* did not owe their position in Frankish society originally to their support for the Merovingian dynasty. One can easily imagine that those who fought alongside Childeric, Clovis and his sons were rewarded with considerable amounts of booty and of land, far outstripping those other, less fortunate, Frankish aristocrats, the unhappy *leudes* of Rag-nachar, Frankish king of Cambrai, for instance, who were, according to Gregory, tricked into betraying their king to Clovis, or the supporters of the independent Frankish kings of Cologne (see above pp. 88–91). Aristocrats close to the king could expect to get grants of land for their lifetimes which, theoretically, would be dependent upon their continuing service and loyalty. In practice, within a generation such grants of land probably became regarded as hereditary possessions, and could be supplemented by property which was acquired independently of royal favour, via inheritance, purchase or marriage settlements. Such land could be geographically extensive (see above p. 215), and carry the interests of a particular aristocratic family far away from the traditional heartlands of the Franks.

We do not have to rely solely on the documentary evidence to be assured of the wealth and importance of these aristocrats. From the time of Clovis through into the sixth century, they followed the fashions of their superiors, and had themselves buried in some splendour. Most of the larger row-grave cemeteries which began in the early sixth century had some rich burials, most of which can be placed in the earliest phase of the cemetery. Archaeologists have paid a great deal of attention to those aristocratic graves which have been found in recent years, in carefully excavated cemeteries, but enough survives from cemeteries dug in the nineteenth century to suggest that it was a widespread phenomenon; in the absence of records or publication it is often only the characteristically aristocratic material in museums which demonstrates the likely presence of aristocrats in a particular cemetery.

Characteristically aristocratic grave-goods, however, swords with gold-and-garnet cloisonné decorations for their scabbard, kidney-shaped buckle-plates, cloisonné purse fittings, horse-bits, and so on, such as are found with Childeric at Tournai (see p. 59), the prince in Cologne Cathedral (p. 153), or the chieftain from Krefeld-Gellep 1782 (p. 90), are not the only things which distinguish aristocratic or privileged burials. The grave itself can indicate status, if it is exceptionally large, or made with a wooden chamber, or placed under a barrow. Status is also suggested if a grave has a special orientation, or is isolated from others, or, indeed, is close to others: Hermann Ament has argued that the apparently poor graves placed very close to high-status graves at Arlon, Flonheim or Morken must be high-status graves themselves. The special privilege suggested by the appearance of horse-bits may be accentuated by the proximity of actual horse-burials. In a very different cultural context, privilege may be conveyed by burial within a church (see above p. 145).

Some of these distinguishing features of privilege may be

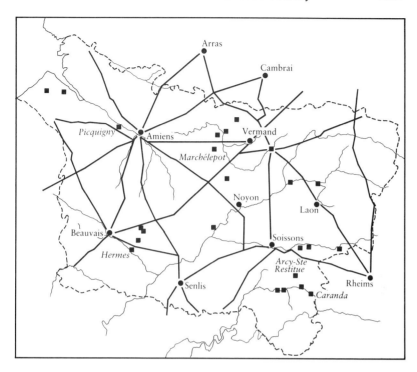

Figure 24 Aristocratic tombs in Picardy from the time of Clovis and his sons.

visible even when a cemetery has been largely pillaged by treasure-hunters of the Middle Ages or later. At Krefeld-Gellep, for instance (see above pp. 56 and 90), there were a number of graves which had been emptied but had once been of enormous size: grave 2268 was the largest known from the Merovingian period, 6.5m. long, 4.2m. wide and 3.55m deep (97m^3.). There were empty spaces around 2268 and another large grave, 2528: it is possible that this represents the space that was once covered by a barrow, which announced clearly the importance of the buried person. Wood which survived in tomb 2268 can be dated dendrochronologically; it was cut in 589. Between *c.* 530 and *c.* 590, therefore, some half-a-dozen important people were buried at Krefeld-Gellep, in burials set apart by their conspicuous expenditure (in terms of wealth of graves-goods or amount of man-power expended, or, originally, probably both) from the other graves in the cemetery.

The aristocratic graves from Picardy have recently been studied by Françoise Vallet (see fig. 24). Many of the classic Frankish row-grave cemeteries are in Picardy – Caranda, Hermes, Marchélepot, Picquigny. Most, however, were 'excavated' in the heroic days of archaeology, by such figures as Eck, Moreau and Pilloy. Vallet has looked for those objects typically found in the well-known aristocratic graves, and they turned out to be significantly distributed. There is a group of four cemeteries yielding high-status graves in the Somme valley west of Vermand. Another group of four is in the valley of the Ourcq, including Caranda with its 2000 tombs and five or six high status graves, and Arcy-Ste-Restitue, which has one of the four long-swords with gold-foil hilts found in France: these are known from a fairly restricted period from the time of Childeric (481) through to 520, and are always associated with very rich grave-goods. There is another concentration of cemeteries in the valleys east of Beauvais, including La-Rue-Saint-Pierre, a sarcophagus burial with another gold-hilt long-sword; Hermes, with some 3000 graves including several very rich ones; and Bulles, the only one of these Picardy cemeteries to have been excavated recently. Finally there are three cemeteries strung along the River Aisne east of Soissons, in which similar rich material has been found. In historical terms what we are to make of these concentrations of cemeteries with aristocratic burials is not clear. We can note that a number of the cemeteries are in fact re-used, or perhaps even continuously used, cemeteries of the Roman period. Some of these cemeteries contained fourth- or fifth-century Germanic, perhaps Frankish, graves (discussed on pp. 44–51); perhaps some of these aristocrats were not newcomers but the descendents of Franks settled in this region for several generations. Rather more significant is the way in which these cemeteries are mostly within 15 kilometres of the Roman towns of Beauvais, Soissons and Vermand. We can add to these the very rich grave of Picquigny, 15 kilometres from Roman Amiens. Since we know nothing of how the Frankish aristocracy acquired its land we can hardly account for this distribution with any certainty. Did Childeric or Clovis, under whom Picardy was incorporated into Francia, give land in these places to aristocratic families for strategic reasons, or did aristocrats themselves choose those of their estates which were closest to towns as their particular residences?

Another attempt to characterize aristocratic graves on an even wider European level has been made by Rainer Christlein. Christlein has distinguished four main quality groups among the male graves of the period, in terms of grave-goods and of grave-construction. He divided his bottom group, A, into those which were without any weapons (A1) and those which had simply a scramasax (A2); his B-graves were those provided with a sword; his D-graves were the very small number of 'royal' graves, as at Tournai, Cologne or Morken. It is the C-graves which correspond to our aristocratic graves. Christlein argued that there were certain objects which were likely to occur in association with each other in these graves, such as horse-bits in male graves, gold disk fibulae and gold cloisonné brooches in female graves, wide bronze bowls of Mediterranean manufacture (often called 'Coptic bowls'), wooden buckets with bronze decorations, gold rings, with bodies of either sex. The suggestion is that these items were placed in graves to symbolize or display or claim status of a particular kind. Christlein has also argued that distribution of these C-graves within a cemetery may be significant: that C-graves scattered throughout a cemetery may indicate rich peasants/farmers who aspire to aristocratic status, while the grouping of C-graves in one place, whether in the centre of the cemetery or to one side, suggests the existence of a wealthy and aristocratic family. Christlein's distinction there, of course, implies a particular view of the Frankish aristocracy: one resembling the nobility of later medieval Europe, in which birth is much more important than acquired wealth. The Frankish aristocracy of the sixth or seventh century may be much less sharply defined and much more accessible to newcomers than he assumes.

It is sometimes possible to work out relationships within these C-graves, or between these and others. A rich male and a rich female grave side by side and roughly contemporary, for instance, are usually interpreted as man and wife. Périn suggests that the three male C-graves at Mézières, dated roughly *c.* 500, *c.* 525, and c.565, represent three generations of one Frankish aristocratic family. In some cases, as at Beerlegem, the C-graves are surrounded by rows of grave-goodless graves, which could be seen as those of servants or dependents.

Most discussion has assumed that the nature of the grave-goods buried has some social significance. Many archaeologists are in agreement that the grave-goods deposited with the dead were not primarily intended for use in an afterlife. The spread of the custom among the royalty and aristocracy in the very generation when it was converted to Christianity makes this implausible (see above pp. 138–141). Another possible explanation is that items closely associated with the dead could not be inherited by their heirs, and had to be disposed of in some way. In later German law there is such a provision for the military equipment of men (*Heergewäte*) and the jewellery of women (*Gerade*), but there is no early medieval evidence for this practice. It seems likely, therefore, that the deposition of grave-goods relates to a social act – homage to the dead person, celebration of his place in society and within the family, or a means whereby the family itself, the survivors, can announce and display their own status. Most discussions of the evidence have assumed one or other of these latter explanations, though frequently without elaboration.

It could be that different types of gravegoods were deposited for different reasons. The vessels containing offerings of food or drink may be a portion of the funeral feast, offered in homage to the dead. The items of dress may be objects which were not heritable, and other objects may reflect a symbolic statement of function, like the croziers buried in the graves of late medieval bishops. In one area at least the symbolic nature of a burial deposit seems likely. This is the case of those boys' graves provided with miniature axes or scramasaxes. Some of these could be toys, or items actually used in some way in life, either for training or for purposes of displaying status, but some were clearly quite unusable – miniature axes without a socket for the haft, for instance – and must surely have been manufactured for symbolic deposition in a grave. Boys' graves also often contain adult weapons: the best example is that of the Cologne 'prince' (see above p. 153), whose helmet would have fitted him, but whose weapons he could barely have lifted. In these cases, weapons can be regarded as representing the free or, perhaps, aristocratic status of the person buried. If one element in a grave has to be interpreted as symbolic, then it is justifiable to ask whether other aspects of the burial ritual are not symbolic as well. The door opens onto infinite speculation.

The Well-Dressed Frank

What archaeologists find in abundance is evidence of the type of clothing worn by the well-dressed male or female Frank – or, at least, what was assumed to be proper for them to wear in their graves. There is still a lot of work to be done on the development of dress styles, but the evidence would seem to be there. What we cannot know is the extent to which this clothing too was redolent of symbolism, as more modern folk-dress in Europe has been. For instance, more imaginative archaeologists have speculated on the particular symbolism of the decoration on the bow-brooches, which have been found with innumerable slight variations in graves not only in Francia, but in the entire Germanic world.

It does seem likely that dress was one indicator of ethnic allegiance (see above p. 113). Einhard, in his *Life of Charle- magne* relates that this Frankish king (crowned Emperor in 800) wore 'the national dress':

Next to his skin he had a linen shirt and linen drawers; and then long hose and a tunic edged with silk. He wore shoes on his feet and bands of cloth wound round his legs. In winter he protected his chest and shoulders with a jerkin made of otter skins or ermine. He wrapped himself in a blue cloak, and always had a sword strapped to his side, with a hilt and belt of gold or silver. . . He hated the clothes of other countries, no matter how becoming they might be, and he would never consent to wear them. . . On feast days he walked in procession in a suit of cloth of gold, with jewelled shoes, his cloak fastened with a golden brooch and with a crown of gold and precious stones on his head. On ordinary days his dress differed hardly at all from that of the common people. (Einhard, 22)

The silk (imported from Constantinople, presumably) and the ermine do not quite sound like the dress of the common people. Aristocrats may, indeed, have stressed their separateness partly by wearing luxury imported items, particularly from the prestigious fashion-setters of Constantinople. Thus Arnegund (see p. 155) wore, in addition to her stockings and chemise of fine wool and a cloak of red wool (both local products), a dress

*Plate 45 The so-called 'chemise de Sainte-Balthilde', preserved since the
seventh century at Queen Balthild's monastery of Chelles.*

of violet silk, and a tunic of dark red silk embroidered at the
sleeves with gold thread, which may well have been imported
ready-made from the East. Rich Frankish women by the late
sixth century also wore Byzantine ear-rings, or imitations of
them; they wore their beads in Byzantine fashion, and may even
on occasion have exchanged their typically Frankish brooches
for imitations of Byzantine ones. A strange relic of these
Byzantine fashions has survived in Chelles, in the fragment of
cloth, embroidered in coloured silks, known as the 'chemise de
Sainte-Bathilde' (see plate 51). We cannot know whether this
actually belonged to Queen Balthild, founder of the nunnery at
Chelles, but it does seem to be from the seventh century. Hayo
Vierck has argued that it was made in Francia, in imitation of
Byzantine products; the embroidery represents pendants of the
type fashionable in Byzantium, right down to a representation
of the chains on which they dangled.

Aspiring to foreign fashions is less evident in male styles, except perhaps in the luxury materials, described by Einhard but usually inaccessible to the archaeologist. Charlemagne himself may have been more conservative than most. The late ninth-century book on Charlemagne, by Notker the Stammerer, describes the traditional cloak of the 'Old Franks', as worn by Charlemagne, as being 'either white or blue, in the shape of a double square. It was so arranged that, when it was placed over the shoulders, it reached to the feet in front and behind, but hardly came down to the knees at the sides'. If we are to believe Charlemagne's complaint about the new mini-cloaks sold by Frisian merchants, the traditional cloaks might be used as bed-coverings too, at least on campaign: 'What is the use of these little napkins? I can't cover myself with them in bed. When I am on horseback I can't protect myself from the winds and the rain. When I go off to empty my bowels, I catch cold because my backside is frozen.' (Notker I. 34)

Both Notker and Einhard describe Charlemagne in his everyday dress, not his dress as a warrior, and we cannot be sure that we have a very clear picture, from the archaeology, of a battle-ready Frank. There are shields in the graves, but few helmets, and only one piece of body-armour, a cuirass built up of 1100 rectangular metal scales, sewn onto leather, from grave 2589 at Krefeld-Gellep (see plate 46). However, both Notker and Einhard describe the sword as if it were an essential item of daily dress. The former says that it was attached to the belt buckled over Charlemagne's white linen shirt, and was 'encased first in a sheath, then in a leather holder and finally in a bright white linen cover which was hardened with shining wax, so that protection was given to the middle of the leg when men drew their swords to kill people.' We have no similar descriptions of dress from the Merovingian period (though cf. Sidonius Apollinaris's description of fifth-century Franks, p. 74), but we do again have the evidence of the graves. Back in the early sixth century the sword did not in fact hang from the belt; it hung from a leather strap slung across the shoulder. And the 'traditional' Frankish warrior carried other weapons which Charlemagne could not have known: the throwing-axe or *francisca*, the short scramasax with the single straight cutting edge, the barbed spear or *ango*. The latter, which the Byzantine

Plate 46 A portion of a cuirass found in the warrior grave no. 2589 at Krefeld-Gellep, which was made of dozens of iron plates sewn onto a leather base.

historian Agathias regarded as one of the most typical weapons used by Franks in the Italian wars, is in fact rare in graves; only some 150 have been found, out of thousands of graves, and by the end of the sixth century it had virtually disappeared. By the mid-sixth century the equally 'traditional' *francisca* had been joined by a variety of other axes. By the seventh century (although the picture is made less clear by the inceasing rarity of weapon graves), angos and axes have gone altogether, and the long-sword is found only in the richest graves. The main weapon now is the heavy machete-like scramasax, hanging from the belt, with a long hilt indicating that it was often used two-handed. Many of them appear heavily used; it may well be that they were indeed used like machetes – an everyday tool as much as a weapon of war. Clearly there was an evolution in burial customs, which may serve to conceal or to confuse an evolution of weaponry and, perhaps, a corresponding evolution in military methods. It is appropriate that the Franks, militarily the most successful of the barbarian peoples in the sixth or seventh century, should apparently have used their weaponry to symbolise their status and power in life and in death. It is also, perhaps, symbolic that by the time of Dagobert in the seventh century they preferred to show their status, in life and after death, by building churches.

Afterword: From Dagobert to De Gaulle

Merovingians and Carolingians

Chlothar II's son Dagobert (622–38) is often seen as the last great Frankish king of the Merovingian dynasty. After him came *les rois fainéants*, the 'Do-Nothing Kings', who peter off into obscurity in the eighth century, and are eventually replaced by the new, vigorous and more Germanic Franks of the Carolingian dynasty. Under Carolingian rulers such as Charles Martel, Pippin and Charles the Great – Charlemagne – the Franks forged a new Empire even larger than that of the Merovingians, stretching from Barcelona and Rome in the south up to Saxony and the frontiers of Denmark in the north. The image of Merovingian decadence stems above all from the vivid description at the beginning of the biography of Charlemagne written by one of his courtiers, Einhard:

The Merovingian dynasty, from which the Franks were accustomed to choose their kings, is thought to have lasted down to King Childeric [III], who was deposed on the order of Stephen, the Roman pontiff. His hair was cut short and he was shut up in a monastery [in 751]. Though this dynasty may seem to have come to an end only with Childeric, it had really lost all power years before and it no longer possessed anything at all of importance beyond the empty title of king. The wealth and the power of the kingdom were held in the hands of certain leading officials of the court, who were called the Mayors of the Palace. . . All that was left to the King was that, content with his royal title, he should sit on the throne, with his hair long and his beard flowing, and act the part of a ruler, giving audience to the ambassadors who arrived from foreign parts and. . .

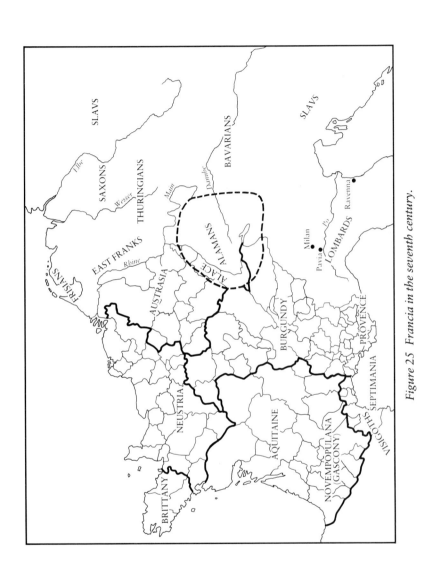

Figure 25 *Francia in the seventh century.*

charging them with answers. . . in which he had been coached or even directed. Beyond this empty title of king, and a precarious living wage which the Mayor of the Palace allowed him at his own discretion, the king possessed nothing at all of his own, except a single estate with an extremely small revenue. . . Whenever he needed to travel, he went in a cart which was drawn in country style by yoked oxen, with a cowherd to drive them. In this fashion he would go to the palace and the general assembly of his people, which was held each year to settle the affairs of the kingdom. . .

It is a passage which has evoked a vast amount of scholarly speculation, ever since Jakob Grimm suggested that the ox cart was a survival of Frankish pagan ritual. Others have argued that it was, on the contrary, a survival of Roman imperial ceremonial. Most have agreed that, whatever one makes of individual elements, the passage as a whole reflects Carolingian propaganda; it was part of their attempt to undermine the mystique of the Merovingian dynasty and to justify their own usurpation.

Nowadays historians would prefer to stress that the Merovingian kings possessed considerable resources of prestige and authority for nearly half a century after Dagobert's death. There were, nevertheless, developments which indicated decline in royal power (although we hardly have to agree with those who equate royal decline with a general decay and degeneracy of Frankish society). There was no more expansion in the seventh century; military enterprises beyond the frontier were few; kings made few expeditions even into southern Gaul. Moreover, the northern part of Francia, Francia proper, was beginning to split into two separate kingdoms. The eastern part, the lands of the Meuse, Moselle, and Rhine, took the name Austria or Austrasia – 'East Land'; these words, and the name of Austrasian, first occur in Gregory's writings. The name for the western part of the kingdom, Neustria, meaning either 'New Land' or 'New West Land' does not appear in our sources until the 640s. This seems to be largely because the Neustrians, who provide us with most of our sources, used *Austrasia* of the eastern kingdom, but used *Francia* of their own. It is the first sign that Francia/France would eventually be a name that was restricted to the western kingdom.

Even as early as Chlothar II's reign – and, indeed perhaps

going back to the time, under Clovis, when the Rhineland Franks had their own kingdom – the Austrasians regarded themselves as distinct and different from the rest of the Franks. In 622 they asked for their own king, and were given Chlothar's eldest son Dagobert himself. It was almost certainly Dagobert who gave the Austrasians their own written law code at this time, the *Lex Ribvaria*; the *Lex Salica* was for the Neustrian Franks. Dagobert's departure westwards to Paris, on his father's death in 629, seems to have been regarded by them as a great betrayal. Before Dagobert's death they had secured his son Sigibert III as their own king. Thereafter, for much of the seventh century, Austrasia was ruled separately from Neustria. Austrasia, and probably Neustria too, were clearly different from the somewhat arbitrary kingdoms into which the Frankish realm that had been divided on the deaths of Clovis in 511 or Chlothar I in 561. There was, to begin with, a genuine cultural difference; Neustria, with its royal residences in the region of Paris, was predominantly Latin (French) speaking, although it also included the Salian homelands of the Low Countries; Austrasia was predominantly German-speaking.

By the late seventh century the Austrasian aristocracy who wanted this separation from Neustria and political autonomy were dominated by the Pippinids. This dynasty was descended from a marriage between a son of Bishop (later Saint) Arnulf of Metz and a daughter of the lay aristocrat Pippin (Pippin I). Arnulf and Pippin were the chief advisors of the young Dagobert I in the 620s; Arnulf was a major bishop as well as a great aristocrat, and Pippin was Mayor of the Palace in Austrasia. The mayor was in effect the king's prime minister, with influence on royal policy and, in all probability, access to the royal treasury. Pippin held the post until his death in 640. Shortly afterwards his son Grimoald became mayor in his turn. Grimoald, it seems, even persuaded the Austrasian King Sigibert III to adopt his son as a Merovingian; when Grimoald forced Sigibert's real son Dagobert to go into exile in Ireland in *c.* 656, 'Childebert the Adopted' ruled for several years. Grimoald and Childebert were themselves deposed, by the Neustrians, and there followed several years of civil strife, in which mayors of the palace seem to have been far more important figures than kings. The figure who emerged as dominant from these struggles was the grandson of Arnulf and Pippin I, Pippin II. He became Mayor in Austrasia, and then, in 687, he defeated the Neustrian Mayor at the Battle of Tertry, and installed his own mayor in Neustria. Soon there was only one Merovingian king, a Neustrian one, but two mayors of the palace, both of them from the Pippinid dynasty. When Pippin II's son Grimoald II was assassinated, Grimoald's own young son Theudoald succeeded him as mayor of the Neustrian palace: a puppet mayor in charge of a puppet king. For a while after Pippin II's death in 715, the Pippinid dynasty was in considerable difficulties, but Pippin's illegitimate son Charles, usually known as Charles Martel, foiled the attempts of the Neustrians to regain their independence. He initiated that great period of military conquest that continued under his descendants, the Carolingians – under his son Pippin III or Pippin the Short, who was crowned Pippin I, King of the Franks in 751, and under his grandson Charlemagne, crowned Emperor in 800.

The history of the words 'Frank' and 'Francia' is not easy to follow after this period of political realignment in the late Merovingian and Carolingian periods. Clearly by Dagobert's time or soon afterwards nearly all the inhabitants of northern Gaul considered themselves to be Franks; 'Francia' was the land to the north of the Loire. Neustrians seem to have considered their part of Francia to be the *real* Francia. But in the period of the Carolingian conquests 'Francia' again expanded, so that at times it included much of the area controlled by the Franks. It was after the Treaty of Verdun in 843, which irrevocably split up the Carolingian Empire, that the word began to have a more restricted meaning again. This treaty established three kingdoms, a western (*Francia occidentalis*), a Middle Kingdom (*Francia media*), which included the Low Countries, Switzerland and Italy, and an eastern kingdom (*Francia occidentalis*). Ninth-century sources often refer to West Francia simply as *Francia*; *Germania* began to replace the term *Francia orientalis*; and the northern part of the Middle Kingdom, after its further partition in 855, came to be called *Lotharingia*, after Lothar II (in German, *Lothringen*; in French, *Lorraine*). Although the kings of Germany continued to call themselves kings of the Franks, in common usage 'Frank' and 'Francia' came to be restricted to the western kingdom – a more restricted area than modern France, but politically its direct ancestor. The kingdom of Germany was made up of Saxons, Bavarians and Alamans as well as Franks; by the twelfth century that portion of Germany where Franks lived came to be called *Franconia* in Latin (German *Franken*) to distinguish it from the 'real' France. That does not mean that every man in the new kingdom of France thought of himself as a Frenchman. Southern France remained fiercely independent until the thirteenth century, and Brittany for even longer. Vestiges of the idea that parts of the Hexagon are not really France still survive; there are Bretons today (I have met one) who speak quite naturally of 'going to France' when they go east of Rennes. Nevertheless, by the year 1000 the meaning of the Latin word *Francus*, after numerous semantic migrations, finally settles down to something approximating to the word *français*. How this happened is, as we have seen, a complex process. Small wonder that over the centuries historians and others have had great problems trying to explain it.

The Frankish Myth

Gregory of Tours had been unsure about the origin of the Franks. He did, however, say that 'it was commonly said' that the Franks came from Pannonia, the Danube province from which, conveniently, Gregory's hero St Martin of Tours had also come. But Gregory's successors as historians of the Franks/French, right down to the eighteenth century, were possessed of much more certainty. It is Gregory's continuator Fredegar who first comes up with, or who first reports, the idea that the Franks were descendants of the Trojans. According to Fredegar some Trojans escaped from the sack of Troy, under their leader Frigia (a confusion with both Phrygia and Frisia, perhaps), and came westwards. The Trojan prince Francion (later 'Francus') brought them to the Rhine. It has been suggested that the notion may have originated with a confusion in the Roman name for Xanten, *Colonia Traiana*, which was close to the home of the early Franks. It is just as likely that the myth was concocted by some erudite Frank, or Gallo-Roman, around the year 600, to give the Franks a dignified ancestry, and one that made them the equal of the Romans. It was impossible to acquire any learning in the sixth century without discovering, from Virgil, that Rome itself had been founded by refugee Trojans; a similar desire not to be seen as inferior later inspired British historians to invent the Trojan Brutus, founder of Britain.

Dignity could also be acquired by more subtle reworkings of history. In the eighth century a prologue was added to texts of the Salic Law which declared that the Franks were not equal, but superior, to the Romans, because they were Christian:

The illustrious nation of the Franks, chosen by God, valorous in arms, constant in peace, profound in wisdom, noble in body, spotless in purity, handsome without equal, intrepid, quick, and fierce, newly converted to the Catholic faith, and free from heresy. . . This is the people who rejected with force the heavy yoke that the Romans had imposed on them and, having received baptism, they covered with gold and precious stones the bodies of the holy martyrs whom the Romans had burnt or beheaded and had torn apart by wild animals.

The Trojan legend continued to develop as well. The first embroidery on Fredegar which we have came in the eighth century in the *Liber Historiae Francorum*, whose author was clearly not very familiar with Virgil; he had Aeneas reigning in Troy during the ten-year siege, and Priam and Antenor being two of the refugee princes who led the Trojans to Pannonia. They built a city there called 'Sicambria'. When the Emperor Valentinian received their help in defeating the Alans he renamed the Trojans 'Franks', 'because of the hardness and the daring of their hearts. . . (for) in the Attic tongue Frank means fierce'. Ten years later Valentinian was rash enough to send tax collectors into Frankish Pannonia. The Franks killed them, and were immediately attacked by the Romans. King Priam was killed (the author obviously imagined the Trojan War to have taken place in the fourth century AD) and the Franks moved to 'the farthest reaches of the Rhine river, where the Germans' strongholds are located'. They had two kings, the sons of Priam and Antenor, but later they decided to 'have one king, like other peoples', and they chose Faramund, Priam's grandson. Faramund's son was Chlodio; Chlodio begat Merovech; Merovech begat Childeric, and we are back in the historical tradition firmly established by Gregory of Tours. As late as the eighteenth century genealogies of the French kings beginning with Priam were still learnt by heart by French schoolchildren.

By the tenth and eleventh centuries the Frankish myth was well established. However, historians then as now still had the problem of explaining how the Franks became the French – in other words, what happened to the inhabitants of Gaul who used to call themselves Romans. A marginal note to a ninth-century manuscript of the *Liber Historiae Francorum* did it in one way, neatly explaining also the problem of why the French should all speak the Roman language: 'Clovis exterminated all the Romans who then lived in Gaul, so that scarcely one could be found, and the Franks at this time are seen to have learnt the Roman language, which they still use, from those Romans who lived there. What their national language was before this is unknown in these parts.' Another solution was found by the tenth-century historian Richer of Rheims, who effectively denies that the Franks existed. Throughout his lengthy history he avoids the word Frank – he calls them *Galli*; the first Christian king of the Gauls, he says, was Clovis. Richer's was the first attempt of many to see the history of France as a continuity, unbroken by the invasions of such peoples as Romans or Franks, summed up later by the phrase 'nos ancêtres, les Gaulois!' – 'Our ancestors, the Gauls!'

In medieval Germany the role of the Franks in national history was even more problematical. The Emperor Charlemagne, king of the Franks, was revered, but there was a general feeling, after the ninth century, that the *Teutones* and the *Franci* were different. At the end of the thirteenth century, Alexander von Roes argued that the Germans were the true Franks; the French were merely *francigenae*, born of Franks, but by intermarriage with Romans. The origins of the cult of racial purity can already be seen. Charlemagne retained his position in the Germanic mythical tradition, but the Franks lost theirs; they were, after all, only one of the Germanic peoples who made up the German nation. *Germani, Teutones, Alemanni, Deutsche* – all these were concepts that had more impact on the development of German national consciousness than *Frank* did.

In France, however, Gaul and Frank continued to battle it out. 'Nos ancêtres, les Gaulois' was first used by François de Belleforest (d. 1583), who solved the problem of who the

French were by arguing that the Gauls returned to power with Hugh Capet in 987; he took the French crown from the Carolingians 'by divine Providence, which purposed to restore to the native Gauls authority over their country and take it away from German and Frankish foreigners who had usurped it until that time'. Jean Bodin resolved it even more succinctly by arguing that the Franks were Gauls: they were Gauls who had been undefeated by Julius Caesar, and who were eventually to avenge the defeat of Vercingetorix by throwing the Romans out of Gaul. A century later, in 1676, another Gallophile, Audigier, addressed a book to Louis XIV which took up those same arguments: 'It will therefore be found, unexpectedly, though undeniably, that our nation had the same origin as that race, the most awesome, the most daring and the most illustrious which the world had ever seen.' It satisfactorily explained the Franks without reference to the increasingly discredited Trojan myth, without reference to the other possibility (by the seventeenth century an even more unpleasant one) that the Franks were actually Germans. In fact, since the beginnings of modern historical scholarship, the debate over the Franks and their role in the origins of France has been closely associated with current political debate.

It was with François Hotman, in his *Francogallia* (1573), that the Franks were first called upon to justify contemporary constitutional debate. Hotman argued that the Frankish people, with their public assemblies, their elective kingship, their role in the government of the kingdom, had replaced Roman rule by something more democratic; it was Hugh Capet in 987 who re-introduced a new and more autocratic system of royal rule. This was very similar to the arguments used in England in the seventeenth century to oppose feudalism and royal autocracy; Anglo-Saxons had known freedom and constitutional monarchy until William the Conqueror had imposed the Norman Yoke.

From Hotman's time onwards the Franks often figured in arguments about the role of the king in French society. Few took the judicious line favoured by Bodin and Audigier, which emphasized continuity and unity. Most would have agreed with Comte Henri de Boulainvilliers (d. 1722) when he wrote: 'There are two races of men in this country'. Franks and Gauls stood

for different things to different men, however. Many, like
Boulainvilliers, saw the Franks as the aristocratic element of
French society, which brought France its greatness: the Franks
were 'the only recognised nobles, the only people recognised as
lords and masters'. Royalists could draw comfort from this; so
could Boulainvilliers and others who believed that the power of
the French aristocracy was being overpowered by the monarchy. Indeed, any attempt to diminish the Franks could be
viewed as a threat to the established order. When Nicholas
Fréret argued in 1714, in front of the Académie des Inscriptions,
that the Franks were not descended from Trojans, and were in
fact a fairly undistinguished group of Germanic invaders, he
earned several months' imprisonment in the Bastille. Even a
critic of the order could admire the Franks. Montesquieu
praised them for their sense of honour and virtue – while
attributing to them, not unlike Hotman, an English love of
freedom and parliamentary democracy. Voltaire was scathing:
'Who were these Franks whom Montesquieu calls our fore-
bears? They were, like the other northern barbarians, ferocious
beasts in search of shelter and of some protection against the
snow. . . Are the House of Lords and of the Commons or the
Court of Equity to be found in the forest?. . . Perhaps the
English owe their fine manufacturing goods to the admirable
habits of the Germans, who preferred living on the fruits of
rapine to working.'

If some were proud to be descended from the Franks, others
were not. The Abbé de Sieyès's renowned 1789 pamphlet, *What
is the Third Estate?*, suggested that those 'who persist in the
foolhardy pretence of being descended from the race of the
conquerors' ought to be sent back to the German forests. 'The
Nation, thus purged, would, I believe, be able to console itself
by the thought that it was constituted of the descendents of the
Gauls and the Romans only'. The French revolutionaries were
indeed consoled by the thought that they were the heirs of either
Brutus or Vercingetorix, and the victors over the descendants of
Clovis. Ducalle asked the administrators of the new department
of Paris to abandon the 'infamous name of French, now that we
have at last thrown off our shackles. . . We are descended from
the pure-blooded Gauls'. Even Catherine the Great participated
in the myth that the French Revolution was a racial war: in

1793 she wrote 'Do you not see what is happening in France? The Gauls are driving out the Franks.'

Racial conflict continued into the nineteenth century to be the historical explanation for the Revolution and for the constitutional conflicts which followed it. In 1823, for instance, after the Restoration and before the bourgeois revolution of 1830, Saint-Simon complained that 'the descendants of the Gauls, that is to say the industrialists, have constituted the money power, the dominating force. . . But government has remained in the hands of the Franks, so that our society now presents the extraordinary phenomenon of a nation which is essentially industrial and of which the government is essentially feudal.'

These ideas were given even more credibility when explained by the new science of race. The nineteenth-century passion for measurement and classification came together with a desire to explain everything, even such things as nationalism, scientifically. Linguists invented the Aryans; physical anthropologists such as Paul Broca found and measured their skulls, and related the measurements to intelligence and ability; theorists like Gobineau refined the concept of race as an historical explanation. French and German scholars debated, with increasing bitterness after the Franco-Prussian War of 1870–71, whether Germans or Gauls best represented the heirs of the obviously superior Aryans. The debate about the contribution of the brachycephalic Gauls and the dolichocephalic Franks (see above p. 109) to the French nation thus came to be explained 'scientifically', in terms of the innate qualities of different races. Broca's successor as the leading French physical anthropologist, Paul Topinard, a good Republican, argued that in his century peace-loving brachycephalic Gauls had triumphed over the war-like dolichocephalic Frankish aristocrats; the right-wing Vacher de Lapouge, on the other hand, bemoaned the way the brachycephalic Gallic revolutionaries had triumphed over the dolichocephalic Frankish nobles in 1789. They agreed over the facts – it was only the interpretation that was in doubt.

After 1871, when French nationalists wished to distance themselves from Germans as much as they could, 'nos ancêtres les Gaulois' were inevitably regarded as the true founders of France, and the Franks were denigrated as the barbarians who had brought Gallo-Roman civilization to an end. Heroic

Plate 47   A modern image of the Frank: a poster for the 1986 celebrations in
Soissons of the conquest of the city by Clovis.

moustachioed figures of Vercingetorix sprang up in villages all over France – never statues of Clovis. The Celtic version of French nationalism has, in recent years, found its ideal parody in the genius of Goscinny and Uderzo and their characters Astérix and Obélix. It is interesting here to note that the popular image of the Gaul, as represented by this comic strip, is remarkably similar to the popular image in modern France of the Frank: the same long blond hair, the same horned or winged helmet. The artist who painted the poster used for the Soissons festivities of 1986 (see plate 47) indeed used the pictures of Gauls he found in a book on military costume as models for his Franks. Another striking feature in the Astérix books is their ambiguity about the origins of the French nation. Astérix is a Gaul, defending his village against the Romans of Julius Caesar. But most Gauls were already Gallo-Romans, living in imitation of the Roman lifestyle. Few Romans are real villains. The Romans troops do not form a hostile army of occupation; when they march, they sing parodies of marching songs used in the modern French army. The barbarians – the enemy – are Germans. The cover of *Astérix chez les Goths* shows the Gallic heroes Astérix and Obélix defending *Roman* Gaul against the Germanic menace. Yet among the various totally anachronistic groups of Germans in the complete *oeuvre* of Goscinny and Uderzo, the Franks are conspicuous by their absence. If they are anywhere, they have been assimilated into the image of the Gauls themselves: the efforts of Richer of Rheims, Bodin and Audigier to argue that Gauls and Franks are the same people have come to fruition in the popular mind.

The ambiguity of the role of the Franks in European history still survives. The title chosen for an issue of *Dossiers Histoire et Archéologie* in 1981, to coincide with the celebrations marking the 1500th anniversary of Clovis's accession, was deliberately intended to be provocative: 'Les Francs: sont-ils nos ancêtres?' The ambiguity results largely from the fact that the Franks figure in the histories of several modern nations, notably France, Germany and Belgium. The French, since the Revolution, have tended to see Franks as foreign invaders who contributed to the destruction of Roman Gaul; Germans have often portrayed them as immigrants into Gaul who helped to preserve much of Roman civilization; the Belgians, since Henri

Pirenne in particular, saw the Franks as fruitfully intermarrying with the Romans to produce a new civilization, a synthesis of German and Roman. Charlemagne has been particularly problematical; each of those three nations regards him as a founder and hero. He is thus to some extent a symbol of unity. The European Community awards the *Prix Charlemagne* 'for contributions towards European unity'. Cynics, remembering Charlemagne's savage wars of conquest, have suggested it could equally appropriately be named after Napoleon or Hitler. Charlemagne is indeed just as much an unfortunate symbol of power and royal might as of unity. 'Was it not this,' asked Léon Poliakov[24], 'that, in our day, prompted Charles de Gaulle, in Germany, to invoke the myth of Charlemagne, the giant, for the purposes of his policy of French *grandeur*? (One may wonder what influence the combination of such a Christian name with such a surname had on the dreams and destiny of General de Gaulle.)'

[24] Léon Poliakov, *The Aryan Myth: A History of Racist and Nationalist Ideas in Europe* (London, 1974), p. 19: I am indebted to this fascinating book for much of the section on 'The Frankish Myth'.

Bibliography

Sources

Most sources used for this book have been edited for the *Monumenta Germaniae Historica*, in one of three series: *Auctores Antiquissimi*, *Leges*, and *Scriptores Rerum Merovingicarum* (although I have used Tranoy's edition for Hydatius and Uddholm's for Marculf). Most of the major historical texts have been translated, and these translations have been used, occasionally slightly amended, in quotations in the text.

Anderson, W.B. *Sidonius: Poems and Letters* (2 vols) (London, 1936).
Bachrach, B.S. *The Liber Historiae Francorum* (Lawrence, Kansas, 1973).
Dewing, H.B. *Procopius: History of the Wars* (London, 1914 – 28).
Gordon, C.D. *The Age of Attila: Fifth-Century Byzantium and the Barbarians* (Ann Arbor, 1960) (collection of texts).
Hillgarth, J.N. *Christianity and Paganism, 350–750: The Conversion of Western Europe* (2nd ed. Philadelphia, 1986) (collection of texts, including the *Life of Amandus*).
James, E. *Gregory of Tours: Life of the Fathers* (Liverpool, 1985).
Peters, E. ed. *Monks, Bishops and Pagans* (Philadelphia, 1975) (texts including Jonas's *Life of Columbanus*).
Rivers, T.J. *Laws of the Salian and Ripuarian Franks* (New York, 1986).
Thorpe, L. *Gregory of Tours: History of the Franks* (Harmondsworth, 1974).
Thorpe, L. *Two Lives of Charlemagne: Einhard and Notker the Stammerer* (Harmondsworth, 1969).

Walker, G.S.M. *Sancti Columbani Opera* (Dublin, 1970) (texts and translation).
Wallace-Hadrill, J.M. *The Fourth Book of the Chronicle of Fredegar* (London, 1960).

Select Secondary Bibliography

This bibliography lists some general works, together with those works referred to in the text which are not mentioned in footnotes. An asterisk indicates a work with an extended bibliography.

Ament, H. *Fränkische Adelsgräber von Flonheim in Rheinhessen* (Berlin, 1970).
Arrhenius, B. *Merovingian Garnet Jewellery: Emergence and Social Implications* (Stockholm, 1985).
Bachrach, B.S. *Merovingian Military Organisation, 481–751* (Minneapolis, 1972).
Böhme, H.W. *Germanische Grabfunde des 4. bis 5. Jahrhunderts zwischen unterer Elbe und Loire* (2 vols) (Munich, 1974).
Böhner, K. *Die fränkischen Altertümer des Trierer Landes* (2 vols) (Berlin, 1958).
Brulet, R. *Archéologie du quartier Saint-Brice à Tournai* (Exhibition Catalogue) (Tournai, 1986).
Brunner, H. *Deutsche Rechtsgeschichte, I. Die fränkische Zeit* (2nd ed.) (Munich, 1926).
Buchet, L. 'Anthropologie des Francs' in Périn 1981 ed., 78–81.
Christlein, R. 'Besitzabstufungen zur Merowingerzeit im Spiegel reicher Grabfunde aus West- und Süddeutschland', *Jahrbuch des Römisch-Germanischen Zentralmuseums, Mainz* 20 (1973), 147–180.
Clarke, H.B. and Brennan, M., ed. *Columbanus and Merovingian monasticism* (Brit. Arch. Reports S-113, Oxford, 1981).
Collins, R.J.H. "Theodebert I, 'Rex Magnus Francorum'" in P. Wormald ed., *Ideal and Reality in Frankish and Anglo-Saxon History* (Oxford, 1983), 7–33.
Courcelle, P. *Histoire littéraire des grandes invasions germaniques* (3rd ed.) (Paris, 1964).
Decaens, J. 'Un nouveau cimetière du Haut Moyen Age en Normandie. Hérouvillette (Calvados)', *Archéologie Médiévale* 1 (1971), 1–126.
Demolon, P. *Le village mérovingien de Brebières (VIe-VIIe siècles)* (Arras, 1972).

*Dierkens, A. 'Cimetières mérovingiens et histoire du Haut Moyen Age, Chronologie, société, religion', *Acta Historica Bruxellensia, IV. Histoire et Méthode* (Brussels, 1981), 15–70.

*Doehaerd, R. *The Early Middle Ages in the West – Economy and Society* (Amsterdam, 1978).

Doppelfeld, O. and Pirling, R. *Fränkischen Fürsten im Rheinland. Die Gräber aus der Kölner Dom, von Krefeld-Gellep und Morken* (Bonn, 1966).

Duby, G. ed. *Histoire de la France rurale*, I (Paris, 1975).

Duby, G. ed. *Histoire de la France urbaine*, I (Paris, 1980).

Duval, N. and Picard, J.-C. ed. *L'Inhumation privilégiée du IVe au VIIIe en Occident* (Paris, 1986).

Ebling, H. *Prosopographie der Amtsträger des Merowingerreiches (613–741)* (Munich, 1974).

Evison, V.I. *The Fifth Century Invasions South of the Thames* (London, 1965).

Evison, V.I. 'Les Francs en Angleterre au Ve siècle', in Périn 1981, ed., 70–7.

Ewig, E. *Spätantikes und fränkisches Gallien* (2 vols) (Munich, 1976).

Faider-Feytmans, G. *La Belgique à l'époque mérovingienne* (Brussels, 1964).

Fleury, M. and Périn, P. ed. *Problèmes de chronologie relative et absolue concernant les cimetières mérovingiens d'entre Loire et Rhin* (Paris, 1978).

Fournier, G. *Les Mérovingiens* (Paris, 1966).

Gaillard de Sémainville, H. 'Burgondes et Francs', in Périn 1981, ed., 56–63.

Ganshof, F.L. 'L'historiographie dans la monarchie franque sous les Mérovingiens', *Settimane di Studio* 17 (1969), 631–85.

Gaudemet, J. 'Les survivances romaines dans le droit de la monarchie franque', *Tijdschr.v.Rechtsgeschiedenis* 23 (1955), 149–206.

Gauthier, N. *L'évangélisation des pays de la Moselle* (Paris, 1980).

Gluckman, M. *Custom and Conflict in Africa* (Oxford, 1965).

Goffart, W. 'Byzantine policy in the West under Tiberius II and Maurice: the Pretenders Hermenigild and Gundovald', *Traditio* 13 (1957), 73–118.

Goffart, W. 'The Fredegar problem reconsidered', *Speculum* 38 (1963), 206–41.

Goffart, W. *Barbarians and Romans, AD 418–585: the techniques of accommodation* (Princeton, 1980).

Goffart, W. 'Old and new in Merovingian taxation', *Past and Present* 96 (1982), 3–21.

*Grahn-Hoek, H. *Die fränkische Oberschicht im 6. Jahrhundert* (Sigmaringen, 1976).

Graus, F. X. *Volk, Herrscher und Heiliger im Reich der Merowinger* (Prague, 1965).

Gregorio di Tours: Convegni del Centro di Studi sulla spiritualità medievale 12 (Todi, 1977).

Heinzelmann, M. *Bischofsherrschaft in Gallien* (Munich, 1976)

Hubert, J., Porcher, J., Volbach, F., *Europe in the Dark Ages* (London, 1969)

Irsigler, F. *Untersuchungen zur Geschichte des fruhfränkischen Adels* (Bonn, 1969)

Irsigler, F. ed. 'Hauptprobleme der Siedlung, Sprache und Kultur des Frankenreiches', *Rheinische Vierteljahrsblätter* 35 (1971), 1–106.

James, E. 'Septimania and its frontier', in E. James, ed., *Visigothic Spain: New Approaches*, (Oxford, 1980), 223–41.

James, E. *The Merovingian Archaeology of South-West Gaul* (2 vols) (Brit. Arch. Reports S-25: Oxford, 1977).

James, E. 'Cemeteries and the problem of Frankish settlement in Gaul', in P. H. Sawyer, ed. *Names, Words and Graves* (Leeds, 1979), 55–89.

James, E. 'Merovingian cemetery studies', in P. Rahtz et al., ed., *Anglo-Saxon Cemeteries 1979* (Brit. Arch. Reports, 82: Oxford 1980), 35–55.

James, E. 'Archaeology and the Merovingian monastery', in Clarke and Brennan, ed., 33–55.

*James, E. *The origins of France: from Clovis to the Capetians, 500–1000* (London, 1982).

James, E. 'Ireland and western Gaul in the Merovingian period', in D. Whitelock et al., ed., *Ireland in Early Medieval Europe* (Cambridge, 1983), 362–386.

Jones, A.H.M. *The Later Roman Empire, 284–602* (3 vols) (Oxford, 1964).

Joris, A. 'On the edge of two worlds in the heart of the new empire: The Romance regions of northern Gaul during the Merovingian period', *Studies in Medieval & Renaissance Hist.* 3 (1966), 3–52.

Kaiser, R. 'Steuer und Zoll in der Merowingerzeit', *Francia* 7 (1979), 1–18.

Kazanski, M. 'Deux riches tombes de l'époque des Grandes Invasions au nord de la Gaule: Airan et Pouan', *Archéologie Médiévale* 12 (1982), 17–33.

Keller, R.E. 'The language of the Franks', *Bulletin of J. Ryland's Library* 47 (1964), 101–22.

Krüger, K.H. *Königsgrabkirchen der Franken, Angelsachsen und Langobarden bis zur Mitte des 8. Jahrhunderts* (Munich, 1971).

Kurth, G. *Etudes franques* (2 vols) (Brussels, 1919).

Lafaurie, J. 'Eligius Monetarius', *Revue Numismatique*, **6** ser. 19 (1977), 111–51.

Larrieu, M. et al. *La Nécropole mérovingienne de La Turraque, Beaucaire-sur-Baïse (Gers)* (Toulouse, 1985).

Lebecq, S. *Marchands et navigateurs frisons du haut moyen âge* (2 vols) (Lille, 1984).

Lelong, C. *La vie quotidienne en Gaule à l'époque mérovingienne* (Paris, 1963).

Lemant, J.-P. et al. *Le cimetière et la fortification du Bas-Empire de Vireux-Molhain (Ardennes)* (Mainz, 1985).

Lewis, A.R. 'The dukes in the Regnum Francorum, AD 550–751', *Speculum* **51** (1976), 281–41.

Lorren, C. 'Le village de Saint-Martin-de-Mondeville (Calvados)', in Périn and Feffer, ed. *La Neustrie*. . . (1985), 350–61.

Lot, F. *Recueil des travaux historiques de Ferdinand Lot* (3 vols) (Geneva, 1968).

Mâle, E. *La fin du paganisme en Gaule et les premières églises chrétiennes* (Paris, 1950).

Maillé, Marquise de. *Les Cryptes de Jouarre* (Paris, 1971).

Martindale, J.R. ed. *The Prosopography of the Later Roman Empire* (Cambridge, 1980).

*Musset, L. *The Germanic Invasions: the Making of Europe AD 400–600* (transl. E. and C. James) (London, 1975).

Nelson, J.L. 'Queens as Jezabels: the careers of Brunhild and Balthild', *Studies in Church History, Subsidia* **1** (1978), 31–77.

Oldoni, M. 'Gregorio di Tours e i Libri Historiarum: letture e fonti', *Studi Medievali* **13** (1972), 563–70.

*Périn, P. (with R.Legoux) *La datation des tombes mérovingiennes. Historique, méthodique, applications* (Geneva, 1980)

Périn, P.ed, *Les Francs sont-ils nos ancêtres?* (*Dossiers Histoire et Archéologie* **56**, 1981).

Périn, P. and Feffer, L.-C. ed. *La Neustrie: Les Pays au nord de la Loire de Dagobert à Charles le Chauve* (Exhibition Catalogue) (Rouen, 1985).

*Périn, P. and Feffer, L.-C. *Les Francs* (2 vols) (Paris, 1987).

Petri, F. *Siedlung, Sprache und Bevölkerungsstruktur im Frankenreich* (Darmstadt, 1973).

La Picardie, Berceau de la France (Exhibition Catalogue) (Amiens, 1986).

Pilet, C. *La Nécropole de Frénouville: Etude d'une population de la fin du IIIe à la fin du VIIe siècle* (Brit. Arch. Reports S-86: Oxford, 1980).

Pirling, R. *Das römisch-fränkische Gräberfeld von Krefeld-Gellep* (2 vols: Berlin, 1966), (2 vols: 1974), (2 vols, 1979).

Prinz, F. *Frühes Mönchtum im Frankenreich* (Munich, 1965).

Riché, P. *Education and Culture in the Barbarian West* (Columbia, 1976).

Rouche, M. *L'Aquitaine des Wisigoths aux Arabes, 418–781* (Paris, 1979).

*Salin, E. *La civilisation mérovingienne, d'après les sépultures, les textes et le laboratoire* (4 vols) (Paris, 1950–59).

Scheibelreiter, G. *Der Bischof im merowingischer Zeit* (Vienne, 1983).

Seillier, C. 'Développement topographique et caractères généraux de la nécropole de Vron (Somme)', *Archéologie Médiévale*, **16** (1986), 7–32.

Selle-Hosbach, K. *Prosopographie merovingischer Amtsträger in der Zeit von 511–613* (Bonn, 1974).

Stevens, C.E. *Sidonius Apollinaris and his age* (Oxford, 1933).

Tessier, G. *Le baptême de Clovis* (Paris, 1964).

Tessier,G. 'Le conversion de Clovis et la christianisation des Francs' *Settimane di Studio* 14 (1967), 149–90.

Thompson, E.A. *Barbarians and Romans: the decline of the western Empire* (Madison, 1982).

Vallet, F. 'Les tombes de chef, reflets de l'histoire de la conquête', in *La Picardie*, 113–19.

*Van Dam, R. *Leadership and Community in Late Antique Gaul* (Berkeley, 1985).

Verhulst, A. 'Der Handel im Merowingerreich: Gesamtdarstellung nach schriftlichen Quellen', *Early Medieval Studies* 2 (1970), 2–54.

Verlinden, F. 'Frankish colonisation: a new approach', *Trans. Royal Hist. Soc.* 4 (1954), 1–17.

Verlinden, F. *Les origines de la frontière linguistique en Belgique et la colonisation franque* (Brussels, 1955).

Vieillard-Troiekouroff, M. *Les monuments religieux dans la Gaule d'après les oeuvres de Grégoire de Tours* (Paris, 1976).

Vierck, H. 'Werke des Eligius', in G. Kossack and G. Ulbert, ed., *Studien zur vor- und frühgeschichtlichen Archäologie* (Munich, 1974), 309–80.

Vierck, H. 'La "Chemise de Sainte-Balthilde" à Chelles et l'influence byzantine sur l'art mérovingien au VIIe siècle', in *Centenaire de l'Abbé Cochet* (Rouen, 1978), 521–64.

Wallace-Hadrill, J.M. *The Long-Haired Kings and other studies in Frankish history* (London, 1962).

Wallace-Hadrill, J.M. *Early Germanic Kingship in England and on the Continent* (Oxford, 1971).

Wallace-Hadrill, J.M. *The Frankish Church* (Oxford, 1983).

Weidemann, M. *Kulturgeschichte der Merowingerzeit nach den Werken Gregors von Tours* (2 vols) (Mainz, 1982).

Wemple, S.F. *Women in Frankish Society* (Philadelphia, 1981).

Werner, J. *Münzdatierte austrasische Grabfunde* (Berlin, 1935).

Werner, J. 'Zur Entstehung der Reihengräberzivilisation', *Archaeologica Geographica* (1950), 23–32.

Werner, J. 'Waage und Geld in der Merowingerzeit', *Sitzungsber. Bayern Akad. Wissensch.* 1 (1954), 3–40.

Werner, J. 'Fernhandel und Naturalwirtschaft im östlichen Merowingerreich nach archäologischen und numismatischen Zeugnissen', *Bericht der Römisch-Germanischen Kommission* 42 (1961), 307–46.

Werner, J. 'Frankish royal tombs in the cathedrals of Cologne and St-Denis' *Antiquity* 38 (1964), 201–16.

Werner, J. 'Bewaffnung und Waffenbeigabe in der Merowingerzeit', *Settimane di Studio* 15 (1968), 95–108.

Werner, K.F. *Structures politiques du monde franc (VIe-XIIe siècles)* (London, 1979).

Werner, K.F. *Les Origines (avant l'An Mil)*: vol I of J.Favier, ed. *Histoire de France* (Paris, 1984).

Wilson, D.M. 'A Ring of Queen Arnegunde', *Germania* 42 (1964), 265–8.

Wood, I.N. 'Kings, kingdoms and consent' in P.H.Sawyer and I.N.Wood, ed. *Early Medieval Kingship* (Leeds, 1977), 6–29.

Wood, I.N. 'Early Merovingian devotion in town and country', *Studies in Church History,* 16 (1979), 61–76.

Wood, I.N. 'The *Vita Columbani* and Merovingian hagiography', *Peritia* 1 (1982), 63–80.

Wood, I.N. *The Merovingian North Sea* (Alingsås, 1983).

Wood, I.N. 'Gregory of Tours and Clovis', *Revue Belge Philol. Hist.* 63 (1985), 249–72.

Young, B.K. 'Paganisme, christianisation et rites funéraires mérovingiens', *Archéologie Médiévale* 7 (1977), 5–81.

Young, B.K. *Quatre cimetières mérovingiens de l'Est de la France: Lavoye, Dieue-sur-Meuse, Mézières-Manchester et Mazerny* (Brit. Arch. Reports I-208: Oxford, 1984).

Zöllner, E. *Geschichte der Franken, bis zur Mitte des 6. Jahrhunderts* (Munich, 1970).

Index

Index compiled by Meg Davis